WHAT CAN'T BE LOST

88 Stories and Traditions from the Sacred City

Made Possible Through a Grant from
LOUISIANA ENDOWMENT FOR THE HUMANITIES
State Affiliate of the National Endowment
for the Humanities

The photographs in this book were not selected to illustrate the writing.
They are meant to be artistic pairings only, inspired by the essays and stories.

No specific individual is receiving any money from the sale of *New Orleans: What Can't Be Lost.*
Proceeds benefit Sweet Home New Orleans, a local 501(c)(3) supporting the individuals and
organizations that will perpetuate New Orleans' unique musical and cultural traditions.

University of Louisiana at Lafayette
P.O. Box 40831
Lafayette, LA 70504

http://www.ulpress.org

ISBN: 978-1-935754-00-8

Library of Congress Cataloging-in-Publication Data

New Orleans : what can't be lost : 88 stories and traditions from the sacred city
/ edited Lee Barclay; photography, Christopher Porché West.
p. cm.
ISBN 978-1-935754-00-8 (hardcover : alk. paper)
1. New Orleans (La.)--Civilization--21st century. 2. New Orleans (La.)--Social life and
customs--21st century. I. Barclay, Lee, 1974- II. West, Christopher Porché, 1958-
F379.N55N46 2010
976.3'35064--dc22
2010027057

This book was printed in Canada on acid-free paper.

We remember.

Contents

Contents (cont.)

Contents (cont.)

Editor's Preface

by Lee Barclay

It might have something to do with the children parading across the street in front of me on their way home from school that day, imaginary horns held high. These are more than passing acts of sudden beauty punctuating our days and weeks in New Orleans. More often than not they are sewn into a story that goes back hundreds of years if you keep pulling the thread. That feather that took to the sky on Mardi Gras Day, the red beans we eat on Monday, and the sash he wears across his chest to dance his last goodbye carry forth generations of storytellers in their deep, wide histories. The story unravels differently every time.

It is on every page in this book, even in the way the words come together. Respect crowns lowercase letters. Uptown is uptown. A poor-boy is the same thing as a po-boy or poboy. You can Second Line or second-line but only when you're behind a First Line. You can parade with Social [Aid(e)] and Pleasure Clubs thirty-nine Sundays a year (says one authority, another says there is no set number). These stylistic expressions speak legends in a long, long story I can't stop chasing.

That feather was never just a feather. The painted coconut on the mantle next to Mary, tiny plastic babies, and the mirror on the door. Just try to catch that floating piece of glitter that, reborn from some masked happiness, passes from cheek to cheek long after the magic has all been packed away. You never will.

This is what we worried about losing when our city filled up with water and then slowly and quietly drained, ring by chalky ring. Suddenly every story behind the workings of our idiosyncratic lives and the traditions that bound us together was more important than ever. Our Kings and Queens and Chiefs and Spy Boys and Grand Marshals and musicians and storytellers meant more to us than we knew how to explain. I should rephrase that.

I wanted that feather to talk.

I followed it from one New Orleanian to another. Along the way I met the bearers of New Orleans culture. They cook our Creole food, design our floats and costumes, give birth to our parades and Social Aid and Pleasure Clubs and publishing houses, protect our historic landmarks, teach our children, honor our ancestors, write our poems and articles and novels and plays, and pass down our traditions in the performance of our culture. These eighty-eight stories and traditions are the piano keys in their love song to New Orleans.

This book is their gift to their city. The proceeds will be donated to Sweet Home New Orleans, a local 501(c)(3) that has distributed millions of dollars into the cultural community of New Orleans by advocating for thousands of our musicians, Black Mardi Gras Indians, and Social Aid and Pleasure Club members. These words were written amid the exhausting demands, distractions, and devastation of a resuscitating city. They made time for this book when there was none to give. These are generous, loving, wonderful people who graciously endured endless interruptions, said, "Thank you," in place of, "You're welcome," and gave me a second family. They endlessly inspire me. I have been asked why New Orleans is worth saving and how it will possibly happen. They are the answer. It is an honor beyond measure to find myself among them.

All of the contributors are those who have lived in and loved New Orleans, save a small handful who have either claimed or have been claimed by the city by a deep love or in thanks for their good and important work. All continue to call New Orleans home.

Which brings me to Christopher Porché West. Whether it's a corner store, a face, or a feather, Christopher draws that something beneath the surface out of hiding. His rare talent—and his studious devotion to New Orleans culture and its people—produced a body of work which is itself a veritable New Orleans storybook. It didn't take long to see how special this pairing could be—these eighty-eight stories and Christopher's photographs—and to wonder where the two might meet. Somewhere between illustration and imagination, there is always a little more of the story to the story, just the way it is in New Orleans.

That feather was never just a feather.

Those children knew it, the ones who crossed the street before me that day, imaginary parade, backpacks keeping time. Maybe they split the sky and the crowd with *March Grandioso* in purple and gold St. Aug uniforms, metronome of bright brass and high steps under the reaching arms of oaks, candy-colored beads like rain from papier-mâché wonderlands rolling behind them.

Maybe they were walking steady for miles on the backstreets, cheeks popping like bubble gum pressed against trumpet, tuba, trombone, bones turned to rubber from the First

Line to the Second Line, singing, "Feet can't fail me now. My feet can't fail me now . . ."

Or maybe those weren't horns at all they were playing but tambourines and drums and cowbells, and they were backing up a Big Chief on Mardi Gras Day, long after the first stitch of his suit in his kitchen, month after month, feather after feather, bead after bead, calling out, "My Big Chief got a golden crown."

Perhaps summer steamed the pleats from their crisp black suits, sashes clinging close in the heat, feet a slow synchronized left, right, left, then the body "cut loose," the sudden rhapsody of "Didn't He Ramble," mourners eddying in the wake behind those joyful horns, giving themselves up to their grief, to their love, to each other.

I saw all of that crossing the sidewalk that afternoon, daydreaming as they danced, knowing I'll be dancing behind them someday soon and wondering where it might be.

That feather, you can sense it even when you can't see it in New Orleans, the way it rides the wind, refusing to touch ground. It brought me here. To you.

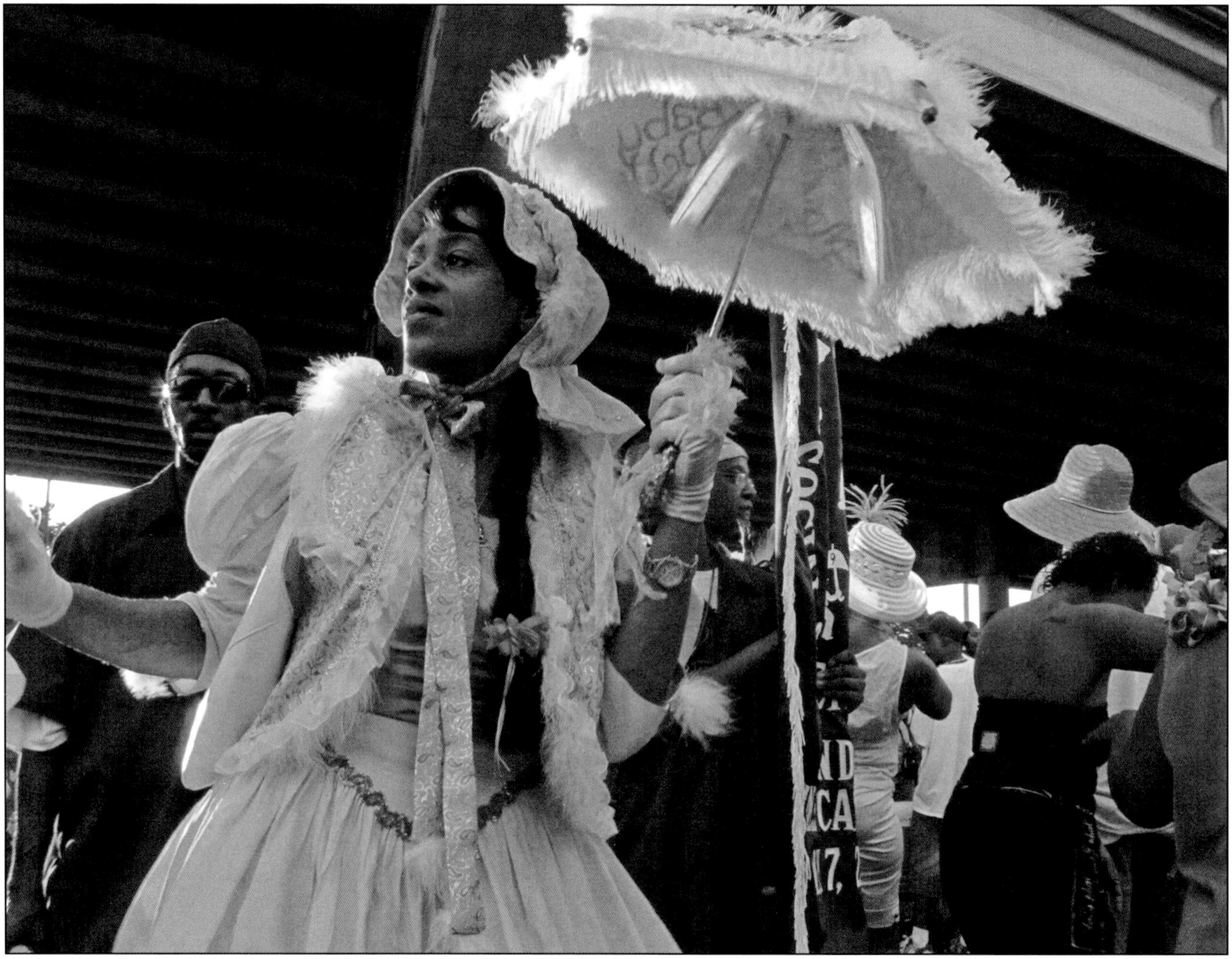

Foreword:
The Indispensable Thing

by Richard Ford

In New Orleans . . . You can't separate nothing from nothing. Everything mingles each into the other . . . until nothing is purely itself but becomes part of one fonky gumbo.

—Mac Rebennack (Dr. John)

All New Orleanians gaze at the future with trepidation and longing now. What that we loved is lost forever? What that we loved is inextinguishable? So much of any culture— its music, literature, its precious art—is the topic of chance, of situation and accident, of who was there for just that moment when it mattered most. Culture is frangible—irreplaceable even—though that quality by which it might never have happened is part of its magic and dream, part of why we, its lovers, feel ourselves illuminated, renewed by its radiance. In this way culture's dilemma is our human, ageless one: poised on the precipice between nothing and everything.

All the more this great tradition of New Orleans writing. In so many ways it's been, over time, the invention of want, of cultural invisibility, of displacement, of those who were marginalized—human states we regret but that seek an audience still, a hearing, a witness to their old longings and answering sounds: Joy. Pain. Hope. Discord. Harmony. From what we lament, sometimes comes the indispensable thing we love.

But then comes a great wind and a great flooding, and everything—the situation and who was in it, the culture, its fabled flowering—is all but swept away, leaving behind the longing. It's hard, so soon after August 29, when all was in place, to think of a day in our future, or someone's—say, twenty years from this one—when a kid could read a story or a poem that's ours, and wonder, "Was it really like that? So alive there? New Orleans? All that great majestic noise and words, coming out of that one place? It must've been some kinda place." That's what happens, though. All of it, and us, swept away on a wind.

The great twin engines of rationality and greed are fired now, beginning to carve up the ground, raze what the flood left standing, dispel those witnessing spirits, do away with their old magic and dream. Those engines hurry along to put up what's earnest and reasonable in the old unreasoning places where the music and writing (and all of art) take root. They plow under our memory, distract us with the new, detach us from our old longings and harmonies and chanciness in behalf of their new *plan*. Those of us left upright, with whatever small gift we're given, must do what we can to hold back our forward-fleeing notice, and even bright new hopes for just a little time, preserve what was in the air and ephemeral, what we might've thought was ours and never-ending, deepen our intimacy with losses new and old, and with what can't be lost. You can rebuild a city, but you can't re*make* it. So, we need a surety, a reminder in the fresh face of disaster, where we're all strangers and unafraid, that when new life percolates out of the dried streets and flooded weed patches, off of the porches and out of the bedrooms—out of whatever's left in New Orleans—that something vital is intact, some marker in our hearts, if nowhere else, by which we can say, "Yes, that's where we were, that's what we heard, what we thought and wrote, that's what we knew was good and worth preserving, that's who we were and are. And that's where we'll start again." There *are* some things you just mustn't lose or life's not life for any of us.

Part One:

March Grandioso

Upon a Photograph by E. J. Bellocq

by Robert Olen Butler

Mattie Treen
23, prostitute

in the Chambre Rouge at Lulu White's Mahogany Hall, Storyville, New Orleans, 1912

Monsieur Bellocq has a crimson scarf tied at his throat and he says in that soft way of his not to move and he disappears behind the camera and the bellows stretch toward me like a hard-on, but with an eye at the tip, like that part of him can go into me and see what's there, and I am naked on the damask sofa except for my black and gold opera-length silk stockings and I let my eyes rise to the cut-glass chandelier catching the morning light, and Annie Two-Ways died in the attic yesterday afternoon trying to have her trick baby and Tenderloin Thelma coughed her way to whatever's next in her dollar crib on Iberville last week and I'm not moving, I just watch the light flutter up there in the cut crystal, and I can smell the morning smell of this place—Lysol and lilac talcum and spent cigars and spilled Raleigh Rye and the leftover smells of our loins and their seed—all the smells of living into a new day—and the fog will rise tonight and it will glow like fire from the light along Basin Street and the men will come and the air will fill with the piano music and the laughter and the cursing and the hissy-screaming and the other sounds through the walls and the men will go, and then there will be the silence and the hot, dark, sweet late night in this city, and I washed these stockings very carefully, very gently, once already, and though I paid six dollars for them, I know the next time I try to wash them they will dissolve into nothing, but for now they feel ever so soft

3

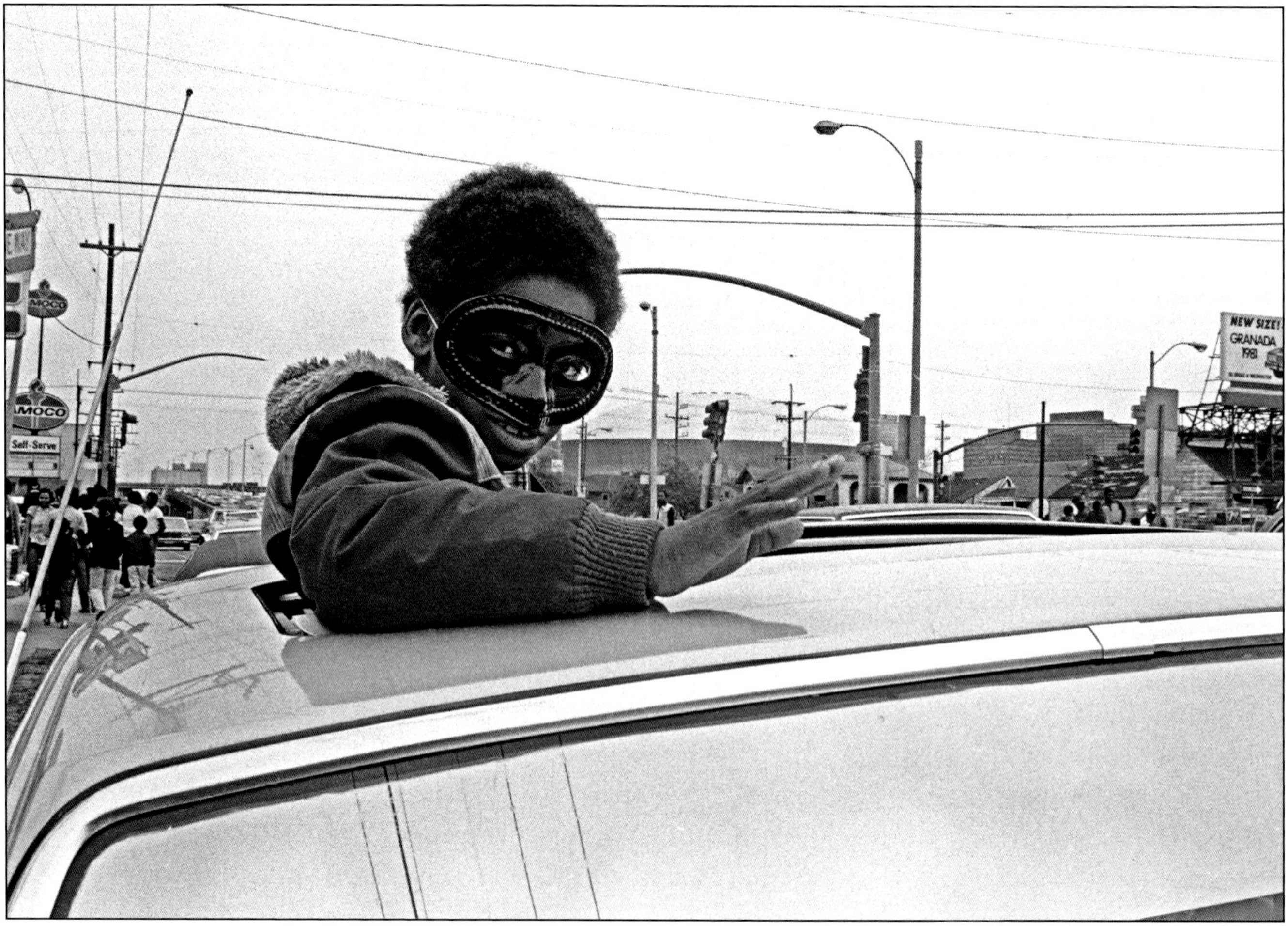
Self-Serve
NEW SIZE!
GRANADA
1981

Everyone Has a Valve

by Poppy Z. Brite

During an argument with her wayward son Ignatius, whose mysterious inner "valve" tends to close when he's under stress, *A Confederacy of Dunces'* Mrs. Irene Reilly asks, "Are you fooling with that valve again? Nobody else got him a valve but you. *I* ain't got no valve."

"*Everyone* has a valve!" Ignatius bellows. "Mine is simply more developed."

John Kennedy Toole employed Ignatius' valve as one of many hilarious traits setting him apart from his fellow New Orleanians. Yet Ignatius is a quintessential New Orleanian himself, unable to survive anywhere else. His one bus trip to Baton Rouge impressed upon him that "outside the city limits, the true heart of darkness begins." At the end of the novel, when that musky *deus ex machina* Myrna Minkoff arrives to sweep him away from the men in the white coats and off to New York, it's hard not to imagine him being pummeled to death on a Manhattan street corner within hours of his arrival.

In his *Journal of a Working Boy*, Ignatius describes New Orleans as "a comfortable metropolis which has a certain apathy and stagnation which I find inoffensive." What Ignatius characterizes as "apathy and stagnation," Gentilly resident Jacqueline Bendtsen rephrases more lyrically: "Because the night is soft. Because in New Orleans, you can walk down the street in costume any time of year and not get strange looks. Because, when I'm not in New Orleans, I always feel like I've just forgotten something."

The costume thing is important, I think, part of that "Mardi Gras mentality" other cities like to chide us for. New Orleans is an intensely Catholic city, but Catholics here seem to be more easygoing in regards to dogma than in some other places. After all, how homophobic can you be in a city where almost every man—regardless of orientation, age, or social status—has at least one dress in his closet? Of course, these gents needn't wait for Mardi Gras. Parades can crop up at any time for any reason and are taken for granted at certain times, such as after funerals. The defining characteristic of New Orleans is surely a live-and-let-live credo, a near-universal belief that as long as that fat man wearing the pirate costume and pushing the hot dog cart isn't hurting anybody, he's not crazy, he's just *interesting*. Let him talk.

There's an old saying about true natives, whether they were born here or have made it their spiritual home: "You know you're from New Orleans if you move anywhere else and feel like you're from Oz and just moved to Kansas." In other words, every true New Orleanian has a valve. We are each and every one of us Ignatius, we diehards who have committed ourselves to this city not because we are especially brave or strong or determined to rebuild—though we may be all of these things—but simply because we have no choice in the matter.

Who We Are

by Chris Rose

Dear America,

I suppose we should introduce ourselves: we're South Louisiana.

We have arrived on your doorstep on short notice and we apologize for that, but we were never much for waiting around for invitations. We're not much on formalities like that.

And we might be staying around your town for a while, enrolling in your schools and looking for jobs, so we wanted to tell you a few things about us. We know you didn't ask for this and neither did we, so we're just going to have to make the best of it.

First of all, we thank you. For your money, your water, your food, your prayers, your boats and buses, and the men and women of your National Guards, fire departments, hospitals, and everyone else who has come to our rescue.

We're a fiercely proud and independent people, and we don't cotton much to outside interference, but we're not ashamed to accept help when we need it. And right now, we need it.

Just don't get carried away. For instance, once we get around to fishing again, don't try to tell us what kind of lures work best in your waters.

We're not going to listen. We're stubborn that way.

You probably already know that we talk funny and listen to strange music and eat things you'd probably hire an exterminator to get out of your yard.

We dance even if there's no radio. We drink at funerals. We talk too much and laugh too loud and live too large, and, frankly, we're suspicious of others who don't.

But we'll try not to judge you while we're in your town.

Everybody loves their home, we know that. But we love South Louisiana with a ferocity that borders on the pathological. Sometimes we bury our dead in LSU sweatshirts.

Often we don't make sense. You may wonder why, for instance, if we could carry only one small bag of belongings with us on our journey to your state—why in God's name did we

7

bring a pair of shrimp boots?

We can't really explain that. It is what it is.

You've probably heard that many of us stayed behind. As bad as it is, many of us cannot fathom a life outside our border, out in that place we call Elsewhere.

The only way you could understand that is if you have been there, and so many of you have. So you realize that when you strip away all the craziness and bars and parades and music and architecture and all that hooey, really, the best thing about where we come from is us.

We are what made this place a national treasure. We're good people. And don't be afraid to ask us how to pronounce our names. It happens all the time.

When you meet us now and you look into our eyes, you will see the saddest story ever told. Our hearts are broken into a thousand pieces.

But don't pity us. We're gonna make it. We're resilient. After all, we rooted for the Saints for more than forty years! That's got to count for something.

Okay, maybe something else you should know is that we make jokes at inappropriate times.

But what the hell.

And one more thing: In our part of the country, we're used to having visitors. It's our way of life.

So when all this is over and we move back home, we will repay you the hospitality and generosity of spirit you offer us in this season of our despair.

That is our promise. That is our faith.

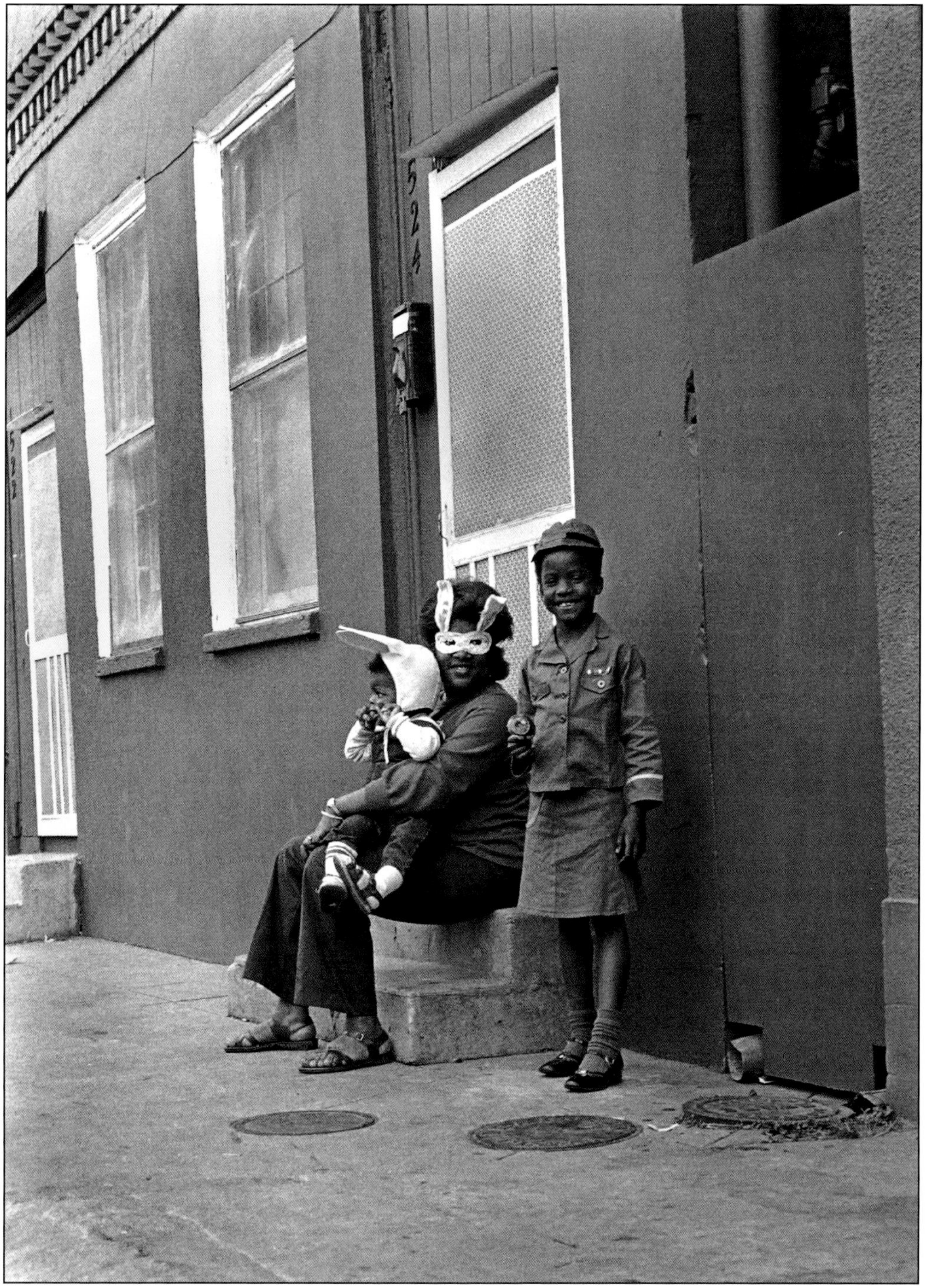
524

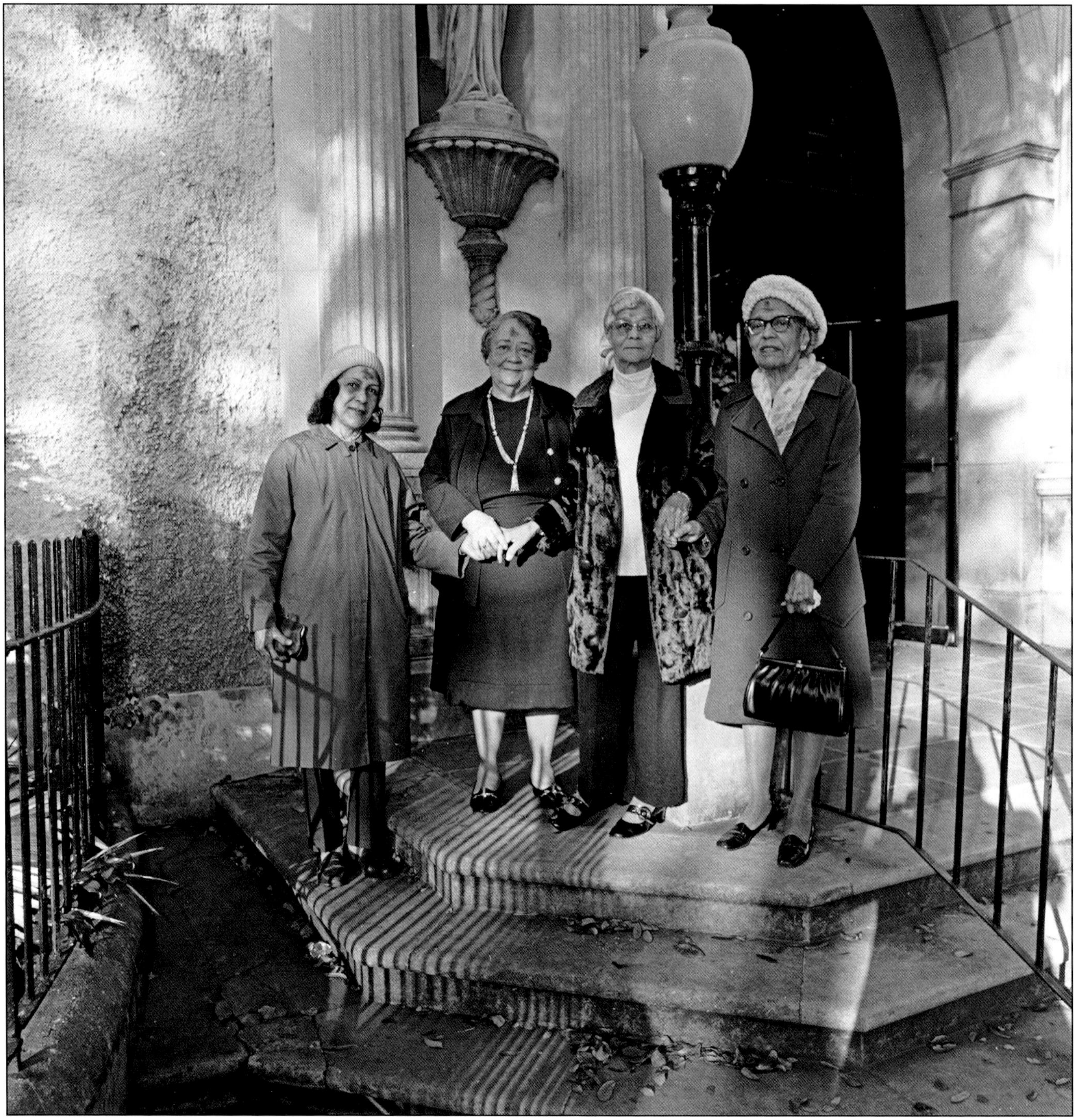

My New Orleans

by Quo Vadis Gex Breaux

Anyone who's lived here has his or her own New Orleans. My New Orleans mothers and embraces. Her waterways calm, her human-scale avenues are art for walkers. Neighborhoods still exist where, until recently, folks felt no need to leave. The neighbors themselves consider your business their business. They know when you leave—when you come. They know that strange man trying to get into your house is not your "Uncle Oscar"—'cause they met him.

The river, bayou, lake have always been balms to my aching spirit. This Scorpio, peninsula town and her people thrive on bountiful, surrounding water.

As a teenager I remember walking the length of Esplanade Avenue whenever I was trying to solve a personal problem. By the end of the walk, I might not have the solution, but I felt like I could, I would, or it just didn't matter as much as I thought it did.

In like manner, I would walk the streets of the French Quarter smelling its myriad conflicting odors, Creole cooking, praline making, free-flowing liquor, and fried beignets topped with diabetic-inducing powdered sugar. As I walked, I'd hear: the sidewalk tapping of a young man dancing for survival dollars; the clacking hooves of horses drawing carriages through the ancient streets; a wafting alto-sax solo that glided over the sidewalk outside a lounge filled with drunken patrons whose loud chatter ate all the room inside and pushed the music out.

A part of New Orleans' beauty is that she is a place where many people, stifled elsewhere, feel safe to be themselves; safe just to be. Whether or not we agree with their politics, life choices, or diets, they are "their business." Of course, being the nosy door-poppers we are, we talk about those choices, just a little, just sometimes.

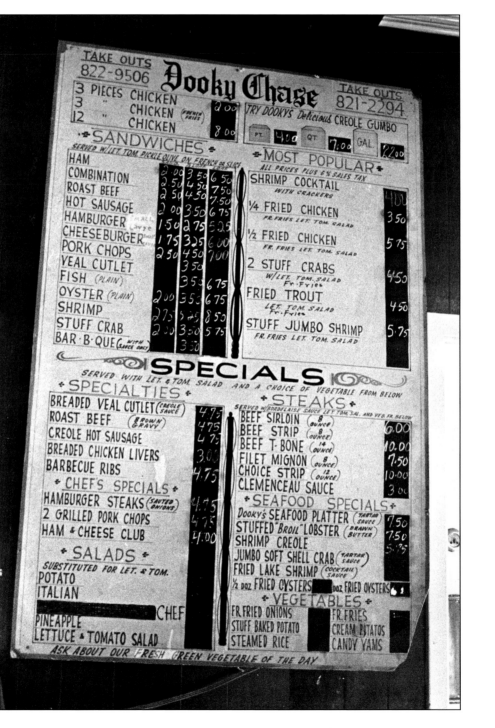

Dooky Chase

TAKE OUTS
822-9506

TAKE OUTS
821-2294

3 PIECES CHICKEN
3 " CHICKEN (FRENCH FRIES) 2.00
12 " CHICKEN 8.00

TRY DOOKY'S Delicious CREOLE GUMBO

| | PT | 4.00 | QT | 7.00 | GAL | 12.00 |

❖ SANDWICHES ❖
SERVED W/LET. TOM. PICKLE OLIVE ON FRENCH OR SLICE

HAM	2.00	3.50	6.50
COMBINATION	2.50	4.50	7.50
ROAST BEEF	2.50	4.50	7.50
HOT SAUSAGE	2.00	3.50	6.75
HAMBURGER (Small)(Large)	1.50	2.75	5.25
CHEESEBURGER	1.75	3.25	6.00
PORK CHOPS	2.50	4.50	7.00
VEAL CUTLET		3.50	
FISH (PLAIN)		3.55	6.75
OYSTER (PLAIN)	2.00	3.55	6.75
SHRIMP	2.75	5.25	8.50
STUFF CRAB	2.00	3.50	5.75
BAR·B·QUE (WITH SAUCE ONLY)		3.50	

❖ MOST POPULAR ❖
ALL PRICES PLUS 6% SALES TAX

SHRIMP COCKTAIL WITH CRACKERS	4.00
1/4 FRIED CHICKEN FR. FRIES LET. TOM. SALAD	3.50
1/2 FRIED CHICKEN FR. FRIES LET. TOM. SALAD	5.75
2 STUFF CRABS W/LET. TOM. SALAD Fr·Fries	4.50
FRIED TROUT LET. TOM. SALAD Fr·Fries	4.50
STUFF JUMBO SHRIMP FR. FRIES LET. TOM. SALAD	5.75

❖ SPECIALS ❖
SERVED WITH LET. & TOM. SALAD AND A CHOICE OF VEGETABLE FROM BELOW

❖ SPECIALTIES ❖

BREADED VEAL CUTLET (CREOLE SAUCE)	4.75
ROAST BEEF (BROWN GRAVY)	4.75
CREOLE HOT SAUSAGE	4.75
BREADED CHICKEN LIVERS	3.00
BARBECUE RIBS	4.75

❖ CHEF'S SPECIALS ❖

HAMBURGER STEAKS (SAUTED ONIONS)	4.75
2 GRILLED PORK CHOPS	4.75
HAM & CHEESE CLUB	4.00

❖ SALADS ❖
SUBSTITUTED FOR LET. & TOM.

POTATO
ITALIAN
CHEF
PINEAPPLE
LETTUCE & TOMATO SALAD

❖ STEAKS ❖
SERVED W/BORDELAISE SAUCE LET. TOM. SAL. AND VEG. FR. BELOW

BEEF SIRLOIN (8 OUNCE)	6.00
BEEF STRIP (8 OUNCE)	
BEEF T-BONE (14 OUNCE)	10.00
FILET MIGNON (8 OUNCE)	7.50
CHOICE STRIP (12 OUNCE)	10.00
CLEMENCEAU SAUCE	3.00

❖ SEAFOOD SPECIALS ❖

Dooky's SEAFOOD PLATTER (TARTAR SAUCE)	7.50
STUFFED "Broil" LOBSTER (DRAWN BUTTER)	7.50
SHRIMP CREOLE	5.75
JUMBO SOFT SHELL CRAB (TARTAR SAUCE)	
FRIED LAKE SHRIMP (COCKTAIL SAUCE)	
1/2 DOZ FRIED OYSTERS DOZ FRIED OYSTERS	

❖ VEGETABLES ❖

FR. FRIED ONIONS   FR. FRIES
STUFF BAKED POTATO   CREAM POTATOS
STEAMED RICE   CANDY YAMS

ASK ABOUT OUR FRESH GREEN VEGETABLE OF THE DAY

Come to Dinner

by Leah Chase

When I first started cooking in here at Dooky Chase Restaurant in 19—what— 45, 46, the things that I put on my menu, like jambalaya, like oyster dressing, mirliton, I didn't see that in any of the restaurants I worked in before. In the white restaurants they didn't have that. They had steak or they had lobster or they had things like that. They didn't have gumbo back in those days in those big restaurants. So that lead you to believe that white people ate one thing, and black people ate another. They had other things than some of those chefs would be making. And they knew how to do different things, but naturally you have to do what your customer wants, you know. If your customer is not coming out eating gumbo, you're certainly not going to put it on your menu, 'cause it won't sell. But then I know I worked in this restaurant, and I did not see gumbo at all.

A man used to fly in here from Boston just to eat. I still have that. And another, he would eat his dinner and just get out of here. Then I had a man who used to come in from Chicago. Call me up on the phone, "I'm coming. Have this ready. Have my gumbo ready. Have this ready." He'd put it in that cooler and get back on that plane and get out of here with it. Had some people in Chicago, too, and New York and all, they would say, "Put me an oyster loaf on the plane, and I'm going to meet the plane." And they would do that. That's wanting what you want to eat. That's wanting what you want to eat.

I'll never forget my daughters. Before they went to college, they went to visit their cousin in Washington, and the big thing is, "Oh, gosh! Just give me some fried oysters! Just please, give me some fried oysters!"

Food is everything to me. A good meal can soften you up. Sitting down, a good meal can really make you think different. In some ways I think in this restaurant that we really changed the course of America, because the civil rights workers planned things in this restaurant. They came, and they ate. Always had gumbo. Always had gumbo. They ate, and then they would say what they were going to do, and then they would go out and do it. Some would go to jail. Some would do this. Then when they got out, they would come back here and eat again. So, when I went to Paris the first thing a man asked me is: "If you had to talk to Mr. Bush and Mr. Chirac," Chirac was then the president over there, "what would you tell them?" I said, "Well, I tell you, in New Orleans, we did everything over a bowl of gumbo. Cook that gumbo, sit down and discuss what you're gonna do, then eat it. And then you go out." I said, "I would invite Mr. Bush and Mr. Chirac to have a bowl of gumbo. They could bring Mr. Saddam along. We would straighten the whole world out over a bowl of gumbo." And as simple as that sounds, sometimes you can do that. Sometimes you *could* do that. If you talked over things. Come to dinner. Sit down to a good meal. And then we'll talk. Sit down. We'll talk.

And I guess most people in New Orleans are real what we call "foodies." They like food. *They like food.* And as many restaurants you have here, you can go in almost any home in New Orleans, white, black, blue, rich, poor, you're going to find somebody in there who can cook you something good. And that makes our city pretty unique. We really don't eat to live in New Orleans. We really live to eat. And I see nothing wrong with that.

Yat

by Christian Champagne

New Orleans has a way of expressing itself through culture that is distinctly different from what, since Katrina, I like to call "the actual United States." So, it is only natural that we have our own version of the English language. For lack of a better word, we call it "Yat." This is derived from the local greeting of "Where y'at?" which is a substitute for "How's it going?" or "How ya doing?"

When I was growing up in New Orleans, almost everyone seemed to use this salutation. Not so much anymore.

Although it seems hard for the actual United States to believe, the New Orleans accent is best described as very much like the New York accent. As an example, the classic mimic of the Boston accent "Pahk yah cah in Hahvahd yahd" in Yat would be "Pawk ya caw in Hawavad Yawd."

Whenever I try to explain this to someone from New York, they resist mightily. The truth is often hard to believe in New Orleans. In fact, I have a friend who, after a lifetime of writing successfully about our local culture, was turned down by a New York publisher because her New Orleans dialects were too close to New York accents, and the publisher thought that the greater world was not ready to believe.

One of the constant irritations we have to put up with in New Orleans is the fact that every time the Hollywood gang comes to town to do a film or TV series, they always manage to do violence to our accent. If it is not a languid Southern drawl with words moving through Jell-O-like air, it's an amazing mangling of Cajun French.

To make a point, I'd like to share the description that I give to a Hollywood producer in a comedy routine I do for locals on how to get the New Orleans accent right: "Ya see, it's kinda like dis: Yat is a lot like Klingon—Klingon as spoken by a baby that wuz raised by crackers in rural Alabama. But to get it jus' right, ya got to stuff French toast in ya mouth and then tawk just like a baby cracker raised in rural Alabama."

This description, as insane as it may seem, is just about as close as any movie has ever come to the correct New Orleans accent. "If ya get ma pernt."

There are several theories as to why our accent is closer to a city a thousand miles away than to the rest of the South. One is that a group of nuns from New York was imported to teach in the Catholic schools in New Orleans, and they brought the accent here. Another reason could be that the waves of Irish and Italian immigrants hit New Orleans and New York with the same impact and at the same time. This is a point I will not argue, because I don't know, and I think no one else does either.

Yat, of course, has its idiosyncratic expressions. To make groceries is to shop for groceries. To make dodo is to sleep. And Yat gives what one transplant to New Orleans explained to me was the perfect phrase for any occasion: Yeahyourite. You see, depending upon inflection, it could mean "I agree" or "I disagree but don't want to argue about it, so I'll just faux-agree." Yeahyourite.

So, that's Yat. Any number of hawts, chawmas, chiefs, caps, dawlins, and chookies will, no doubt, continue to argue the point. 'Cause, "Cuz, dat's de way it is."

I do have a theory that may be mine alone. I think that New York must have stolen our accent. Yeahyourite!

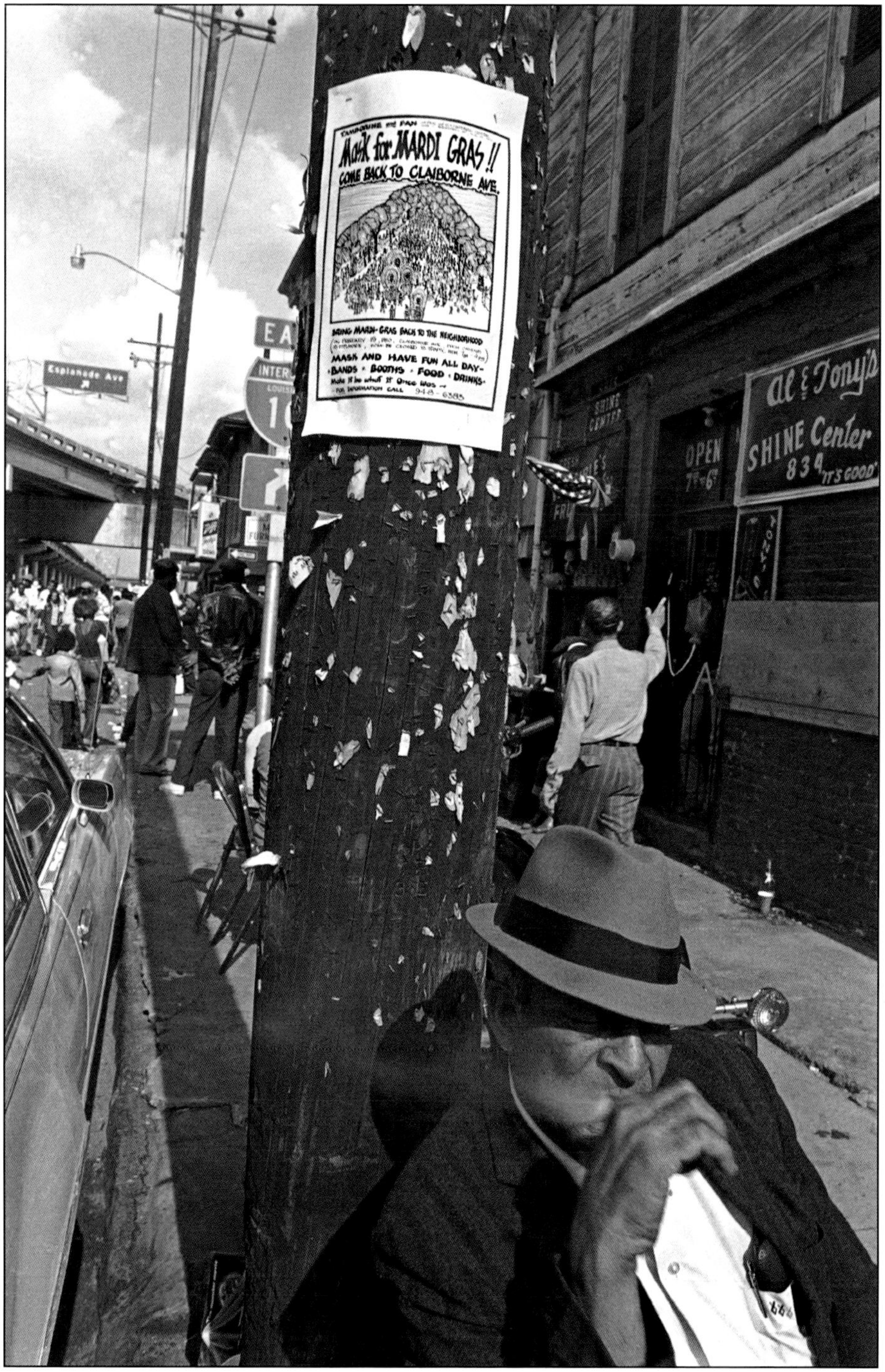
Mask for MARDI GRAS !!
COME BACK TO CLAIBORNE AVE.
BRING MARDI-GRAS BACK TO THE NEIGHBORHOOD
MASK AND HAVE FUN ALL DAY
BANDS · BOOTHS · FOOD · DRINKS
FOR INFORMATION CALL 948-6385
Esplanade Ave
Al & Tony's
SHINE Center
834 "IT'S GOOD"
OPEN

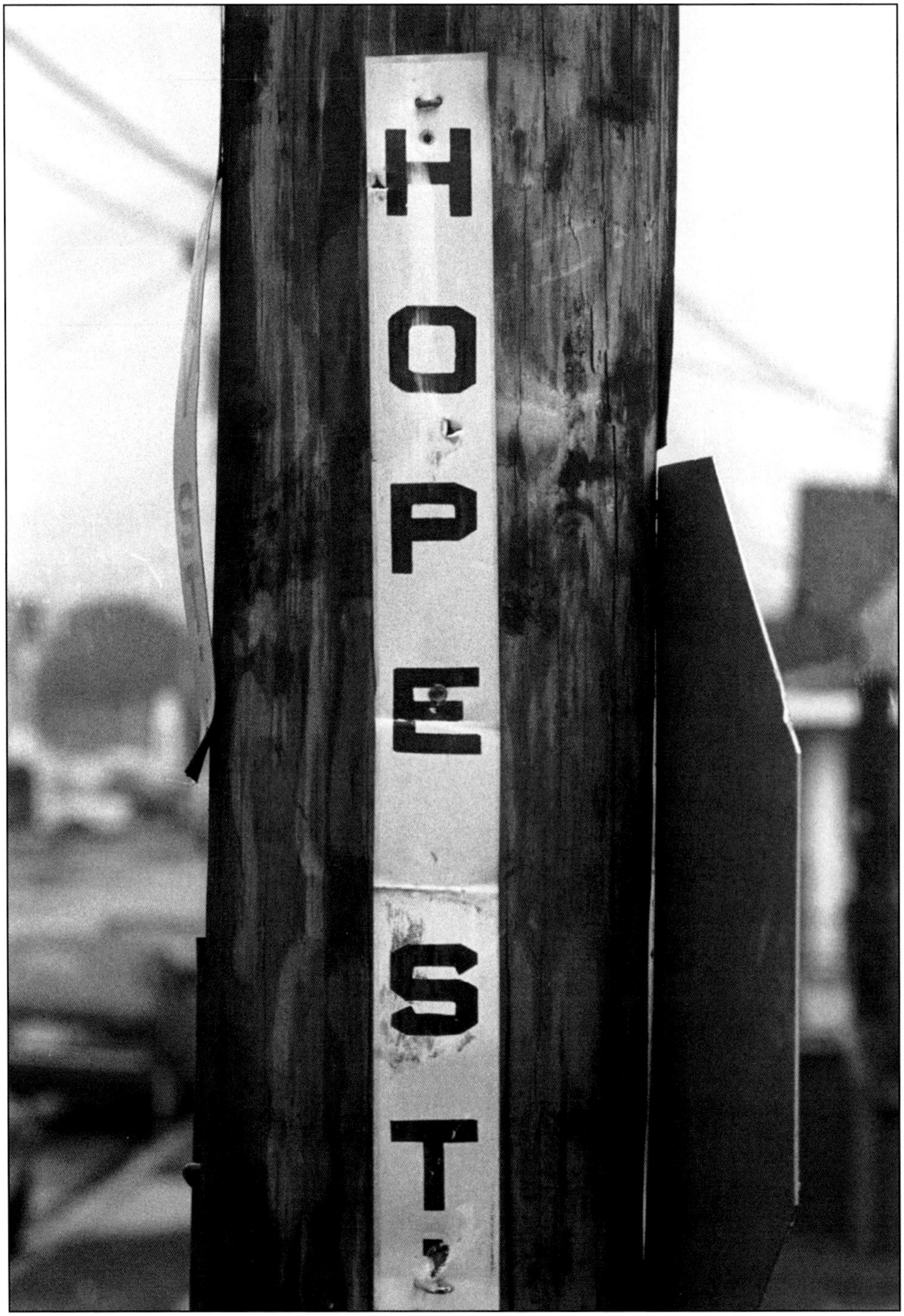
HOPE ST.

New Orleans Street Name Pronunciations

by Kami Patterson

Just as the streets curve and meander unexpectedly due to our unique geography, the singular history of New Orleans lends itself to some distinctive street names. Many seem French or Spanish at first glance but are pronounced with a peculiarly local twist. Uptown, there's Burthe Street, pronounced BYOOTH, and Cadiz Street is KAY-diz. Dufossat, unlike your French teacher would have you believe, is pronounced DOO-faucet. The street sharing a moniker with the Italian fashion mecca is pronounced MY-lan, not Milan.

The Garden District boasts streets named after the classical Greek muses—but as a local babe, Calliope is known as CALLY-ope, while her sister Euterpe becomes YOU-terp. In the Ninth Ward, Mazant Street is MAY-zant, and you may even hear the characteristic local accent that turns Royal Street into RERL, Poydras into PER-dras. Across the river in Algiers, Socrates Street is—you guessed it—SO-crates.

Then there is the French Quarter. It's guaranteed to confound when a street sign that looks like BUR-gundy is pronounced Bur-GUN-dy, and one bearing the name of a French cathedral is pronounced Chart-ers instead of Shart. A visitor mystified the bus driver by asking how to get to DEK-a-tur Street, until a helpful local offered: "It's Da-KAY-tur, baby." And it's more proper to prom-e-nade up Es-pla-NADE than promen-ahd up Esplan-ahd.

I live on a street with the mother of unpronounceable, un-spellable names—Tchoupitoulas. Here's a hint: ignore the initial T and the extra vowels and just let it roll off your tongue as Chop-i-TOO-las. Running from downtown at Canal Street along the curvaceous bottom of the Crescent City to Audubon Park, Tchoupitoulas, like many other New Orleans street names, is a kind of local shibboleth—if you can pronounce it AND spell it, you must be from around here, or at least in the know.

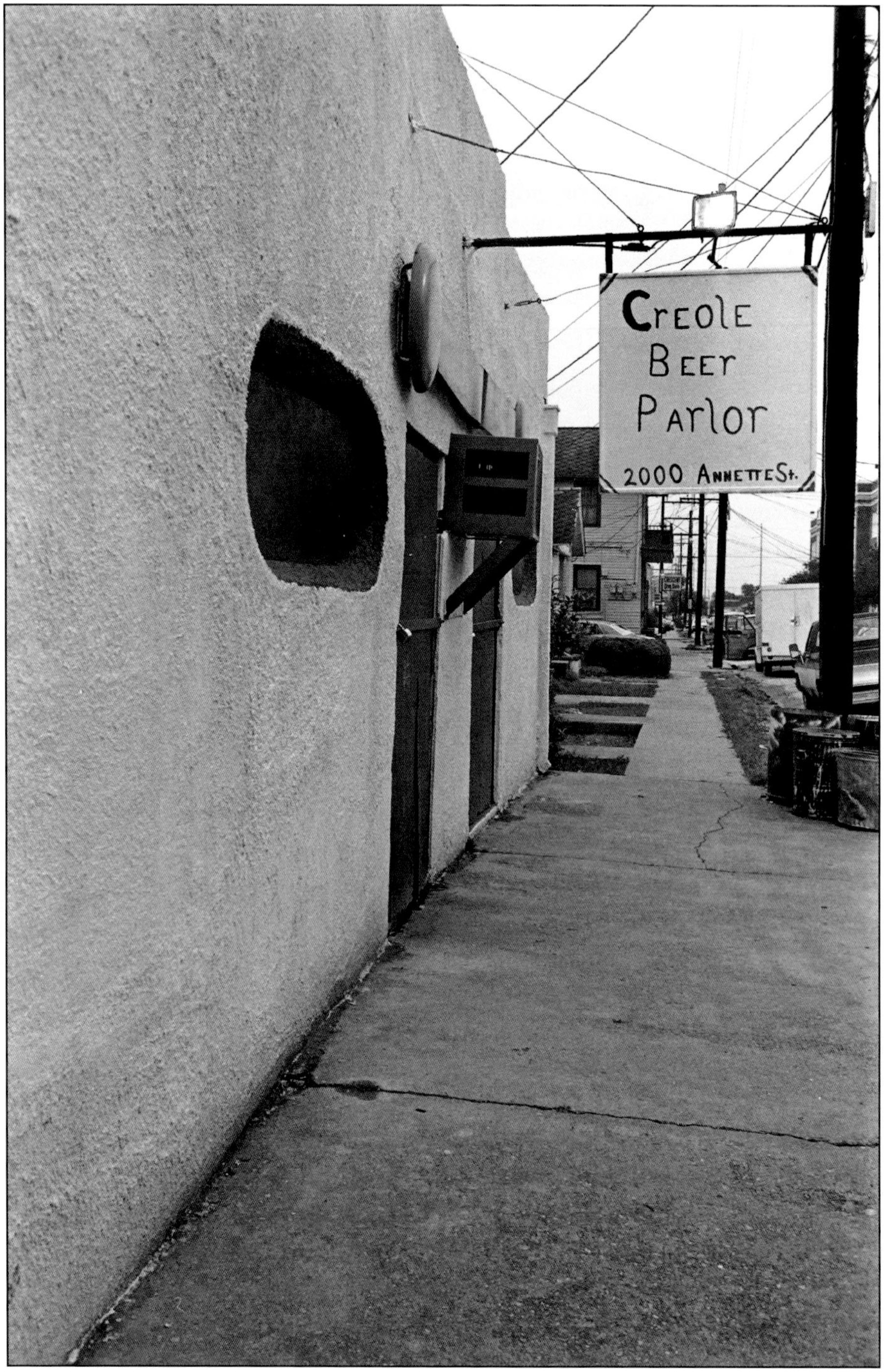
Creole
Beer
Parlor
2000 Annette St.

The River and the Lake

by Missy Wilkinson

Each fall, hordes of college freshman, mostly from northeastern states like Connecticut and New Jersey, descend onto Tulane's campus. They're completely unprepared for New Orleans' heat, its grifters, its weird little idiosyncrasies, its well, *New Orleans-ness*. One year, a program was devised to serve as a kind of cultural ambassadorship. A lecturer stood in Dixon Hall before several hundred freshmen. He would give them a test, he said, to demonstrate the difference between their mindsets and the New Orleans' mindset.

"Okay," he challenged them. "Point in the direction of the river."

A brief pause. Then, hundreds of index fingers pointing hundreds of different directions.

His point was this: if you're from New Orleans, the Mississippi is not only a fact of life, it's how you orient yourself. Every single New Orleanian knows where he is in the city with relation to the river, all the time. Uptown and downtown get their names because they're located upriver and downriver, respectively. And if you get lost, don't expect anybody to tell you which way is north or south. Lakeside or riverside is all you're likely to get, as in,

"So, you're driving down Carrollton—"

"Which direction?"

"Towards the lake."

These two massive bodies of water left their footprints on our psyche. They shaped us, figuratively and literally, as the city grew up nestled in a crook of the river's arm. Yet we always knew the risk. We knew it when we looked *up* at tugboats that sailed above our heads because the city was lower than the river. Everyone understood what could happen if "The Big One" hit. Nobody believed it actually would.

So we bought another round. And the water in our drinks, the water that poured freely from every tap and quenched the city's collective thirst, that came eventually to flow through our very veins: this was from the Mississippi River, too.

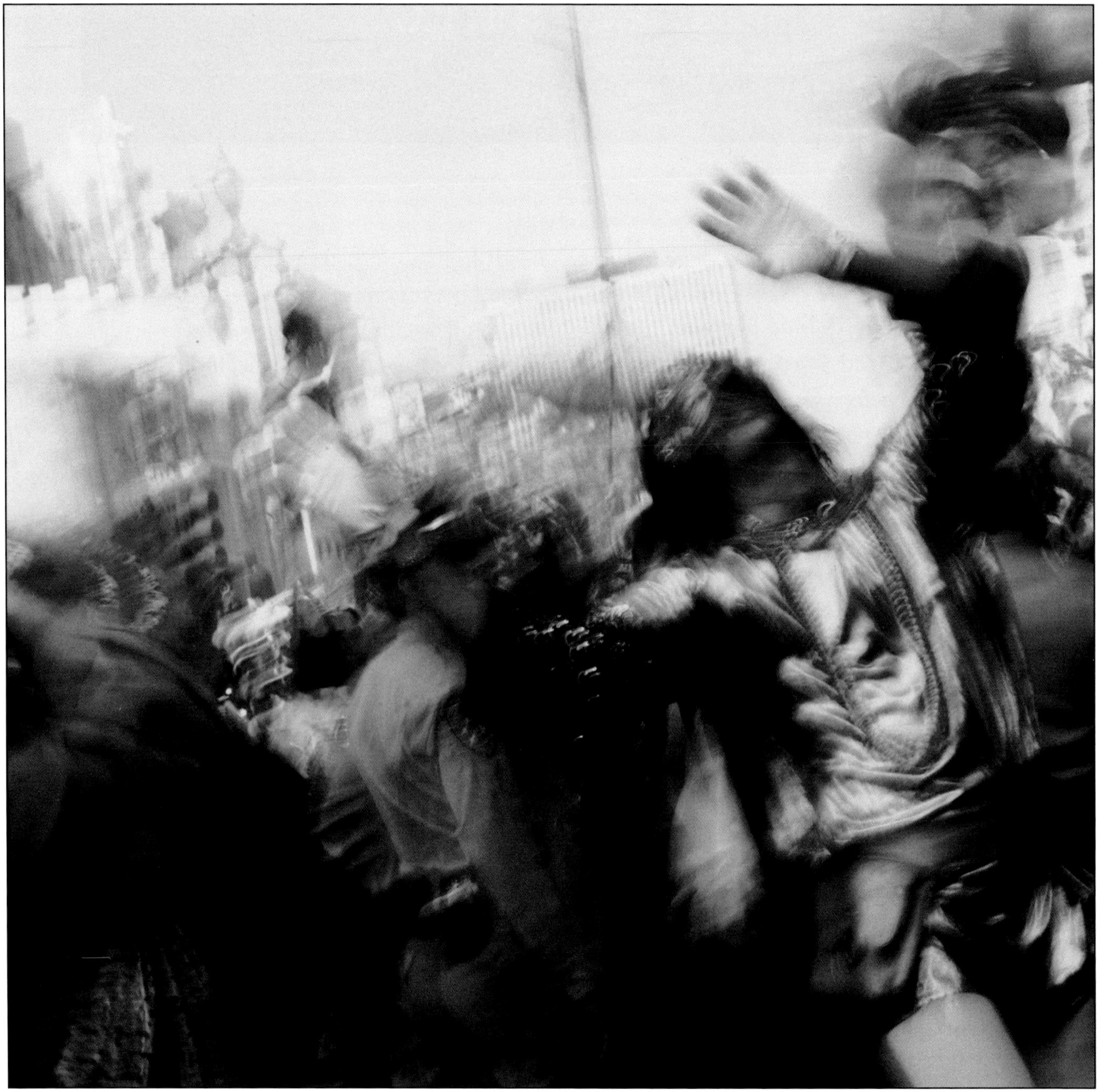

Olive Oil and Alligator Pears

by James Nolan

Olive oil was part of our Sunday ritual. After the adults drank their demitasses of coffee and chicory, dinner dishes were cleared with a clatter from the dining room table and shutters closed against the oppressive afternoon sun. Mémère would heat a saucepan of olive oil and, returning to the dining room, massage the warm, pungent oil into my scalp. Then her sister, Marguerite, would pomade my grandmother's hair, and so on around the table. There was really not much else to do, after vanilla ice cream and *crème de menthe* on an endless Sunday afternoon in my childhood New Orleans. And as in many French Creole families, this is how we passed the time, chattering all the while like parakeets.

Another ritual was, after the beach, when we children were splashed with vinegar to soothe a stinging sunburn, then rubbed all over with olive oil until we smelled like little salads. Swimmer's earache was cured by warm olive oil poured into the ear. And a famous beauty treatment not wasted on the young was smoothing the skin with olive oil to prevent wrinkles. It is not surprising that Creole women were famous for their long, beautiful tresses and lustrous skin. The men almost never went bald and, they say, were always youthful and dashing.

You must understand that these rituals took place on land reclaimed from a snake-infested swamp. The Mediterranean cult of the olive was transplanted to the New World, often to inhospitable planets where not a single olive tree has ever bloomed. Spanish and French colonists, and later Italian immigrants, created among Louisiana bayous a subtropical variation on a Mediterranean culture-in-exile. Along with the Virgin Mary, Carnival, and corrupt politics, came the first barrels of olive oil.

Louisiana was too chilly to cultivate the Caribbean coconut for its oil, and too humid for the Southern peanut, so olive oil remained one of the few imported staples. Too far north to be real Caribbeans, and too far south to identify completely as Southerners, to this day, in our hearts, we feel like misplaced Mediterraneans. We announce this with flowering courtyards, three weeks of Mardi Gras, and an ongoing obsession with food.

Whatever was imported we put to original uses, needless to say. Take that American fruit we call the "alligator pear" for its dark green bumpy skin, a variety of avocado. We slice it in two, remove the slippery seed, then fill each side of the indented moon with a small pool of olive oil, on which we float a spot of wine vinegar. Then flesh and oil are mashed together with a spoon, and we eat it like green ice cream from its alligator skin.

While well-fed French colonists introduced olive oil as a beauty treatment, health remedy, and condiment, hungry Sicilian immigrants made it a central ingredient in Louisiana cooking. With them, the Sicilians brought those ubiquitous flowered cans of olive oil with the lithe art-nouveau maidens on them. Growing up, I fell in love with the girls on the olive oil cans that lined the towering wooden shelves of corner groceries, smelling of Parmesan cheese and dried cod.

The tomato, eggplant, artichoke, and stuffed dishes of Creole cuisine are drenched in olive oil and are of Sicilian origin. "Those Italians even fry their eggs in olive oil," Mémère once told me with some distaste, as she plunked another tablespoon of butter into her roux. But thanks to Sicilian grocers and chefs, the use of olive oil has become one of the distinguishing factors between Creole and Southern—or "soul"—food, cooked in fatback or bacon grease.

Despite this Mediterranean influence, wine never entered Catholic Louisiana with the popular impact of olive oil. Irish and German immigrants introduced beer, better suited for the heat, and Southerners their beloved bourbon whiskey. So it was olive oil, not the grape, that became a symbol of Mediterranean Louisiana, a fierce region of alligators and cypress swamps far from the sun-dappled olive groves of Tuscany, Catalonia, and Provence.

Our Corner Store

by Amanda Boyden

We've screwed the remnant menu-board into the wood of our kitchen wall: HO CHEESE, LUNCHN MEAT, SALAM, WE TAKE FOOD STAMP. The board is missing letters like teeth, but it's still intact. In our new-for-us but quite old house, we feel the sign belongs to the building.

We own what used to be a Cuban corner grocery store in Mid-City turned into a home, a skip away from Bayou St. John. It's our imperfect, beautiful place. Sizing up the walls, vertical isn't exactly that, horizontal even further away. But the front room, open to the second-floor rafters, makes the best library around. And our mixed-bag neighbors seem happy we're here.

As a kid, I came up in Chicago. I snuck to a corner store with my weekly allowance to buy taffy that pulled at my fillings. My parents never knew I made the trip or crossed four lanes of traffic without their permission, but the place equaled sugar and childhood consumer freedom. How many kids have purchased and pilfered candy from a place on the corner? Later, so many of us had more important items to grab. Condoms. Pregnancy tests. Formula.

When I first moved to New Orleans—my hometown now for longer than any other earthly place—I lived in an Uptown rental. If you somehow had a reason to go to my Prytania corner store with your eyes closed, you'd smell it before you walked in the door: old grease, cleanser, frying shrimp. I smoked still, then. As a graduate student, I went to the corner store for generic cigarettes and po-boys. Bags of rice and pens and gum and old onions sprouting green tops. The corner store delineated my new Southern parameters in a way nothing else could. I didn't yet understand I should always say hello to strangers on the street. I didn't understand the pace of New Orleans or how to accept the lines at the bank, the post office, the red light, the corner-store deli counter. But I know now.

Years later, my husband and I lived kitty-corner to a, well, corner store on Magazine

Street. We were the only residency left on the block amid art galleries and clothing shops, and the corner store was almost as much of an anomaly, a run-down place carving out a business from six-packs and sandwiches on day-old bread. The owner, a woman no bigger than my ten-year-old niece, shouted at the clustered neighborhood kids in Vietnamese. We bought cold 40s sometimes, the occasional pack of toilet paper. The owner eventually recognized us as neighbors. She smiled and never charged us tax. After a month away one summer, we returned to hear that she had been murdered, shot in the back by a repeat customer. Her family couldn't bear keeping the store, and so it closed. With it went a piece of our community, a place that was at once the bearer of all things necessary and completely extraneous. Nothing, and everything, essential.

Competing with Walmart and Rite Aid can't be easy. There's a reason owners like us now live in buildings that used to serve a neighborhood. Aspirin, sugar, hamburger buns. We need them, but, of course, we don't. In the past, we might have met up with the people across the street more, said hello and found out what they were having for dinner, but the necessity for community corner stores has long since gone.

Still, I have the sixth-sense feeling that someday our home will revert back to what it was intended to be, a place that feeds the neighborhood, but with a menu-board that isn't so full of holes. Maybe, I like to think, something that will better reflect what calluses we've accumulated as a city amidst storms and murders, partial recovery, and reinvention: GOOD EATS, FOOD STAMPS WELCOME, and PLEASE TALK AND LINGER. THIS IS YOUR PLACE.

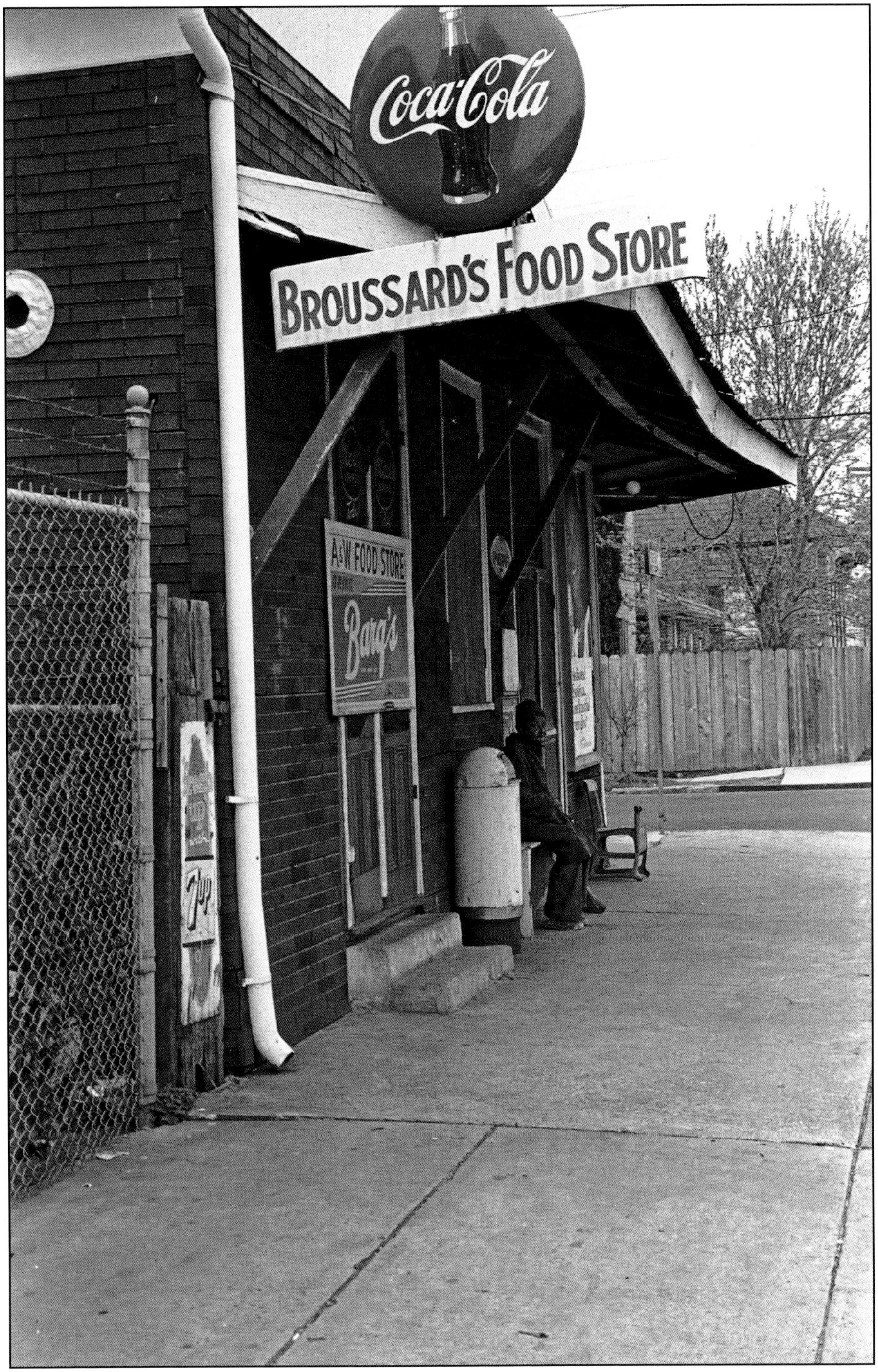
Coca-Cola
BROUSSARD'S FOOD STORE
A&W FOOD STORE
Barq's
7up

New Orleans Music

by Anders Osborne

New Orleans music has no fear; it has no rules to keep it small and no boundaries to hold it down. New Orleans music is not a scale or a beat that can be taught in a class or learned from a book. It is not a myth or an era. It is as alive and well today as it ever was.

The music of New Orleans . . . is as rich as the smoke of fifteen kitchens cooking at the same time on one block; it is as deep as ten thousand years of culture merging on one square; it is as joyous as the birth of a child and can be as mournful as life without any hope or faith.

New Orleans music is an attitude that carries Monday through Sunday. It's a conversation amongst friends; sometimes it's how arguments are resolved. It's a way of talking; it's a way of walking; it speeds up and it slows down; it stretches out and it bends around. It's proud and respecting, always warm and accepting. It's full of love that brings you to the heavens above. It blows up like nothing else, but it is always the fiber that holds the city together . . .

Oh, yes! . . . The music of New Orleans is as unashamed as the little kids walking home from school around Mardi Gras never hiding, but always raising their old "hand me down" or borrowed horn way up to the sky, filling every neighborhood with that familiar stumblin' serenade to being alive.

If you are a native or a visitor, a complete stranger or a dear old friend, an experienced musician playing your instrument, or an untrained listener trying to figure out these magical sounds, if you are black, white, rich or poor or anywhere in between, there is no escaping, when you are in New Orleans, YOU ARE New Orleans music.

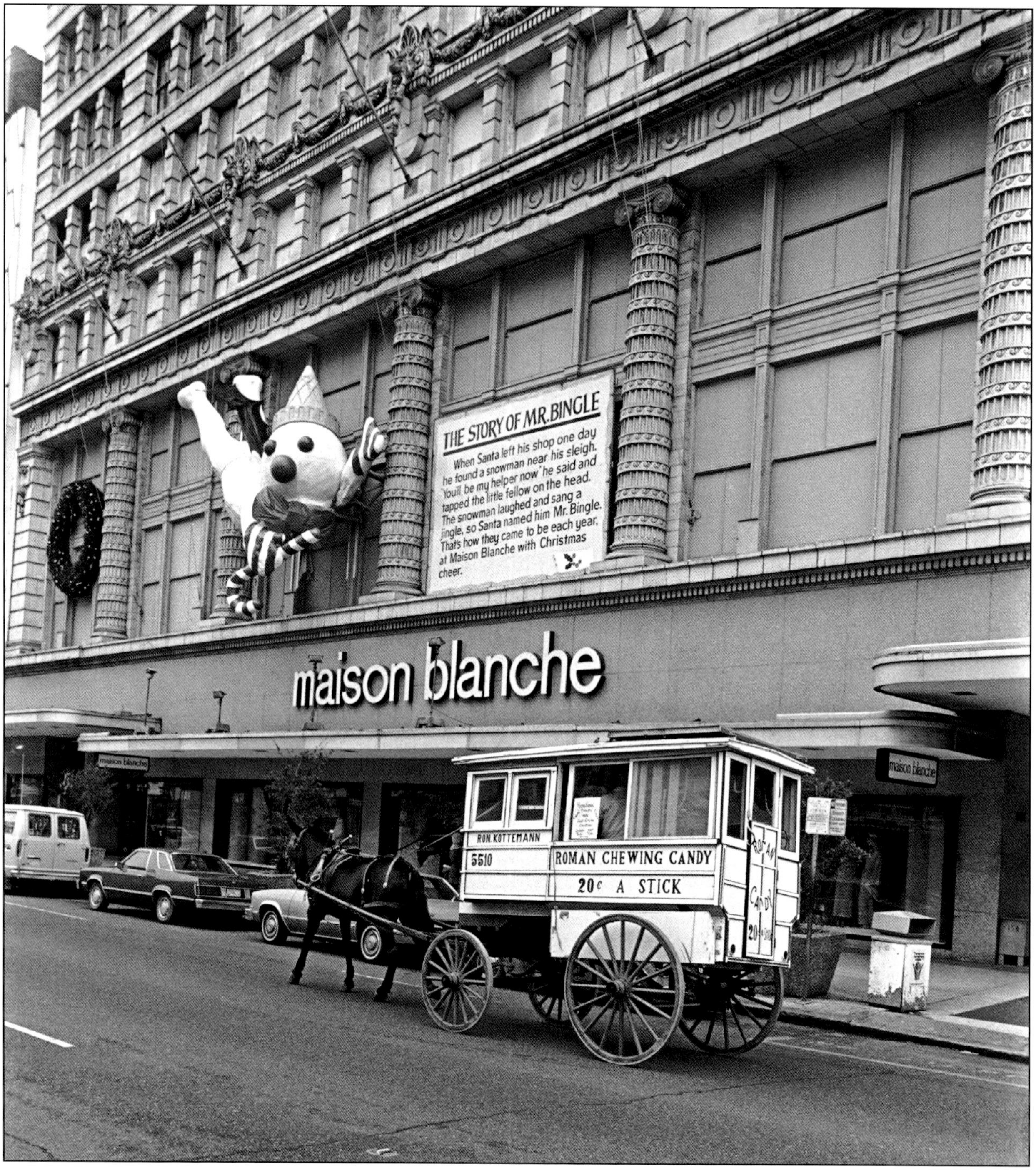
THE STORY OF MR.BINGLE
When Santa left his shop one day
he found a snowman near his sleigh.
'You'll be my helper now' he said and
tapped the little fellow on the head.
The snowman laughed and sang a
jingle, so Santa named him Mr. Bingle.
That's how they came to be each year,
at Maison Blanche with Christmas
cheer.
maison blanche
maison blanche
maison blanche
RON. KOTTEMANN
5510
ROMAN CHEWING CANDY
20¢ A STICK

Lost Names

by Errol Laborde

Because New Orleans is a city with such a distinctive past we need to revisit that past occasionally. Here, in ascending order, are six especially missed (by me) business names. (Note please: Contemporary New Orleanians often tend to associate most everything as being linked to Hurricane Katrina, yet none of these losses can be linked to the disaster. There was, we must remind ourselves, life, and decline, even before the storm.)

1. Krauss. Its name was straightforward and not flowery, and that captured the spirit of the last of the locally owned department stores. Krauss was not grandly decorated, but it was a good place to find notions, drapes, fabrics, and even ball wear. The Krauss building at Canal and Basin Streets has since been converted to condos, but the name was not kept. What a loss. I would have been proud to say that I was going home to Krauss.

2. D. H. Holmes. Meeting "under the Holmes clock" was part of the ritual of the downtown shopping experience. The Holmes name was also a blessing for ad-copy writers who put forth inevitable slogans such as "there's no place like Holmes for the holidays." In New Orleans, Holmes was where the heart was. The clock at least is still ticking. The former Holmes Building on Canal Street is now a hotel, and the clock is now in its bar. Meeting under the clock might now mean buying a drink. A Sazerac please.

3. Maison Blanche. Holmes and Maison Blanche were the city's retail twins. Downtown customers would move easily across the side street from one to the other. Once the suburban malls came, they were identified by whether they housed a Holmes or an "MB." The Maison Blanche name had a tad more local flavor because of its Frenchness and because of its resident elfin Christmas snowman, Mr. Bingle, who shared his initials with the store. Bingle is working the burbs now where he has become a symbol for Dillard's Department Stores. Maybe he should now be called "Dingle."

4. Hibernia Bank. This is the one name that lasted past Hurricane Katrina, though it was already endangered. The bank that had the most outlets throughout the state was at its most important during its last days before being merged under the Capitol One name. Displaced New Orleanians stood in line at far-flung Hibernia branches hoping to withdraw money to finance their evacuation. The familiar green Hibernia logo was an appreciated symbol of home. The tower atop the downtown New Orleans building that was once Hibernia's headquarters still glows with different colors to reflect the seasons. No matter what the official name may be, the "Hibernia Tower" is still guiding New Orleanians.

5. Schwegmann's. If any locally owned retail outlet seemed like it would be the conqueror rather than the conquered, this was it. In its prime, Schwegmann's ruled, not just through its stores built across South Louisiana, but also through some of its family members who ruled politically. The Schwegmanns built a political base from their stores having a reputation for low prices. That was parlayed into their being thought of as consumer advocates. A Schwegmann endorsement printed on a shopping bag could be political gold. In its pricing and its politics, the Schwegmann's name had a populist appeal.

6. Katz & Besthoff. Gone forever is the familiarity of a local name that had been whittled down in the native lingo to simply KB. The drugstore chain's oval purple sign became part of the urban streetscape. There was a time when New Orleanians routinely shopped at the two Bs—MB and KB. But, as Shakespeare might have wondered, why have we gone from two Bs to not two Bs? That is the question.

Another question is: what will survive? Blessed are some old names including Whitney Bank, Rubenstein's, Hubig's, Adler's, CDM, and Antoine's that still exist. New Orleans remains a city in which much of its future remains in its past.

Dominican Nuevaorleanos

by Lucas Díaz-Medina

In the spring of 1977, a Dominican man named Tomás Díaz, my father, immigrated to Louisiana. Something about the climate, the people, and the food felt familiar to him, so he set up a home for his family on the West Bank of the Mississippi, a rifle shot away from Uptown New Orleans. We joined our father shortly after, never to return to either the Dominican Republic or Puerto Rico until long after we'd already become local New Orleanians. His arrival was the start of what resulted in a modest wave of Dominicans making their way to the New Orleans area.

We moved into a mixed neighborhood in Gretna, and my mother's brothers, sisters, and mother joined us. They bought homes within the same neighborhood, and my father's friends bought homes close enough to drive over for Sunday domino games. Until my father's death in 1985, our home became the central stop for a large number of Dominican men, who eventually brought their families, as well. These men imported their natural habits from their homeland, which played out in our driveway almost every Friday evening and Sunday afternoon. The quiet little street on which we lived would periodically wake up with the sounds of Merengue, Son, and Boleros blasting out of my father's stereo system (speakers on the windowsill pointing out). Our Cajun neighbors never seemed to mind, and over time they even walked over and joined us, drinking rum and coke and Presidente beers with us.

The children of these immigrant adults, such as myself, took in these last vestiges of the country we came from while at the same time steadily joining the new world in which we lived. Over time, the edges of our Dominican identity slowly dulled. The men stopped coming over to play Brisca. The women stopped roasting entire pigs for parties and Christmas. Sunday domino games were replaced by NFL games. We accepted turkey for Thanksgiving and opted for frozen chicken from the large supermarket down the road over freshly butchered chicken from the chicken market in Mid-City.

Despite these changes over time, we have remained Dominicans at our core. Most of us have become U.S. citizens. The majority of us hailed from low-income rural lives, and we brought with us a keen sense of family and duty that is still alive in our first- and second-generation U.S. born today. We are part of the Dominican Diaspora, which saw over one million Dominicans leave the economic hardship of our country for better opportunities in the U.S. Those one million Dominicans headed straight to New York City, but a small number found a home in the New Orleans area and stayed here. True to our nature as vivacious, outgoing people, we have embraced New Orleans life. We have married across racial and ethnic lines, brought a never-ending menu of Merengue and Bachata parties, and added a Caribbean perspective to our personal circles of influence among our friends and neighbors.

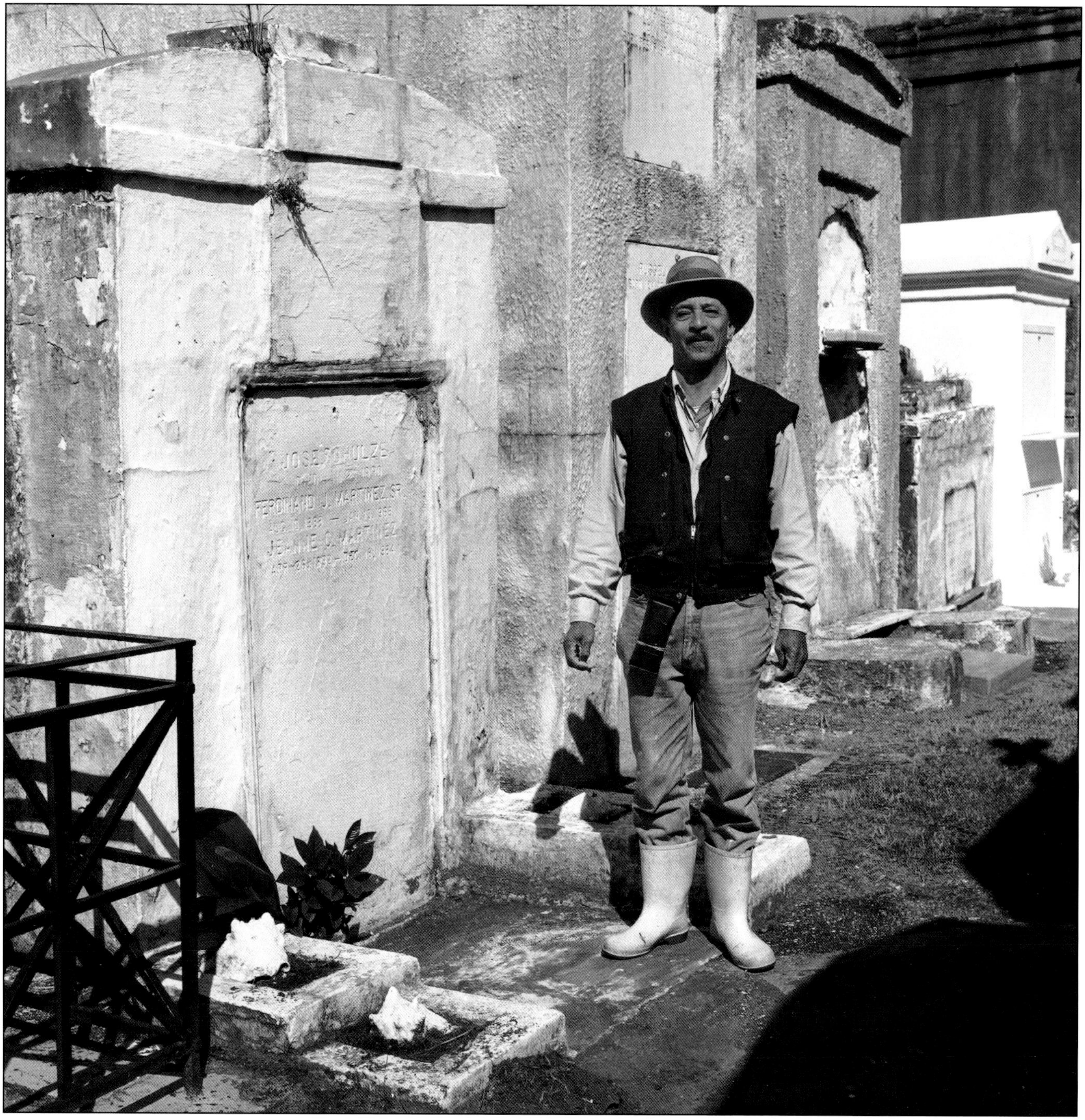
JOSE SCHULZE
FERDINAND J. MARTINEZ SR.
JEANNE C. MARTINEZ

What Matters Most

by Valentine Pierce

Under the rise over the Harvey Canal, newly installed lights remind me of fountain lights from summers at the lakefront. Memories flood my mind of days when I was still young enough to wear lace ankle socks and sandals, frolic in the grass and be awed by rainbow-colored shoots of water. Days when Westwego was so far away I hardly believed it existed. It had to be a fairy tale, right?

Today Westwego is next door. What seems a fairy tale are Sunday drives and warm holidays on the lakefront. Did we really brave the scorching July sun and September's con-stricting humidity? Didn't mosquitoes own the night then like they do now? Was May as sweet and temperate as my recollection, or is it only the fondness of childhood memories that obliterates its flooding rains?

None of that matters, really. What matters are eight children frolicking in the grass on the lakefront, pork-chop bones used to lure crabs into nets, and my mother's talent for stocking a picnic basket, stuffing an ice chest, and packing the trunk of whatever beat-up old car we may have had.

I'm grateful for those cars that took us from the confining bricks of the projects to the other side of Lake Pontchartrain on unhurried Sunday afternoons. And to the wide-open spaces of the lakefront on warm holidays where we could run, roll in the grass, eat—endlessly. No stepping over dice or card games to get in our front door. No need to mop and disinfect the outside hallways and porches so we could sit on the steps and eat watermelon. Those cars worked well enough for Mom to trust staying out late enough to see the fountain and its rainbow of lights illuminate the night, turning the lakefront into a wonderland.

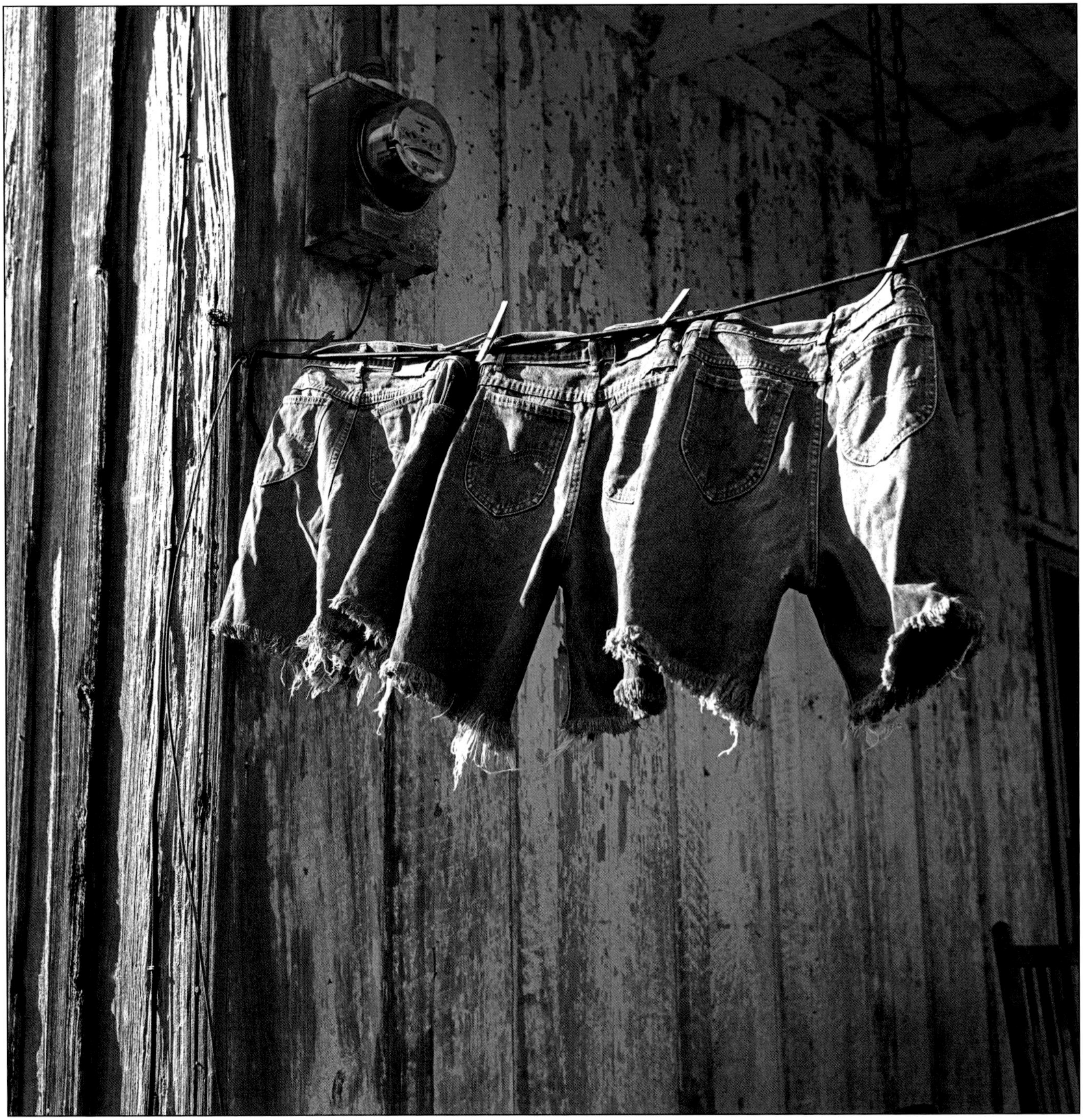

On the Batture

by Lee Meitzen Grue

Uptown, at the end of Oak Street, is a flood wall. There, if you take a sharp left turn onto a shell road which runs up and along the levee, you'll find yourself in the country. On the batture, the land between the levee and the river, are twelve houses built on high pilings; some were built there before World War II. When we came, some thirty years ago, the house we bought was simple, but the vista was superb. The back deck of the house looked to the sandy riverbank with leaning willow trees and pin oaks, and to the river, where huge ships pass with a throb that enters your body like a heartbeat.

The front yards have roses and impatiens; the people who tend them are good solid working folk. Some ten years ago, my son, a tugboat captain, renovated our original house and built his own. He lives there now with his wife and son and daughter. There are also artists, most who built or added on to existing houses. It's a close-knit community of friendly people who have crayfish boils in the front yard or dinners on the back deck. The home owners have built redoubts of concrete and rubble which strengthen the back of the levee. They're good land stewards who keep the big drifting logs pushed out into the river.

When the water is low batture children have huge yards to play in with cable slides, land boats, and tree houses, but in the spring the water rises until it is directly underneath the houses, most of which have long catwalks to the levee where joggers and cyclists take advantage of good weather. The houses built by home carpenters have been reinforced with strong beams and hurricane roofs. It's a peaceful place to live. The city seems far way on the batture, but under the levee, uptown New Orleans is right down Oak Street.

These houses have long been spared by hurricanes and tornados. The houses on their stilts belong to the people, but in the spring the land belongs to the river.

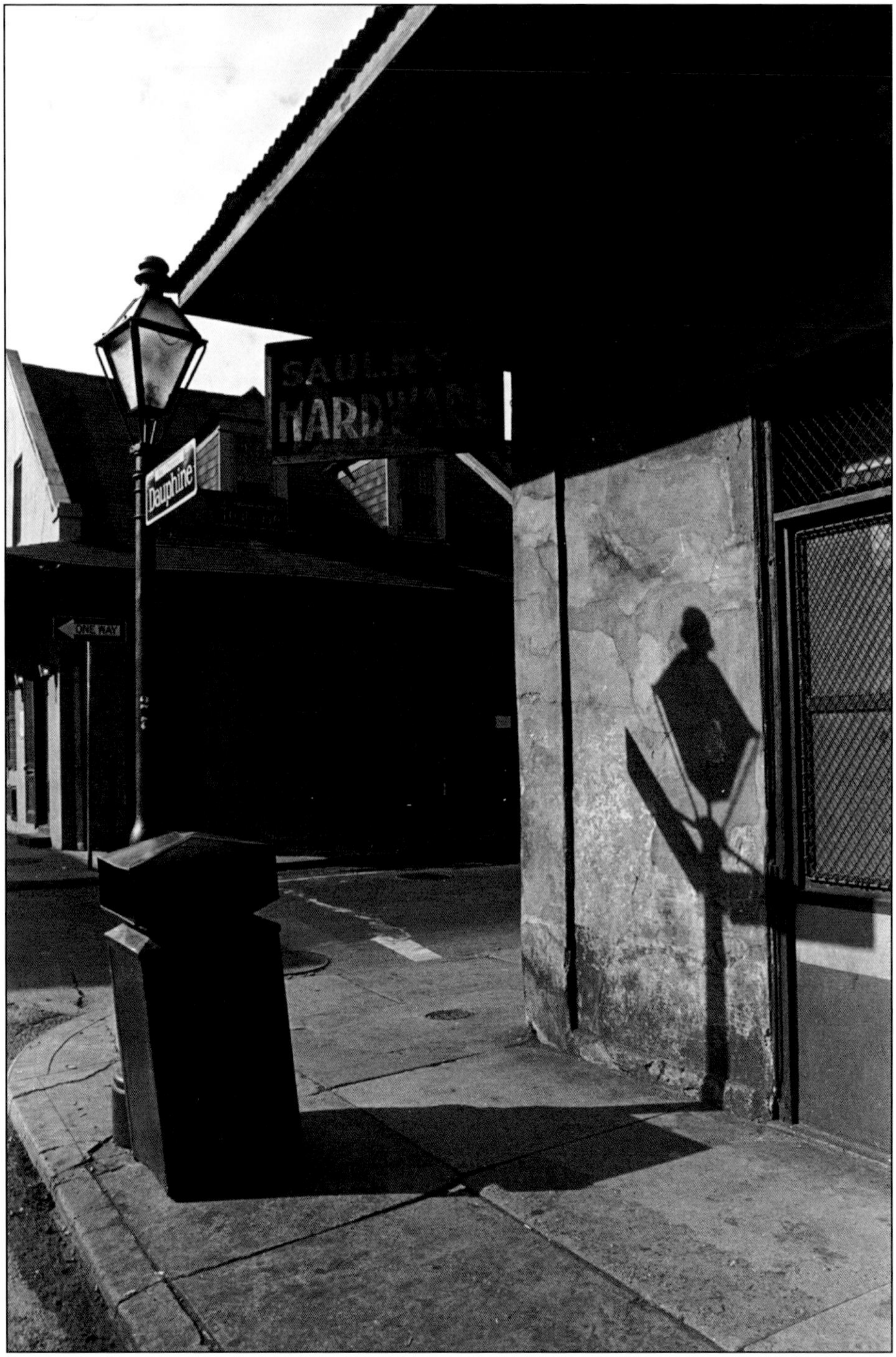
Dauphine
ONE WAY

Chi Chi and the Man

by Alex McMurray

There's a hardware store on St. Claude. You know the one—it's right by the light on Desire, across from the PNT grocery. They're never open past three. By "they," I mean the owner and his Chihuahua, Chi Chi. The owner is somewhere in his seventies, and the dog is probably about that in dog years. I've been working on a property for a friend around the corner on Congress for the past seven months or so and wasn't too surprised to see that he still wasn't open a year after the storm. I got to know the store when I was doing some work for the same friend at another property on Gallier Street. This was a few years ago and even then their inventory wasn't the most up-to-date. But they kept regular hours and usually had sandpaper and caulk and were right around the corner, so you'd always try there first before going all the way down to Elysian Fields.

The work over on Congress Street is over, really, but I go over there a few times a week to do little finishing jobs to make the place more attractive to potential renters. Last week I was hanging a new door on a closet and finishing it with trim. I bring no radio with me because I enjoy the peaceful feeling of the springtime afternoons and the light coming through the windows when I take the plywood off of them. After the chaos of the past months, I can stop and look at what's been accomplished here. Soon there will be people living here. But now and then I still need something from the hardware store.

The place on St. Claude is open now. Chi Chi lives on the counter and demands attention from the customers paying for their things. The dog makes people relax and chat a little. Several times I've overheard the old man tell his story to a customer. He's selling off the inventory and closing. He's not sure when, but soon. "I been at it fifty years at this store," he says. "I seen it all. I got a little property." He picks up the Chihuahua and hands the man his change. "We gonna go sit down for a while."

Remembering Plessy

by Shirley Elizabeth Thompson

Whenever I drive uptown on St. Charles towards Tulane and cross Rosa Park, I always think to myself: "Rosa *Park*? Shouldn't there be an 's'?" I imagine the street to be a tribute to the Montgomery, Alabama, seamstress who in 1955 would not be moved. Fitting, I think, that New Orleans should honor this woman of propriety and strength with a lane such as this. Grand oaks and flowering trees shade both sides, and elegant mansions anchor sprawling lots.

In reality, though, Rosa Park is just a street. In New Orleans, civil rights memories linger in an altogether different place—on the edge of Faubourg Marigny, in the weeds at the corner of Royal and Press. A block riverward on June 7, 1892, Homer Adolphe Plessy boarded an East Louisiana Railroad train bound for Covington forty miles away. The train lurched along Press Street to Royal where Plessy—a man of one-eighths African ancestry— was ejected from a whites-only car and placed under arrest.

This was a scene months in the making. Here was a genuine race drama—more pro- vocatively staged than any minstrel show! The year before, eighteen men of color had formed the *comité des citoyens* to test the constitutionality of Louisiana's 1890 Separate Car Act. With surnames Martinet, Desdunes, and Mary, they were heirs to French revolutionary cries of *liberté, égalité, and fraternité*. Heirs also to Haiti, they perhaps prized *liberté* above all. Segregation was a "badge of servitude" they would not abide. Anyway, segregation would never work in a place like New Orleans. Their forefathers had argued as much during the Civil War: here "there are nearly as many black whites with wooly hair as there are white people of color with silky hair!" Plessy was the perfect test case. Once aboard the train, the silky-haired Plessy cast aside his "thin disguise" of white skin to reveal the drop of black blood beneath. The *comité* had hired the arresting officer. Even the railroad had been privy to the plan.

I would like to have seen it. I imagine being there, though I could have been present only as a white child's nurse. The *comité* had worried about what people like me would think of their high-minded quest for public equality. My folks had been slaves, some of them owned by *gens de couleur libres* like them. I would remain inconspicuous, watching from my first-class berth, shifting the weight of the curly-headed baby from one arm to the other. But I would try to catch Plessy's eye with a silent *thank you.* Even so, Plessy would masquerade until his death in 1925. He was frequently "colored," sometimes "black," "white" to vote.

In May of 1896, the United States Supreme Court insisted, against the *comité's* efforts, that "separate" *could* be "equal," that the "legal distinction" between the races "must always exist." Nonetheless, we often pick up the *comité's* mantle. In the years before and since Katrina, a group of African-American students from nearby Frederick Douglass High School have labored to create Plessy Park at the now-overgrown intersection. They envision railroad tracks linking Plessy to Rosa Parks and others and a public stage for their own dramas of protest and liberation. Their simple but evocative design has hovered ghost-like in an atmosphere of red tape and cautious reconstruction.

The Culture of New Orleans Can Never Be Lost

by GiO

The definitive slice of New Orleans culture is the work of visionary, self-taught folk artist Robert "Dr. Bob" Shaffer. Most well known for his ubiquitous "Be Nice or Leave" signs, the idea was originally designed as a signature piece of art, affordable for all. Art for the people, the signs have been his bread and butter for more than twenty years, yet have become an anathema, labeling him as a sign painter, when there is so much more. His work hangs in courthouses and has been acquired by the Smithsonian.

Almost all of Dr. Bob's art includes some element of recycled found objects, from bottle caps to architectural salvage. The finders-keepers habit began as a boy, when he was rewarded with a trip to Six Flags over Texas by winning a grocery store dumpster-diving contest. His first attempts at producing decorative objects began with wood carvings of animals, particularly alligators, given as gifts to family and friends. This interest started to overwhelm him in his twenties, working as a forest ranger in central Louisiana. Returning to the coast, driftwood became birds, highlighted with paint.

Dr. Bob's menagerie in paintings and carvings breathes anthropomorphically, sometimes with only gestures of paint. This applies not only to flora and fauna, but also to the wondrous variety of indigenous architecture, the corner stores, tire repair shops, juke joints, and shotgun houses, of the region. The paintings have grown into a distinctive style of layered spray paint, house paint, precise brushwork, pointillist paint pens, and aforementioned gesture, teeming with the life tapestry that is the New Orleans experience we may kinesthetically feel and are filled with delight when the artist coaxes us to see the visual music with new eyes.

Some of Dr. Bob's work can appear deceptively simple, so much so that one might hear a "My kid could do that" from a father who winces at a twenty-five dollar price tag as easily as a five thousand dollar one. Current carvings display a virtuosity of technique that may begin with a chainsaw, move though various carving tools, secret pattern/texture skills, and

45

finish with jewelry-weight sandpaper, shoe polish, and dry pigment. One can hardly resist touching the work, especially children, who are encouraged to do so. An upside-down wheelbarrow that became a giant turtle with carved head, limbs, and tail was a particular favorite at a recent Mirliton Festival. (Pronounced mella-tone.)

Beyond the signs, paintings, carvings, and assemblages, the artist's personal installations are probably the most fragile in terms of exposure and his obsession to constantly alter his own visual environment. The oldest outdoor piece, a mural on corrugated fence tin in his studio yard, spray-painted a few years before Katrina, features twenty feet of bayou garden with a large, dark gator, watching over the space. The most current installation can be seen across the street from his 3027 Chartres studio. A low-slung, abandoned concrete-block building with multiple security gates covering what were front windows has been gleefully painted pink and yellow, adorned with graphics, sophisticated tattoo-type graffiti, three-dimensional sculptural items, and an ersatz white picket-fenced "front yard" growing bowling balls on sticks of rebar.

It almost makes up for the multiple-dashboard-Jesus, DayGlo-reflector-covered, windmill "Gone Pecan" camp sign, pre-Katrina, at a Lake Catherine party place. The site wiped clean now, of course, because nothing ever stays the same, and the always-evolving installations were never meant to be permanent. Some of Dr. Bob's visual vocabulary, developed by years of literally pawing through the swamps and hoods, and honed by years of perfecting his craft, will continue to be evidence of extraordinary talent. The appetite for representations of the depth and history of New Orleans culture will never be lost.

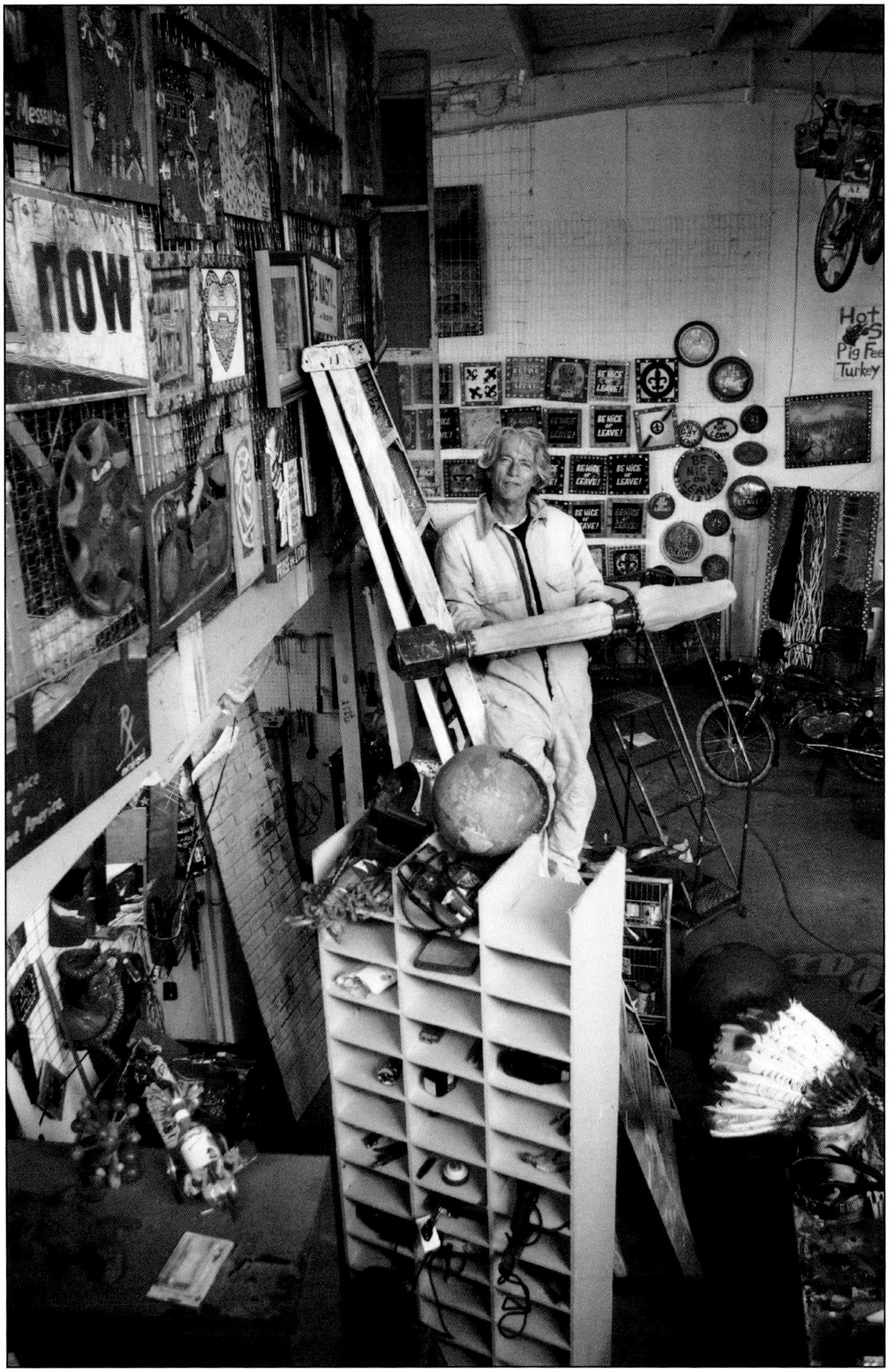
now
BE NICE or LEAVE!
Turkey

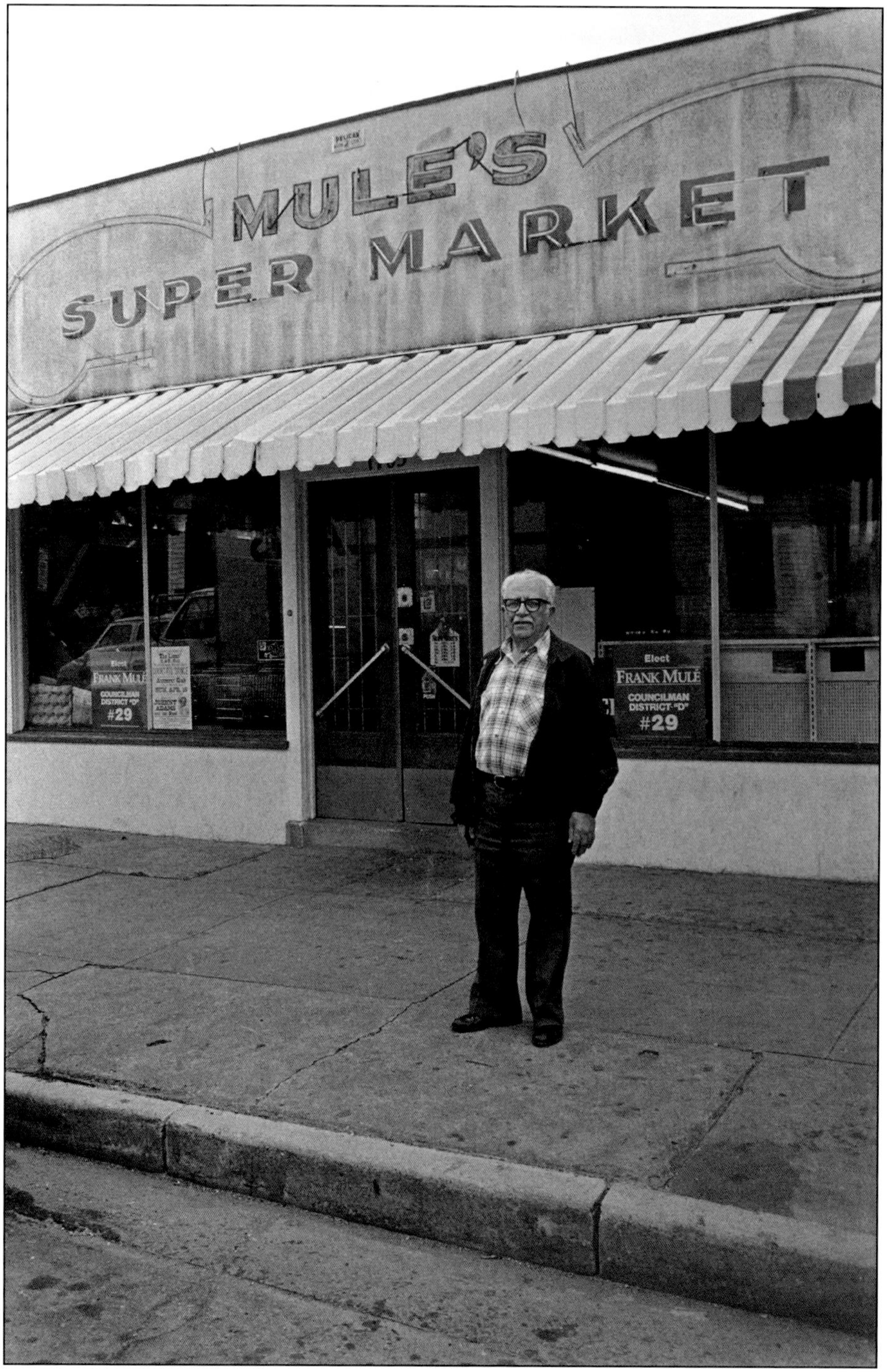
MULE'S
SUPER MARKET
Elect
FRANK MULE
COUNCILMAN
DISTRICT "D"
#29
Elect
FRANK MULÉ
COUNCILMAN
DISTRICT "D"
#29

Alligator Man

by Julia Carey

There's a man at the Uptown Square Farmer's Market on Tuesdays named Jo Jo Rouchard. He likes to park his oil-burning 1992 Ford F-150 next to the dairy farmer who names and pets his cows. Jo Jo's big harvest moon eyes welcome every stranger to his booth where he sells alligator sausage, Des Allemands catfish, and gumbo crabs. Old denim overalls with muddy thighs hang over a thin white t-shirt made transparent with his sweat. A brunette sheepdog mustache conceals most of his mouth, making it that much more difficult to decipher his Cajun-French accent. The farmer noticed Jo Jo's right hand wrapped in an old Ace bandage and asked what had happened.

"Yesterday morning I caught two alligators, first day of the season." He gestured his right hand as though he were ninety-years-old and exasperated. "Still young, both of 'em, 'bout six feet. One of 'em yanked the chicken pole straight from my hands, and just as I picked it up to get back in the game, the fella thrashed with the bait in its mouth, and the base of the pole ripped my palm open." The farmer gasped appropriately to acknowledge the wound, but didn't seem too alarmed at the cause since he asked,

"How's the meat look?"

"Molly skinned 'em both yesterday, and I've gotten the fat off from one of 'em, but I'm definitely working slower than usual with this hand all wrong, so I turned it over to Trey today to finish up so I could come to the market. I've already sold the meat from both of 'em if I can just get the butchering done."

They were interrupted by a regular of theirs, and as her red head approached with her young son, Jo Jo called out,

"Hello, *ma chérie*! I saved some fresh filé for you! Pounded the sassafras this morning."

"Thank you, Jo Jo! I am running low. I was hoping you may have some fresh alligator meat? I know the season opened yesterday . . ." She eyed his right hand with a knowing look.

"For you, I'll go home and catch another one."

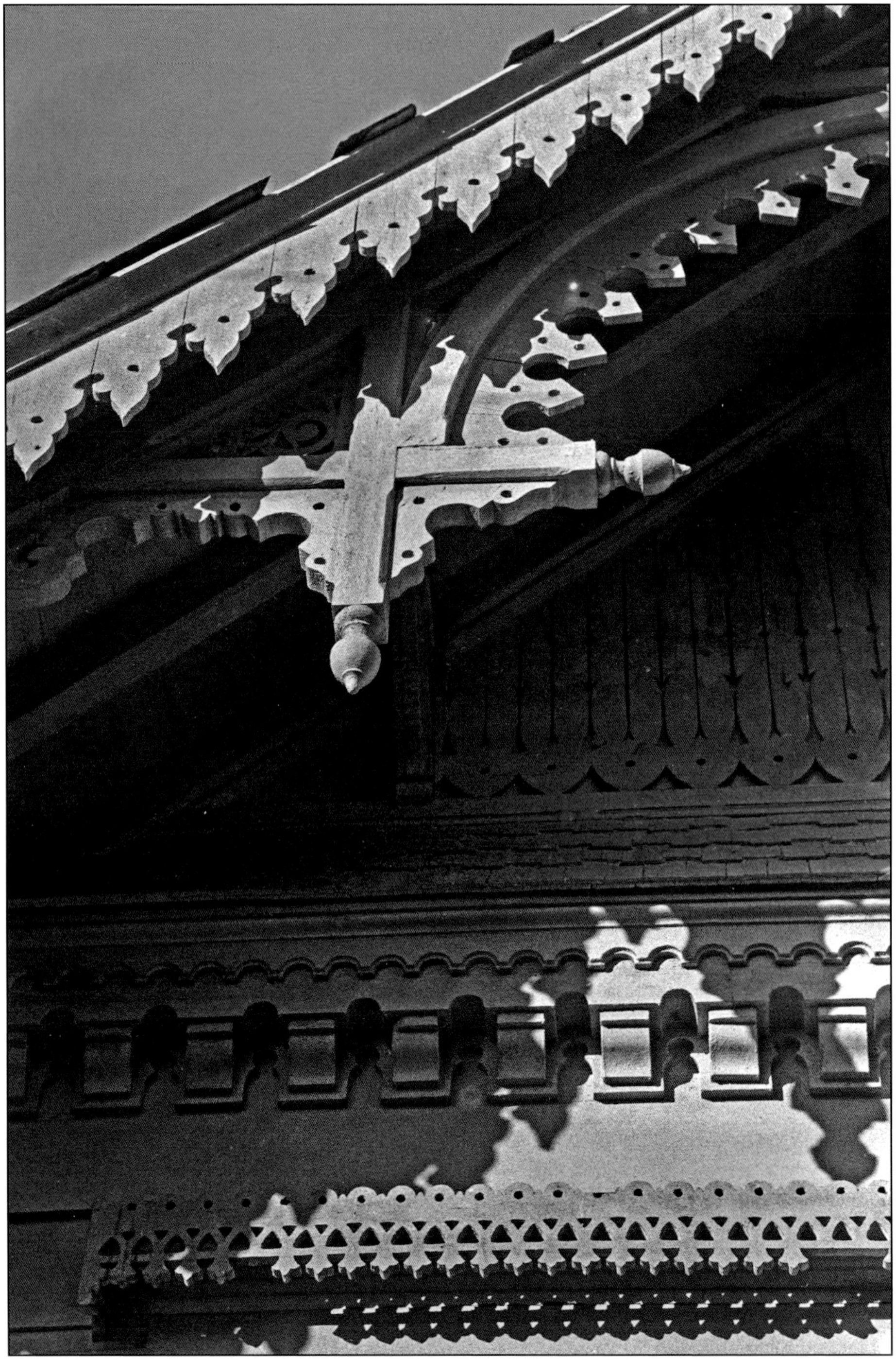

Architectural Distinction and Identity

by Michael Sartisky, PhD

In a world more characterized by conformity than innovation, stereotype than originality, my adopted city of New Orleans arguably stands alone among American cities for the distinctiveness of its architecture. Blindfold a tourist and deposit him on the corner of Royal Street and Toulouse in the French Quarter, or St. Philip and Coliseum in the Garden District, or Esplanade and Bayou Road, let alone St. Charles Avenue between Jackson Avenue and Riverbend, and a nickel will get you a dollar he will know it's not New Jersey, not Iowa, certainly not Texas.

Nor is it only our most distinguished houses that are noteworthy. True, houses in New Orleans, like its chefs, have identities known to the populace at large, like an accounting of first cousins or maiden aunts: the Hermann-Grima House, Gallier House, Pitot House, the George Washington Cable Cottage on Eighth Street. But many of the most blighted and neglected sections of New Orleans, such as Central City, boast a housing stock that, while anonymous, would eclipse the historic districts of most cities in the United States.

Like our cuisine, music, and even our complexions, our architecture evolved through a complex process of cultural influence and adaptation to the environment in the eighteenth and nineteenth century, one characterized by its Creolization, as documented by such writers as architectural historian Lloyd Vogt. Our earliest styles: French plantation houses, Creole cottages, shotguns, shotgun doubles, bracket shotguns, camelbacks, and Spanish *entresols*, define the urban landscape. Individual features reveal the myriad adaptations made to the environment: brick piers, *bousillage*, bargeboard, *briquette-entre-poteaux*, center halls, louvered shutters, high ceilings, hipped roofs, wrought iron, and extended galleries.

Whose heart would not sing at the sight of the visual music of our architecture from the graceful arabesques of wrought and cast iron to the finely turned jig-work and carved brackets and paneled doors, no two the same? Many architectural adaptations of European forms to the tropical climate were imported from Saint-Domingue as the city doubled in population from the influx of immigrants fleeing the Haitian Revolution. Some of the very best adaptations to the flood-prone terrain are embodied in such houses as Madame John's Legacy on Dumaine Street, built in 1788, or the raised nineteenth-century townhouses on the 700 block of Girod Street which today have carports on the ground level, simultaneously resolving both flooding and parking congestion in a dense business district. Every lesson we needed to know about adapting our European lives to the tropical milieu is embodied in Madame John.

The architect Andrés Duany provided context to the significance of our architectural heritage, pointing out that "the key to your future is embodied in the wisdom of your ancestors," and explaining that where our twentieth-century slab houses were perpetually vulnerable to the ravages of flooding, future safety lay in the raised-masonry pier construction of the nineteenth-century homes, not just due to their height, but because even the mortar and paint were lime-based—processed from our indigenous seashells—and lime was a mold-inhibitor.

Subsequently, like layered and intermarried relationships, other cultural influences superimposed themselves on the original forms, but with an inventiveness, profligacy, and exuberance unknown in other more staid and restrained cities. These extended from the nineteenth into the early twentieth centuries, especially in our residences: Greek Revivals, Italianate Mansions, Gothic Revivals, Queen Annes, Georgian Colonial Revivals, Spanish Colonial Revivals, even a few International Style houses. But even many of these styles, whatever their distinct embellishments, incorporated the structural features of the earlier period in order to accommodate the prevailing high water, heat, and humidity, and contribute to the character that makes New Orleans unique and endearing.

Vieux Carré

by Karissa Kary

Ferries, barges, and riverboats glide by on the horizon. Streetcars, mule-drawn carriages, bicyclists, and walkers meander along history-lined streets. Card readers, artists, and street performers offer their magic in the shadowy coolness of Saint Louis Cathedral in Jackson Square. Lace iron balconies drip with plants and Mardi Gras beads, and every step brings a different site, sound, and smell.

Stranger-than-fiction moments come and go with great frequency in this small but distinct rectangular neighborhood along the almighty Mississippi river. Down that street two colorful cowboys stroll past antique shops walking miniature horses like puppies. Down that one, two men dressed and painted all in gold and silver share a trajectory as they walk down a vine-laden lane. They stop frequently to let onlookers admire their regalia.

This is life in the French Quarter, and for those who frequent its streets what should be exceptional is often reduced to a footnote on days blurred by circus-like attractions. Here people come to play, pray, party, work, visit, eat, drink, and live.

Each image in this oft-photographed site is worth much more than a thousand words.

Over there, behind that wall, is a secret garden joining past to present. There, a nun in her habit standing in a doorway. And there, of course, is Bourbon Street filled with famous and infamous bars, clubs, and music. This is a fanciful reality where dishwashers run to work past vampire tours and voodoo shops. "Dixieland, gospel, blues, or jazz?" asks one trumpeter who plays on a corner where cigar, perfume, and candy shops compete for your nose's attention.

Up near the river the smell of chicory coffee from Café Du Monde overtakes you 'til a river breeze blows it away. Locals and tourists alike sit in a powdered-sugar haze dipping their beignets in strong coffee. Nearby restaurants and bars offer a delectable slice of life in the form of muffalettas and po-boy sandwiches to be washed down by a Hurricane or Sazerac. Keep walking and you will see the French Market where you can find local pralines, Creole tomatoes, seasoning, and boiled peanuts, as well as crafts and wares from all over the world.

So much is intoxicating in the heart of this old city . . . . Here in the French Quarter.

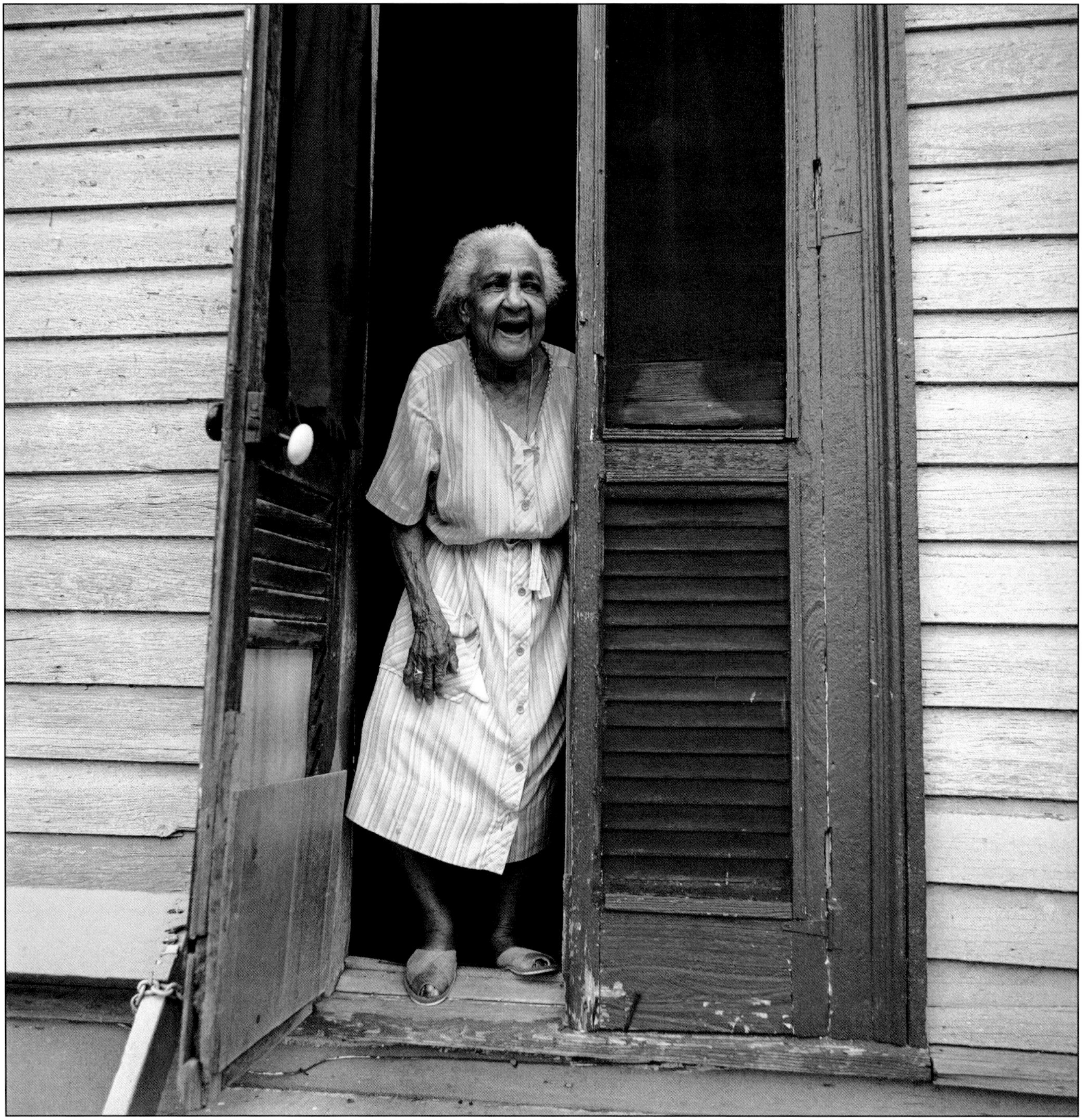

Here Lies a Great Leviathaness

by Dave Brinks

Had there been nothing more than a sandbar in that bend of the river,
Bienville would have urged his settlers to camp on it.

— Garvey and Widmer, on Jean Baptiste LeMoyne, Sieur de Bienville's arrival by ship
via the Mississippi to the old Indian portage where New Orleans stands today.

Cartographers tell us the Crescent City is located at 30° latitude and 90° longitude. However, the hodgepodge mix of this creatured ergosphere is less a geographical certainty than it is a grand *mystère*. In fact, the ancestral heritage of this forbidden *paradis* owes as much to the countless cypress tree knees erupting through busted sidewalks and streets as it does to the pure sensate of Mythos itself. What hungers, what treacles here is a multispectrum of sleepless moons whose menses puddle like fresh blood on the hands of the dreamer. Here lies a Great Leviathaness swathed in an archaea of sludge and slime so rooted in chaos, misrule, and anti-aesthetics, she is at once the mother of her own birth. On the other hand, as a personification of culture, our lady is more like an orphaned kid tossed aside by an unworldly world. She is more attuned to *feeling* than she is to thinking, which is likely one of her greatest attributes. She looks banefully upon the empire of mores oft celebrated by her American counterparts. Her countenance is stalwart in its disapproval of unheresiarchal ruses. Her aliveness is never to be confused with pusillanimous forgiveness. As a shaman, she descries the rise of verisimilitudes unfathomable to messianic humans. The ocean is her cloister. She quaffs only the most prescient pearls. Her parfum is a putrid smelling yoke. To chart the origin of her ABCs is to track down the abecedarium of sublunary goo cooing from the roots of her upside down tree. We can only wish to grasp, as the Chapitoulas-Choctaw Indians once did, the infinite variance of her reptilian aviary while treading ankle deep with the stars. Consider for a moment the alchemy necessary here. Try recounting the story of your lover's face for a thousand and one nights as though your very soul depended upon it.

This bioregion aches with big life. There is no egg-shaped equivalent to its existence. Actually in the big bang of things, if our galaxy were an inch across, I'd be tempted to say Baby Nola formed the warp and weft of its womb. Furthermore, I seriously doubt her deepest secrets, which the history books might fail to record, will remain out of reach of her poets' hearts. What is embodied in the people of the city of New Orleans is a richness of natural being so unparalleled and mystifying that it has become a living opus of wonderment. Of course her ever-changing narrative always ends and begins alongside a river that serves as a symbol of her enduring presence—the Mississippi, or more properly the Mesechabe, as it was called by the Choctaw (meaning "Father of the Waters"). Not surprisingly I recently encountered a word with almost the same phonetic signature thousands of miles away on the western coast of Africa—Masechaba, which comes from the Sotho, a narrow Bantu language belonging to the Niger-Congo family (meaning "Mother of the People"). Mere coincidence? I'll let you handle that one! What is certain is that the relationships between words and water serve as natural a bridge as any between all people, estranged or not; and throughout the ages, this is precisely why the motley assemblage of New Orleans' citizenry is so profoundly singular in their *joie de vivre*.

Part Two:

My Feet Can't Fail Me Now

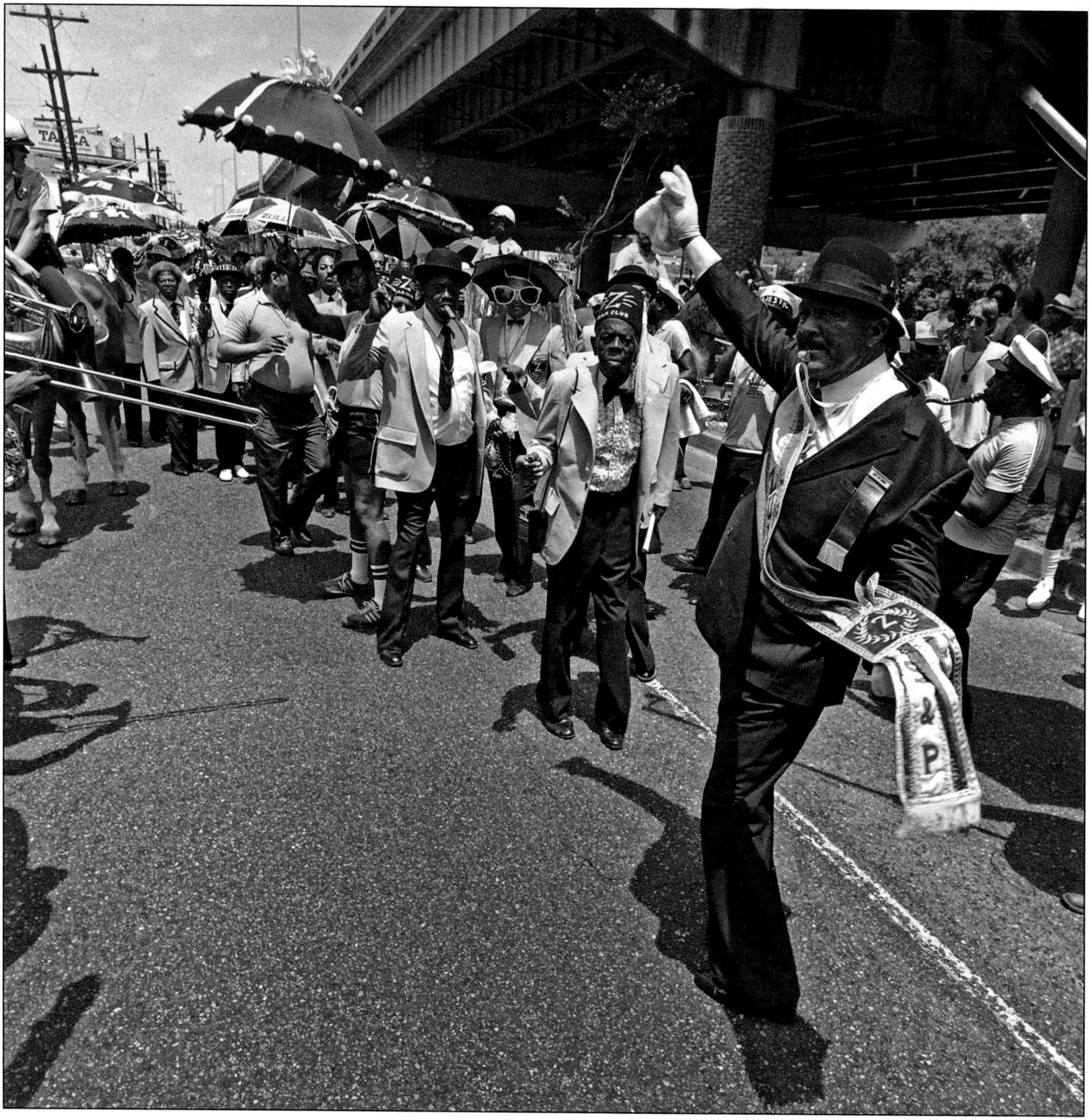

Beneath the Bridge
(A Eulogy for North Claiborne Avenue from Canal Street Down to Elysian Fields)

by Kalamu ya Salaam

[NOTE: this is an excerpt, ain't but the half of it—maybe next time we'll have time to run down the whole nine]

beneath the bridge on claiborne avenue, there,

where once tall oaks grew spreading magnificent branches that embraced whole families of revelers joyfully enjoying a home-cooked holiday brunch, iron horseshoes clanging as poppa p threw a dead ringer and junior dug a serving spoon into aunt juanita's mustard-colored potato salad while ambrose sat with his latest girlfriend snuggling in his lap, lying through his gold-capped teeth about how much money he won betting on the ponies late last week and how he was paying for this whole shebang out of just a small portion of the purse he achieved when he selected a horse whose number was the same as this girlfriend's birth date or was it the thirty-something double digit that was the measurement tape of both her bust and her butt?;

where the mardi gras indians used to go and offer up their colorful vows to never bow down as they trodded around mean streets, freely treating our eyeballs to the most prettiest, feathered, multi-hued suits that any man could ever hope to sew and wear in any given lifetime, they hollered the chants of saints, their eyes burning with the fire of the guardians of the flame sounding out sacred syllables in a language without name, words whose meanings we could not specify but whose dynamic intentions none of us could deny;

where along either side of the street used to thrive haberdasheries (which offered everything

61

worth wearing, from congressional sky pieces and cobalt blue prom tuxedos to tailored peg-legged pants dyed a diversity of tints and shades selected from a rainbow of pigments that made technicolor seem dull, not to mention stacy adams shoes whose shine was so gleaming you did not need a mirror);

where doctor offices and pharmacies, grocery stores and mortuaries, flower shoppes and butcher stalls testified to the urban industry of a neighborhood community still shaking country dust off its boots, run right up next to passé-blanc dynasties that had been resident in these homes since the slavery time plaçages that produced their pale-skinned lineages;

where houston's school of music was on one side and the negro musicians' union was on the other, and barbershops and hair salons hosted weekly informal town hall gatherings at which every manner of contemporary problem was advised and analyzed in betwixt the salacious shoo-shoo of who did what to whom and why;

where protest marches and marcus garvey celebrations, spring festival carriage and limousine processions featuring little freckled-faced future creole queens shyly waving a gloved hand at ruffians with holes in their pants as their manhood throbbed at the thought of a chance at knocking the little man out of those young girls' boats;

where fleets of second-liners have carried so many of us off to the great beyond in ceremonies during which coffins were sat on bars and shots of scotch were poured atop the casket, a libational commemoration of another man who done gone to glory or how the unforget-tably gorgeous sight of a mother dancing atop the box that held the remains of her son was a socially sanctioned and totally acceptable way to both memorialize a life as well as say her last goodbyes accompanied by the bravado of some young dimple-cheeked trumpeter duel-ing with an elegant grey-bearded cornetist, each of the both of them trying to out blow the other, one could have been named joshua and the elder might have been called gabriel, as their brass notes rang out the strains of one bright morning when this day is over i'll fly away, oh lordy, i'll fly . . . ;

there, beneath the bridge, on north claiborne avenue didn't us ramble, didn't we ramble, til the waters cut us down . . .

The Other Caribbean City

by Marlon James

If Miles ever did run the Voodoo down he found her in New Orleans, a city like my own Kingston; one perched on the ledge between desirable and dangerous, black and white, independent and colonial. With lines of distinction as thin as skin or as thick as the levees, which turned out to not be so thick after all. There are other similarities so obvious they barely need mention, but striking enough to lead more than one Caribbean adventurer to snatch the city for his own. My friend Garnette went to New Orleans for college and stayed there five years more. Like me he recognized the ghosts on the street, avenues paved smooth by the stomp of enslaved Negroes. He saw something else as well that called for a Caribbean sensibility. Beauty and menace could not only come from the same place, but as Miles would testify, be essential to each the other.

Race plays out in New Orleans in ways unlike anywhere else in America. It's very much a Caribbean thing to be beyond history yet caught in its undertow. To mix and match personal space in Mardi Gras even as everybody remembers their place. Sexuality plays differently as well. Mississippi sissies would look at the flare of Cubana queens and seven-foot Jamaican divas (they exist) and be both jealous and proud. New Orleans is a mulatto city, a branded one, but there is more to our separated-at-birth resemblance than a beautiful, terrible history. After all, with its narrow streets, Spanish balconies, and surprises at every turn, New Orleans looks like what many Caribbean cities, including Kingston, used to be.

Maybe it's the heat or maybe it's our bounce. We children of the race rarely got a chance to move on up, so instead moved sideways. Call it dance, but we who deal in feetspeak know better. That's why I lost and found myself in the Second Line. Carnival, of course, but also call and response. The Second Line is more journey than destination because we all know where we're going anyway. Not much is different between your wards and our garrisons, and both of us on Sunday afternoon try our best to chant down Babylon. The Second Line is our Bruckins, our Dinki-Mini. The Voodoo is our Pokumina if you're the light, Obeah if you're the darkness. And at even those terms we both laugh because we know it's all dark.

Perhaps what's most Caribbean about this city, or Maracaibo, or Aracataca, is that they all kiss the sea that brought them Africa, Europe, and the Far East. My friend Ned Sublette would say that it's not a Caribbean city at all, but a port one. But being near the sea produces a kind of latitude, one that allows you to accept that Fat Tuesday colours can burst from one corner while a glock bursts from another. African Diaspora dances with the European in a different way than it does anywhere else. Call it gumbo logic. Perhaps what's most Caribbean about New Orleans, especially for a Jamaican there for the first time, are two feelings at once: that you've come home and that you've never left.

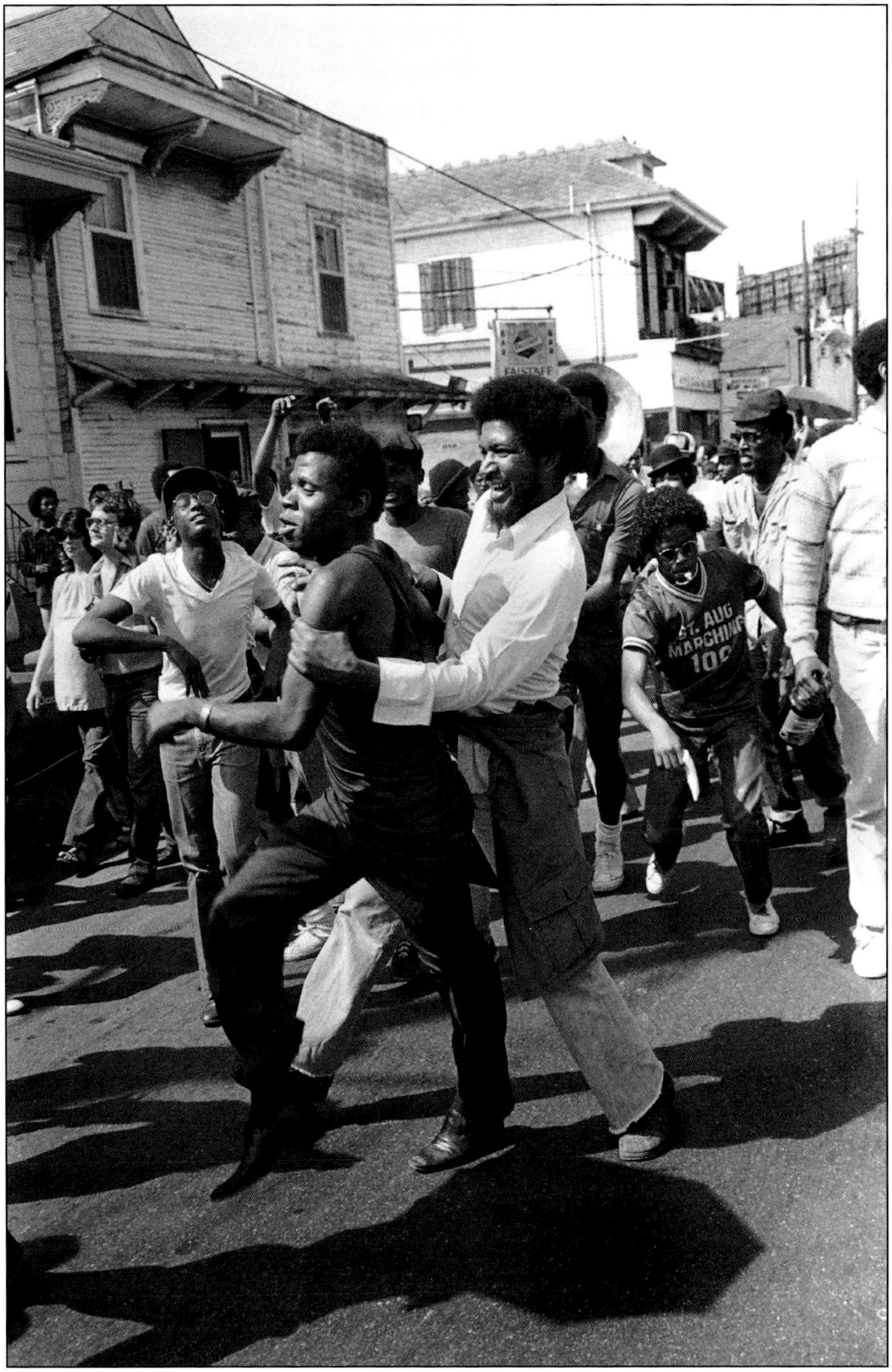
ST. AUG
MARCHING

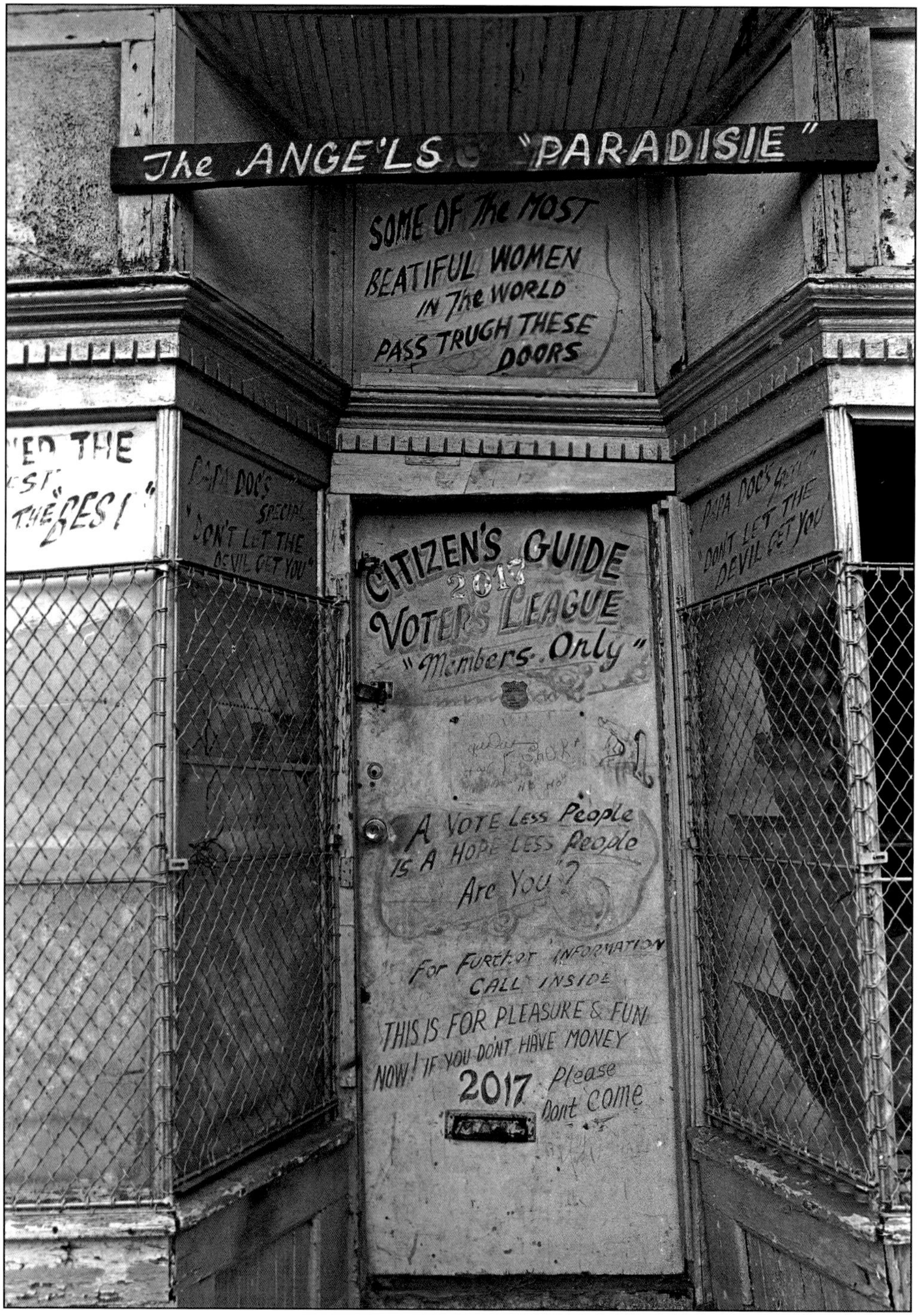
The ANGE'LS "PARADISIE"
SOME OF The MOST BEATIFUL WOMEN IN The WORLD PASS TRUGH THESE DOORS
"DON'T LET THE DEVIL GET YOU"
CITIZEN'S GUIDE
VOTERS LEAGUE
"Members Only"
A VOTE LESS People IS A HOPE LESS People
Are You?
For Further INFORMATION CALL INSIDE
THIS IS FOR PLEASURE & FUN NOW! IF YOU DONT HAVE MONEY
2017
Please Dont Come

New Orleans Immigration

by David Kunian

Although other cities have greater numbers of different ethnic groups or greater populations, all the ethnic groups in New Orleans have contributed to a unique culture in the Crescent City. Before Europeans came to the land that became New Orleans, there were Native American tribes living here who included the Bayougoula, Houma, Tangipahoa, Colapissa, and, soon after Iberville founded the City of New Orleans, the Choctaw. As Iberville and Bienville, the founders of New Orleans, carved out a rough town on the (relatively) high ground near this bend in the river, other French immigrants slowly made their way to the colony of Louisiana. When the colony was ceded to Spain in 1763, many Spanish immigrants made New Orleans their home and brought it their distinctive architecture which is most prevalent in parts of the French Quarter. New Orleans was mostly French and Spanish colonists and African slaves until Toussaint Louverture and his rebel band rose up in the revolution in Haiti starting in 1791. From 1791 until 1810, over 15,000 refugees both white and black fled the violence from the island of Saint-Domingue. This doubled the population and permanently changed New Orleans' way of life. With them came their traditions of food (a combination of French and Caribbean to match the African/Louisiana cooking already here), music, architecture, and culture. Many of the refugees were free people of color who formed their own Creole culture here that was politically active and musically savvy. (Hairdresser and voodoo priestess Marie Laveau and Ferdinand LaMothe, better known as Jelly Roll Morton, were products of this culture.) After Napoleon sold the Louisiana Territory to Jefferson, intrepid Americans came south to find their fortune in New Orleans. This caused tension at first between the "cultured" Europeans and Creoles and the "uncouth" Americans to the point where there were two separate municipalities with the Americans being Uptown and the Europeans and Creoles being Downtown, but this did not last past the first third of the nineteenth century. By that point, there were also Germans moving here avoiding the unrest in their country and Irish who came here fleeing the potato famine. The Irish were used as inexpensive labor on the docks and digging many of the canals that ran throughout New Orleans. Many of those Irish were felled by the yellow-fever epidemic. The population of Irish immigrants in the numbered streets Uptown near the river gave that neighborhood the name "The Irish Channel."

After the Civil War, there were many Sicilians who immigrated here in increasing numbers until 1910. Many of them settled in the French Quarter which was called "Little Italy" or "Little Palermo." The Sicilians brought a recipe for a particular sandwich of olives and meats with them that became known as the muffaletta. Central Grocery on Decatur Street, famous for their muffalettas, is one of the few businesses that remain from that time.

Immigration continued in the twentieth century with many Hondurans coming to New Orleans because of the strong ties between the United Fruit Company, which was based in New Orleans, and the banana growers in Honduras. There have also been many families from Vietnam coming to New Orleans during the last half of the twentieth century. New Orleans is attractive to Vietnamese due to the similar climate, similar topography, a fishing industry, and the French influence.

In the same way that the mile-wide Big Muddy of the Mississippi combines the Ohio, the Arkansas, the Des Moines, and the Wisconsin rivers in its long journey down America before passing by the Crescent City, the many nationalities that have called New Orleans home have contributed unique culture that is Caribbean; European; Mediterranean; North, South, and Central American; and Asian. Visitors and natives alike walk through the French Quarter, eat Sicilian muffalettas, dance African dances in Social Aide and Pleasure Club parades, visit the Irish Channel, sip hot *phở*, and commemorate Creole Homer Plessy's decision to sit in an illegal seat that led to *Plessy v. Ferguson*. It all comes together in New Orleans, the soul of America.

Child of the Bayous

by John P. Clark

The swamps, marshes, and bayous of Louisiana have had a deep meaning for me since my childhood. I recalled this recently when I looked over some writing I did as a child in school.

When asked to do the obligatory "How I Spent My Summer Vacation" essay, I always seemed to gravitate to the theme of my favorite places, the Louisiana wetlands, and my favorite activity, fishing. One essay begins: "Last vacation was one of the best I've ever had. We went fishing every week!"

I described the thrill of getting up at 3:30 in the morning to prepare for the trip. I remember the hum of the big window fan above as we sat in the kitchen drinking dark, hot chicory coffee, as my grandmother fixed breakfast.

Then my father, my grandfather, and I would make the short trip to the French Market. Where boutiques now stand, we bought shrimp from big bins filled with crushed ice and got the "tripe" to bait our crab nets.

Then we headed out from the city. I remember vividly the feeling of the cool early morning air streaming in through the car window, and my increasing excitement, as I began to smell the rich, pungent, organic fragrance of the subtropical vegetation of the marshes and swamps.

According to my childhood memoirs, we always had good luck. Once we caught thirty fish. Another time we caught none, but I commented that, nevertheless, "we had lots of fun, and I think that's enough!" The whole experience was utopia to me.

I was struck most by the spectacular sunrise over the wetlands on our early-morning trips. I described being entranced: "I would look out of the car window into the swamps and see reddish-orange sky with a few white clouds. For miles I would look at it."

Later, I came to appreciate these bayous, marshes, and swamps more deeply. Though I've traveled fairly widely, it's not often that I've encountered anything like the sublime solemnity of sunrise and sunset over the Louisiana swamps. It is not without reason that such great natural places have been called "Cathedrals of the Spirit."

Later, I also found out how crucial these rich ecosystems are to the life of our city. I learned that each several miles of coastal wetlands protects us from a foot of storm surge. I discovered that if the marshes, swamps, and bayous that I knew as a child still existed as they did fifty years ago, much of the disastrous flooding that we recently experienced would not have occurred.

Knowing how fragile and endangered our wetlands are, and knowing how precarious is the very existence of our beloved city, I can still say as I did as a child: "I hope that next summer I'll again be able to see the sun rising over the swamp."

I now know how necessary these magnificent wetlands are—both for our spirit and also for our survival.

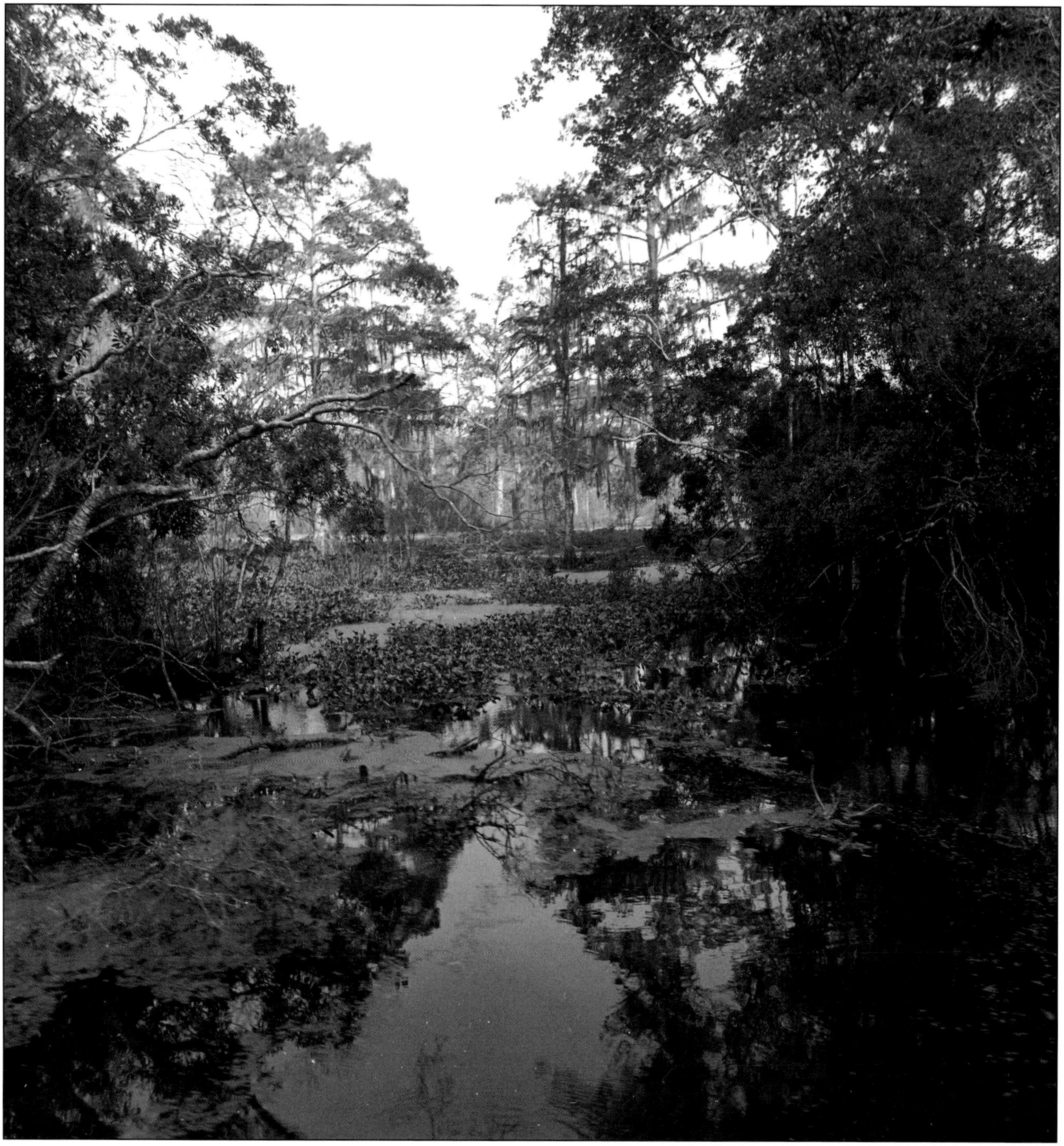

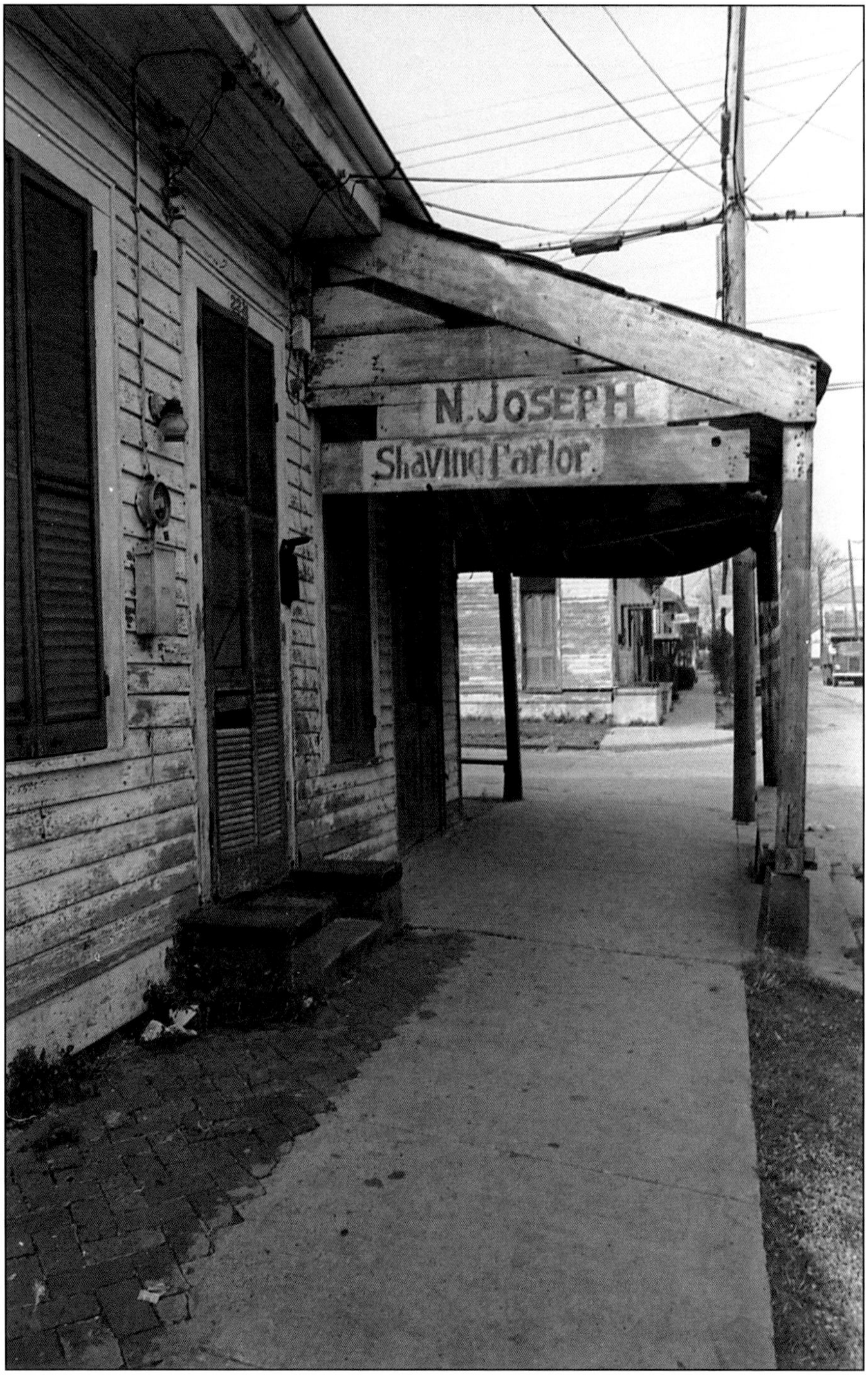
N. JOSEPH
Shaving Parlor

The Barbershop I Used to Go To

by Ester "Humphrey Standard" Hitchens II

The barbershop on Caffin Avenue or the Lea & Purvis Hair Center. It doesn't matter how the words are mentioned. In the minds and hearts of its patrons, this place is solace. In the Lower Nine, this is a place where whole families have come weekly or biweekly to get their haircut first and learn some lessons of comedic timing and procedure next. In this barbershop, the barbers are as follows: Mr. Purvis is a straight shooter. Mr. Lea is a born comedian, who just happens to cut hair. Mr. Youngblood is the youngest of the three and blends both characteristics of his counterparts effortlessly.

Meet some of the patrons. Mr. Amos is a man who was always in the barbershop, but oddly enough, I never once saw him get a haircut. He is a man of honest opinion and has no qualms about telling you or informing you about the differences, both positive and negative, about race relations in the U.S.A. Sam Green is a guy who worked with my father at one of the Winn-Dixie locations in the New Orleans area, and he too had comedic leanings. Squash was a former felon who always used his experiences as teaching moments for the youngsters who frequented the shop, myself included. The list could go on. I simply gave you an overview of personalities who frequented the barbershop. All the wonderful people who knew my father and my family.

Around the shop, my brothers and I are known as Collin's boys, or individually by our names. Our first professional haircuts were done at this barber shop. They all watched us as we matured into young men.

In the shop that I used to go to, history was made. Both Mr. Lea and Mr. Purvis sit on the Licensing Board of Hair Dressing and Barbering of the State of Louisiana: the first African-Americans who garnered that honor. Two bronze plaques that hung on the wall in my barbershop. The barbershop on Caffin Avenue. A Lower Ninth Ward fixture that over the years became so much more than just a hair trim. It was our refuge, steam room, advice column, and fraternity, where all it took to join was to enter, sit down in one of the orange folding chairs that were aligned against the wall, and listen for everyone to call your name.

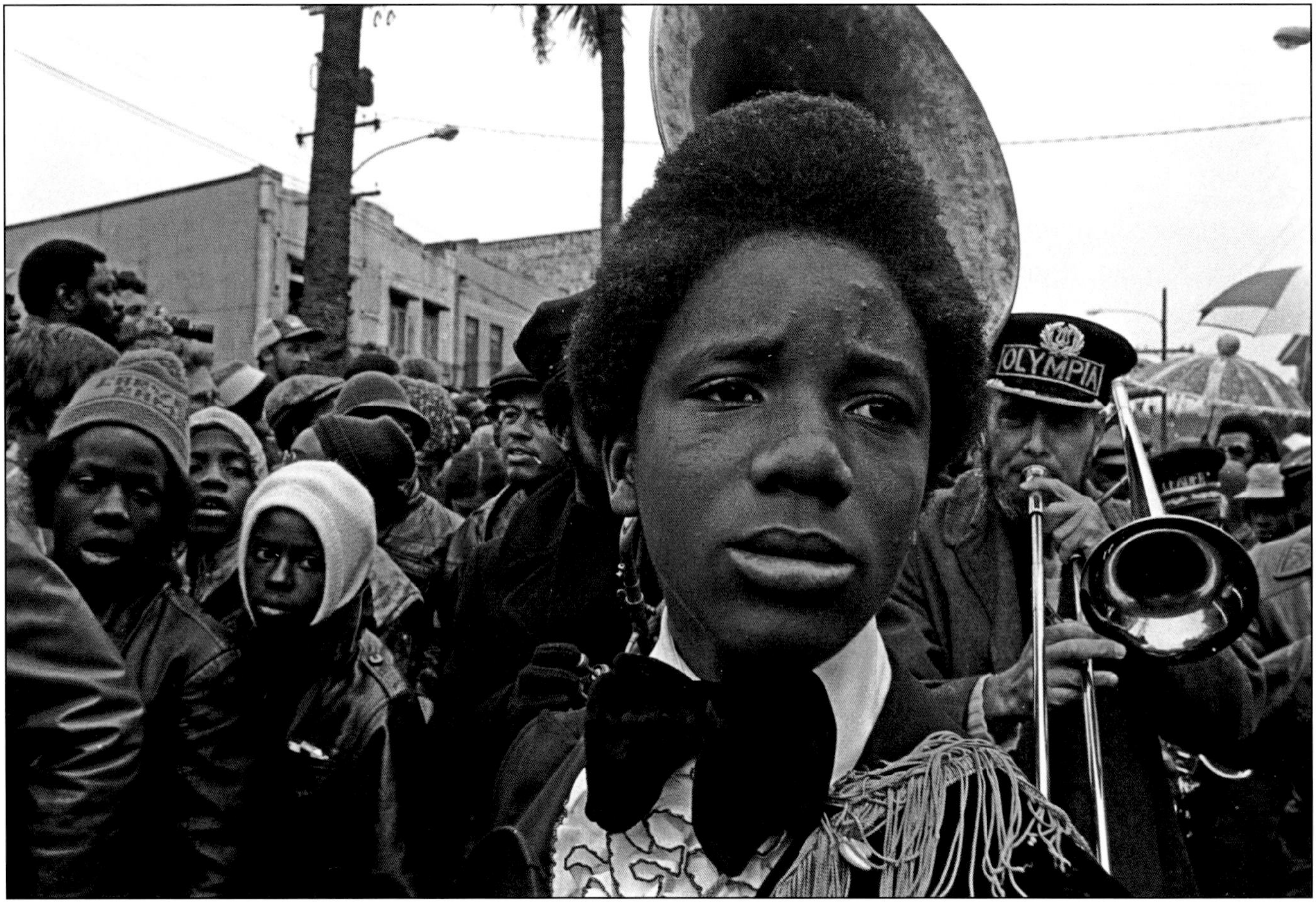
OLYMPIA

Ode to Tipitina's

by Jason Berry

Professor Longhair's ghost roams benevolently in the club named for his signature song. The gods await some blues-struck couple to name their baby Tipitina. "Three times seven girl, knows what you want to do."

Actually the girl in the song is named Luberta: Tipitina is a mellifluous scat-prelude to a thin lyrical story line. But the female place-name is paired with memories of the crusty bluesman whose followers opened it in '77 as Fess' home base.

Fess (Henry R. Byrd) was fifty-nine then. His performances were epic. When the self-effacing hipster took his seat at the keyboard during carnival, you felt the quivering of so many dancers pitched for the burst as he launched into "Big Chief" on igniting percussive rhythms. His music was steeped in the human comedy. In "Baldhead," the guy taunts his galpal when her wig falls off: "She ain't got no hair!" Fess did not have chemotherapy in mind. The woman had a naked head.

Fess' funeral in 1980 was one of the largest, worst-managed jazz ever; the Neville Brothers kept the club going with years of showstopping performances that rarely began before eleven.

The club had a sui generis downhome funk. One night James Booker sashayed in, wearing a dusty tuxedo coat, white collar shirt, pin-on black tie and that patch over his eye with the inset diamond gleam. Jessie Hill leaned at the bar in a rhinestone-studded coat of shimmering green (stones bought in Vegas). Earl King was inspecting the maze of photographs set under glass on the bar as Booker, stoned to the moon, smiled like a gentlemanly confederate: "I just thought I'd come down to the club tonight and see what the fellas were up to!"

Oh, Booker, genius at the keys. Poor, manic, broken Booker, who sat in a waiting room at Charity Hospital in 1983 dying of a low-grade coke dose.

The best show I saw at Tip's was by Nigeria star Sonny Okosun. He had three women as background vocalists and partners in a spinning gyre of stage dancing—pure magic. Another summer night, the AC system conked as Fela, Yoruba pioneer of Afrobeat and a political firebrand, began a speech. His band uncorked a long groove. Cigarette in hand, index finger upright, he said: "Do not worry about the air, people of New Orleans. Fela has come to speak to you!"

In another summer Ernie K-Doe put on a rhythm-and-blues review with Jessie Hill, Tommy Ridgley, and usual suspects. This was before K-Doe met his beloved Antoinette. The self-styled Charity Hospital Baby was having women problems. One of them showed up along past midnight with the band on a break. She came in a cab, told the cabbie to wait by the side door, walked in, pulled out a gun, and *pow!*—shot the other K-Doe woman. In the thigh. She just started shooting *pow pow pow!* at the floor. No one else was hit; everyone scattered like rats on Ray Nagin's roof. She left in the cab. Within minutes NOPD arrived. The wounded woman lay on the stage as the ambulance siren grew loud. K-Doe talked his retinue out of a seriously messy situation. There were no useful eye witnesses. No one was arrested. Nothing appeared in the *Times-Picayune*.

Tipitina's is vastly more tranquil today.

The Rhythm of the City

by Christine Wiltz

At five o'clock, as was her habit, Delzora left work at the big house on Convent Street. She was picked up by the same young man who dropped her off every morning. He drove up in a gleaming white Cadillac with custom Continental kits built into the front fenders and spiked hubcaps that looked dangerous. He was wearing tight, bright blue leather pants and a matching vest without a shirt on underneath it.

He opened the back door for Delzora as she came down the walkway in front of the house.

"Don't you never come pick me up again without no proper shirt on, Dexter, do you hear?" Delzora said to him.

"Yes, ma'am."

"You look like a pimp from the Quarters, all got up like that."

Dexter held the door for her silently while she settled herself like a queen on tomato red crushed velour behind dark-tinted windows. Then her carriage pulled out, traveling a stately ten miles an hour down Convent Street under a canopy of graceful oaks. Behind the oaks were the houses of the rich, set back from the clean street and surrounded by emerald green lawns and artful landscaping. The white Cadillac was as out of place here as an Iowa prize pig on a stroll.

The canopy of graceful oaks was broken as the car reached the intersection of St. Charles Avenue. The avenue was the buffer zone between the very rich and the very poor. Across it the canopy resumed. A block farther the Convent Street Housing Project began.

Delzora didn't think about it because she'd been this way too many times before, but across St. Charles, Convent Street was darker. The houses on one side, the project units on the other, were set closer to the street and to each other; there were no green lawns for the sunlight to filter through oak leaves and sparkle upon. The oaks themselves were brooding and scary instead of graceful over here. They weren't so much a canopy as good cover—for crime, for poverty, for sadness, for the darker side of human nature. The droppings of the oaks fell to the street and were never swept away by the city or the residents. They stayed, messy, dank, and filling the air with the sweet odor of decay.

Delzora, her head resting against the velour, her eyes closed, knew when the car crossed St. Charles. From dense silence the Cadillac slid into the sounds of people on the street, kids shouting to each other over rap music blasting out of boom boxes, and across the street from the project, rhythm and blues coming in a wave from the open door of the Solar Club, a saxophone riff swinging out over the street and gone.

This continued for a while until there was another wide avenue, another buffer zone. The Cadillac could roll straight across New Orleans on Convent Street, through the inner city with its random and opposite elements that blend into a sort of symmetry, elements dispersed in a rhythmical flow of dark to light, sounds to silence, rich to poor, black to white. This is the rhythm of the city.

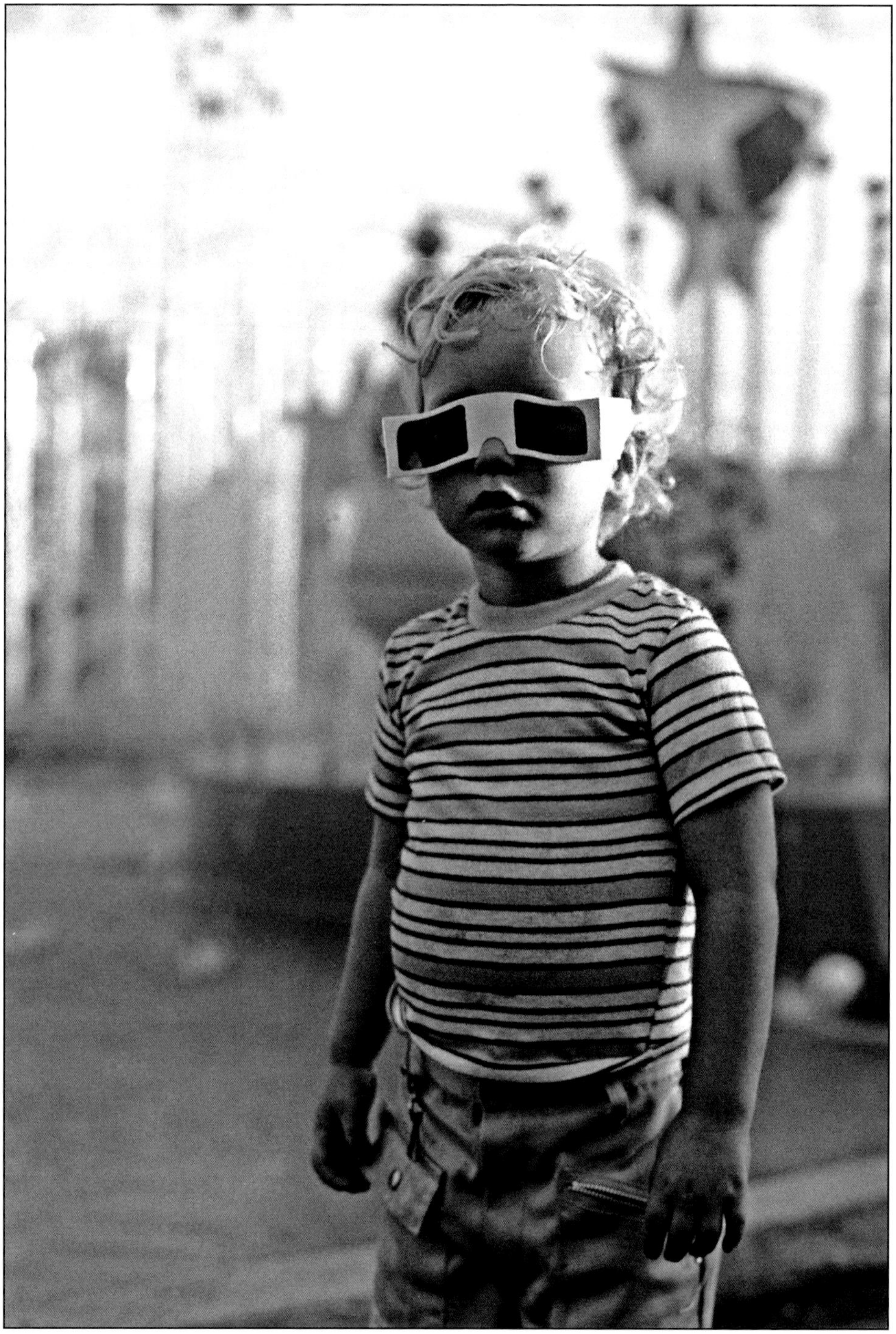

Where Hip Goes to Die

by James Nolan

One day my hard-drinking cousin announces that after a brief sojourn in California, she's "gone macrobiotic." I roll my eyes and hand her a plate of my jambalaya.

"It's macrobiotic," I tell her.

"Hmmm good," she says between mouthfuls. "This tastes better than the macrobiotic food I ate out West. But I thought it had to be covered with miso, or something Japanesey."

When I moved home from San Francisco, a vestige of my childhood New Orleans was still visible, though as pale and fleeting as moth wings around a porch light. Yet in these past few years, Japanesey food and everything else in California I was running away from have turned up to haunt me: real-estate speculation, political correctness, psychobabble, Internet evangelism, nouvelle cuisine, veganism, lattés and muffins, gangsta rap, dreadlocks, anti-smoking laws, jogging, French theory, and—the icing on the cake—language poetry, a form of literary Alzheimer's that took Berkeley by storm twenty years ago, when I was still in graduate school there.

Local friends are astounded I don't swoon along with them at all this second-hand hipness. But I was there when these fads were born, and except for the new-car smell, found them no more exciting then than I do now, as they die a slow death on Magazine Street.

The good news is that by the time these hip phenomena make it to New Orleans, you can rest assured they are over everywhere else. New Orleans is where national trends go to die, dumped like those tee shirts of defunct American rock groups sold on the cheap in Mexican markets. Just today, on a café bulletin board, I noticed a flier about a masochistic massage therapy called Rolfing. Nobody has been Rolfed in California since that nasty spate of personal injury suits two decades ago. Even EST, the self-help seminar founded by those gurus of greed all the rage during the 70s in Los Angeles, has changed its name, moved to New Orleans, and opened an art gallery on Bourbon Street.

"Look," I explain to my cousin, already on her second plate of jambalaya, "macrobiotic just means eating what grows around you. These shrimp, crawfish, tomatoes, andouille sausage, and rice are all from right here, so it's macrobiotic. In San Francisco they think you have to eat like Japanese fisherman to be macrobiotic. But we're not Japanese fishermen. That's food for people who don't come from anywhere. But we do. So enjoy."

"New Orleans doesn't do San Francisco very well," my friend Charles Suhor observes in his book on postwar New Orleans jazz. We're macrobiotic and do New Orleans well, another style of hip to our own Mediterranean beat.

Yet insecure in our parochialism, New Orleanians are often the worst offenders when it comes to adopting some Californian fad to feign sophistication, never realizing we're so far behind the times our dated hipness reads as retro. We have a natural talent for caricature, and tend to turn every national trend we touch into something garish and larger-than-life, a Mardi Gras float. The last jogging vegans in dreadlocks who can recite language poetry, and make a living by feng-shuing condos on the Internet, will probably wind up dressed as gigantic papier-mâché lattés and muffins with their own Carnival parade through the French Quarter.

Then the twentieth century will finally be over.

Meanwhile, in the pressure-cooker meccas of hip, people are so bored and frustrated with homogenized America that, every moment they can, they spend down here, drinking, smoking, dancing, and sucking on crawfish heads. You can spot them at Mardi Gras and Jazz Fest—there's Harry Shearer from Los Angeles and Francis Ford Coppola from San Francisco—those cool Californians we're supposed to be imitating.

And guess what? They've gone macrobiotic, and are imitating us.

Swing Street

by Cristina Black

You really shouldn't have worn those shoes. It's never an easy thing walking around Uptown New Orleans in heels that high, your round hips teetering over every crack and hole in the pavement. But you make it look easy for the benefit of the slacker boys looking on as you make your way up Magazine Street. Your jeans are stuck to your thighs, your blouse is stuck to your back, and your bangs are stuck to your forehead. Sweat is the glue, but that's normal too.

It takes a long-ass time to get to Rue de la Course because first of all, you can't walk that fast in this heat. Secondly, you're feeling a little bit queasy, but that's your own fault, isn't it? And thirdly, like so many things in New Orleans, Magazine Street is crooked. No, it is. It's a simple fact dictated by nature: Magazine, just like Prytania, St. Charles, Tchoupitoulas, and Claiborne, submits to the curve of the Mississippi. The whole town never really had a chance at straightness, which explains the sloping sidewalks, which you must now concentrate on negotiating without breaking an ankle because you had to wear those goddamned shoes.

When you do get to the Rue, you'll order a bagel with cream cheese and a medium blend, which you'll drink black. Your lips will leave a greasy red stain on the mug, the same one you left last night on little plastic cups of free wine while pretending to stare at sculptures in some gallery on Carondelet. You'll get the paper and stomp over to the table by the window. The front page will have a picture of a panting beagle with the oft-recycled August headline "Dog Days." You might think this is a dumb-ass bit of journalism, but it isn't. It's an act of mercy. See, nobody wants to read about murder right when they get up, so they save that stuff for the second page.

By the time you get to that point, you're only pretending to read because he has walked in the door, the one you were looking for last night. Isn't he the whole reason why you wore your Betsey Johnson dress with you bra straps showing, drank all those cocktails, did all those little bumps in the bathroom, and ended up at Big Daddy's way down in the Marigny? You were waiting for him to show up somewhere, weren't you? And now here he is, that skinny, bed-headed boy who tends bar at CAC parties. You keep pretending to read the paper, but you're really listening to his conversation. In your peripheral vision you can see him nodding while the guy behind the counter brags about his road trip to a death metal show in Pensacola.

You clear your throat and try to think of a reason to go up there. You must pretend to need something, extra cream cheese maybe. But you can't. You suddenly feel like you're going to throw up, don't you? And isn't your face covered in sweat chilled by air-conditioning? You're frozen, baby. By the time that boy walks back out the big glass door with his large iced coffee, you've been staring at a Winn-Dixie ad for five minutes straight.

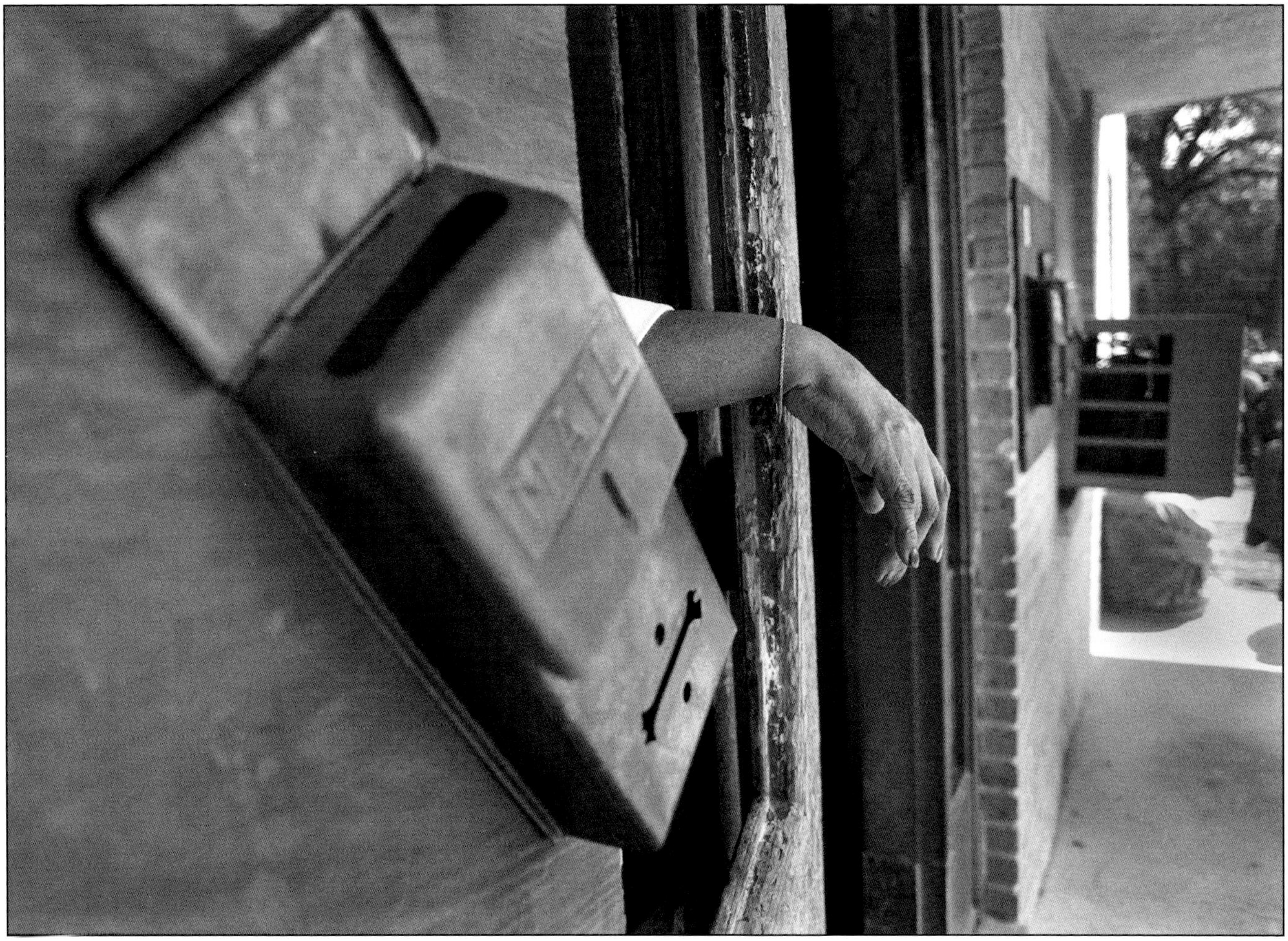

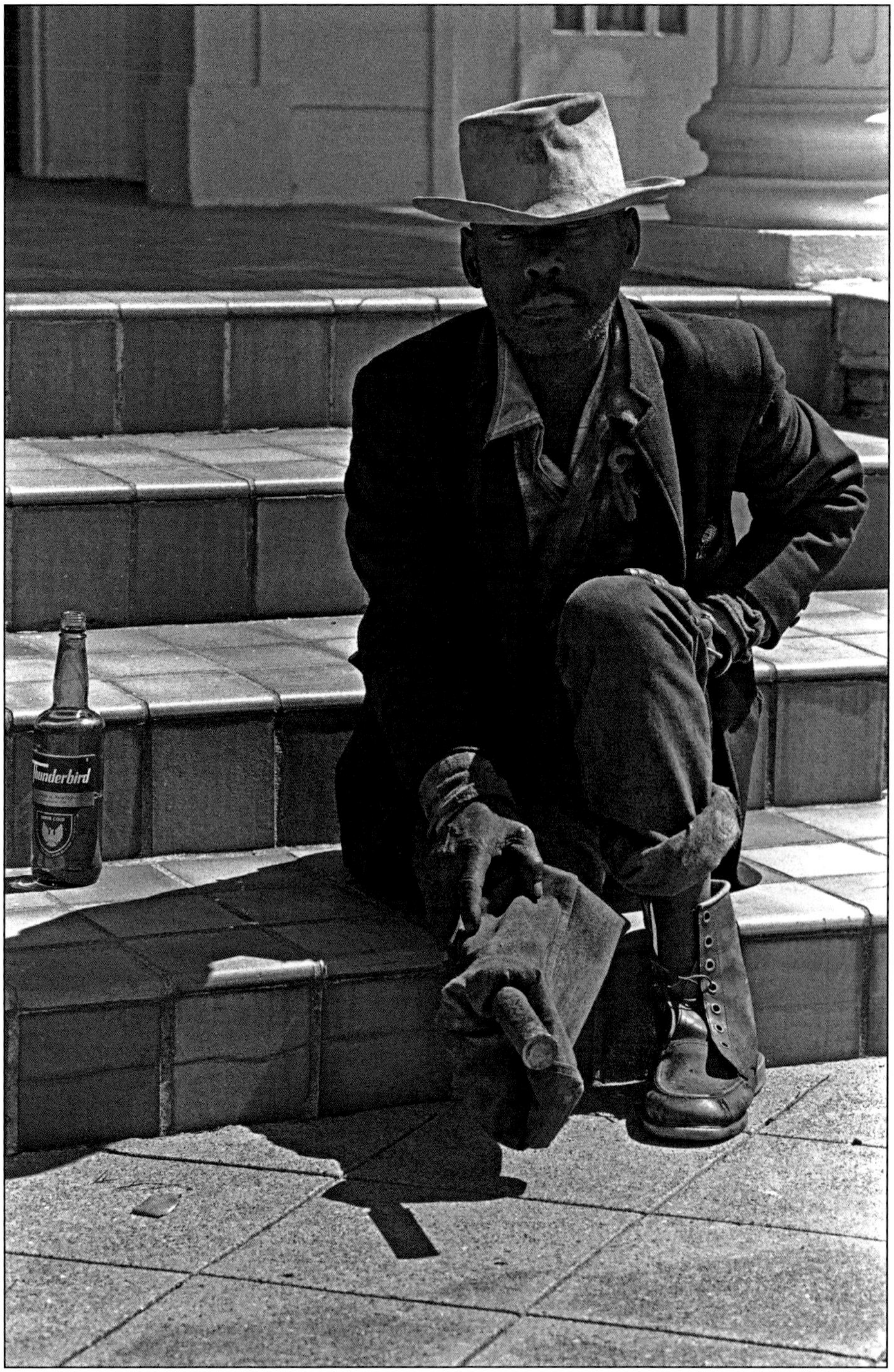
Thunderbird

What a Mind

by Sarah K. Inman

In walks the foursome, their skin shiny from beer sweat. The air hangs heavy and warm in this uptown shack called Snake & Jake's. With only one exit apparent and low ceilings, the bar is cozy and damp like a sarcophagus. The two women plop rumps on a worn couch as the men retrieve cold drinks. Facing one another, the sun-kissed woman speaks.

"He thinks of things I would never contemplate," she beams. Having delivered their pints, the men return to the bar, below the Christmas wreath and lights, and talk loudly about music.

The door opens, and a man with a three-inch Afro enters. He wears tennis shoes without socks and baggy shorts. Meanwhile a tabby cat rubs its cheek against an end table, then slinks between bar stools. The paler, more tired woman dressed in a red skirt with a slit up the side puckers her lips, making the universal cat kiss. The orange animal regards her for a moment and then continues to press its face against the furniture. But the man in the baggy shorts jerks his neck in response, seeking the culprit of the sound.

"I'm just calling that cat," she explains, sliding one knee on top of the other.

"You want what?" he asks.

She shakes her head and turns her attention back to her companion who is still talking. "He comes up with these ideas, like about DNA. Supposedly we all have the same DNA. Right? And if that's the case, then why are we different? Why don't people look more alike? Why aren't we all the same?"

The tired woman nods and calls again for the cat.

At the sound of her kiss noise, the sockless man scoops up the animal in one arm; in the other he holds a bottle of beer. Then he stutter-steps from side to side, jerking his shoulders and head as if trying to out-hustle some invisible opponent. He shuffles and moves forward toward the couch. "I'm O. J. Simpson," he says.

His small stature and slender limbs reflect nothing of the famed football player. The cat is pinned to the side of his paunch, indifferent to the man's imaginary game.

"Now is that something you would ever think of?" the young, sun-touched woman asks. "I mean, my God, what a mind."

The tired woman nods at her companion and watches as the self-proclaimed O. J. Simpson dances about the bar holding a tabby cat to his hip.

Channeling the Spirits on Dauphine

by José Torres-Tama

I lived at 1427 Dauphine in the Faubourg Marigny Triangle from October of 1987 until December of 2004, seventeen years of two houses and a corner to the maison of Charles Laveaux, father of Marie Laveau—the iconic voodoo priestess.

I chopped garlic a thousand times and over again in this house of ghost erotica, performance salons, mild orgies with poetry, catfish barbecues over open flames, and salsa strutting until three a.m., or when the neighbors called the police once more because they were clueless to our collective intent of challenging the spirits to join the "live art" cavorting.

The many lips of long, drunken kisses merged here, sometimes clumsily. The hundred inches of red orange velvet couch circa 1949 was a centerpiece in an electric yellow parlor, enhancing my magical-realist, Latino, voodoo aesthetic. Decorated dramatically, *la casa de amores brujos* was my revamped version of the Creole brothel it once was.

My Jamaican Yoruba scholar friend confided there were numerous souls of women crowding the stairs to the bedrooms on the second floor, going up and down for their duty, making a clamor when I was alone. When my wife was my girlfriend and moved in, she sensed their hostility.

I often channeled visions of myself as their Madame in some century before, caring for these courtesans hungry for nightfall and the price of their company. I made love to them all in different rooms. I petitioned their passage from the other realm, becoming naked easily as was my customary ritual in the company of intoxicated strangers, bedding friends who became lovers, and some who still remain friends. Some couples can trace their first exchange of saliva to this house of altars and apparitions.

Gede, lord of sex and death, ruled the first room, announcing the house's disposition as my own red light district. Centered on the fireplace mantle, the crystallized-sugar skull

89

with black stove-top chapeau was flanked by a shot glass filled with Puerto Rican Rum and an authentic Cuban cigar, smuggled back from Havana as contraband *regalitos* by our resident Romanian poet.

La Virgen Maria and Yemaya had their place of worship above the rustic mahogany dining table inside the azure sea kitchen walls. The altar to Ganesha in my art studio of lavender hues was the repository of many prayers to help me control my lower-chakra appetite. Lakshmi, the goddess of fortune, reigned from my bedroom, and I prayed to them all asking for mercy when I almost buried myself inside this house, feeling the exhaustion of my vampiric thirst while inebriated by multiple *tequilas* in the middle of the two front parlor rooms.

Maybe Marie entered through these pocket doors, and she was back again in charcoal contours filled with pastels of caramel flesh and Prussian blue aura bordering the overcooked red of her negotiations against an ivory *tiant* headdress.

The soft earth of yellow ochre markings above the brows lifted her ebony eyes from the Arches paper that contained her. Crimson highlights juxtaposing her deep black snaking shawl evoked the secret wisdom I beckoned in the many *duende*-possessed mornings spent to draw out the elusive mythic priestess. She is the most famous of her hybrid caste, *les gens de couleur libres*, born of mixed pigment and *plaçage*, African-French-Spanish.

I began my first Laveau portrait at 1427 Dauphine wondering if I could capture something of her occult soul through time on paper, freeze her conviction, and channel the spirit of a *santera* who later lived seven blocks from where I slept for seventeen years in a house built in 1847.

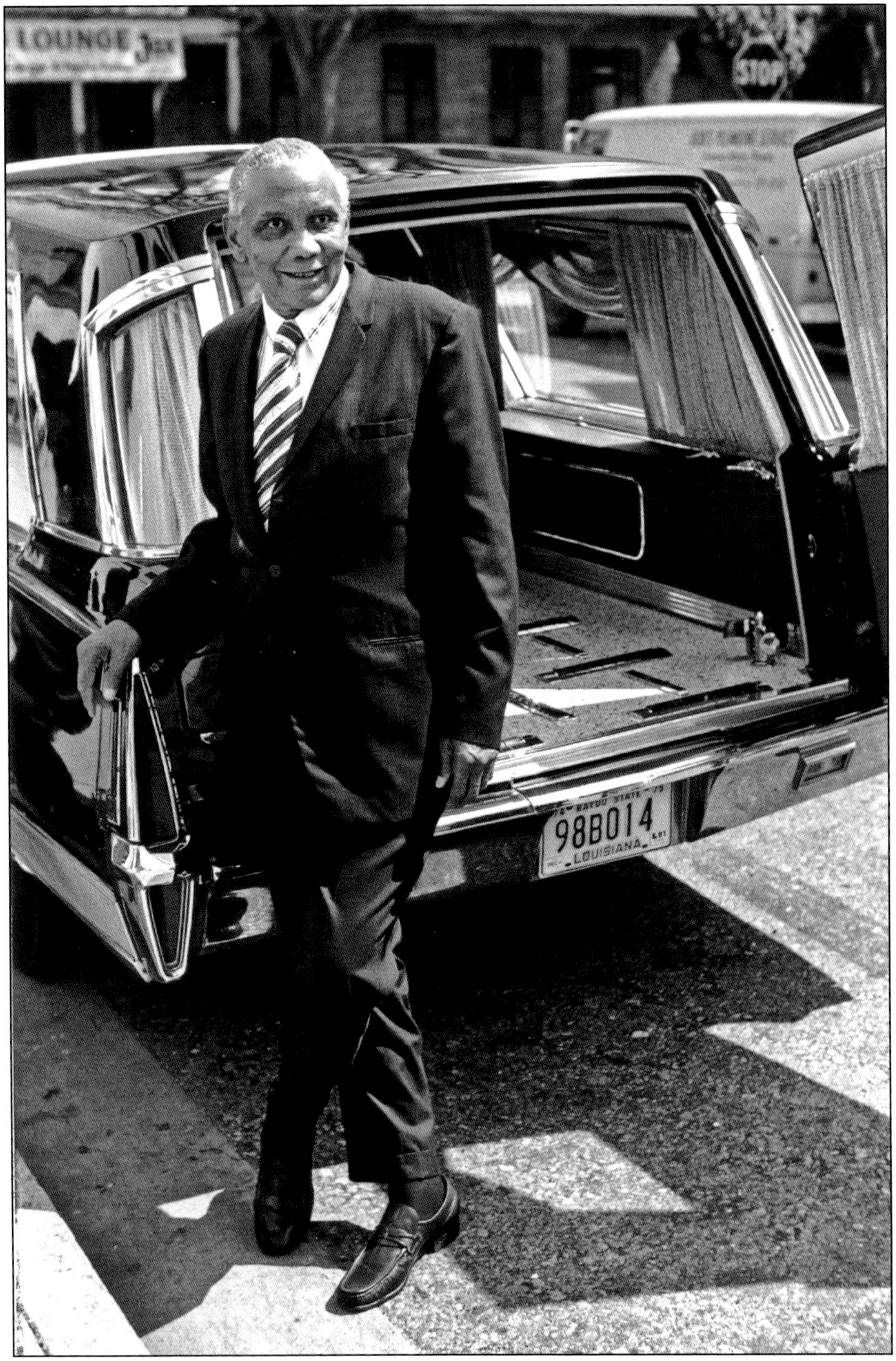
LOUNGE
STOP
98B014
LOUISIANA

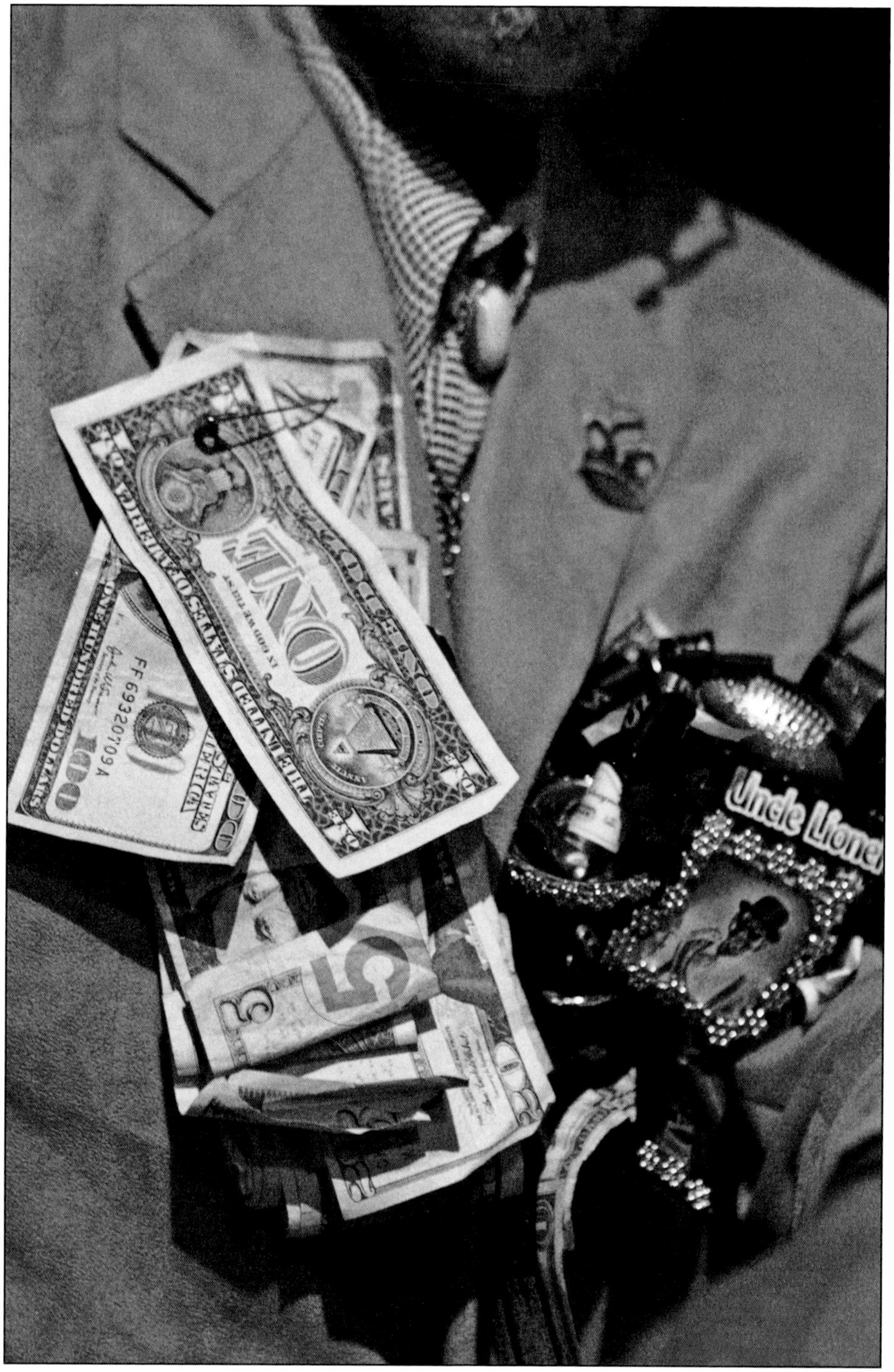
Uncle Lionel

Wearing the Money

by Tara Jill Ciccarone

"But what will you do on your birthday?" my ex wails in the parking lot of the Discount Zone Gas Station on Claiborne and Esplanade Avenue where I've agreed to meet him. He claims he can't live without me in the same parking lot where, months earlier, unable to put air in my tire alone, I suffered a slow leaking of the eyes.

There is nothing as lonely and deviant as stretching a Friday paycheck to get as fucked up as possible on gas station liquor and street drugs.

"What will you do this September 11th?" he asks as a gritty dusk settles. "You'll be thirty-four and I'll be forty."

A doppelganger has emerged before me; this thin, gray-haired man who's been delivering poetry to me at inappropriate hours and can spell my last name barely resembles the guy who I figured I was bound to by coincidence when we both blew out candles on a single ice-cream cake. He almost convinces me that we are two lonely souls and without him, when I turn thirty-four, I'll be looking down at that cake with our two names melting beneath all those candles, or worse, sealing photo albums with wax because as he implies, I'll have nothing to do.

But then I know.

It's 2001, and I draw airplanes on the brown paper that covers my workstation in photography class. My brothers in New York do not have cell phones, and even though I awoke to my grandmother's voice singing Happy Birthday on my answering machine, I think only of the photograph of my siblings that for some reason I've been using as a bookmark. My friend already had the five dollar bill attached to the pin, she explains, and I wear the money for a few hours before spending it on a dry gin martini because it is not my birthday that year.

It would have been an indifferent kind of day until I found my neighbor passed out on her porch, and alarmed, I rushed towards her only to see the money pinned to her black halter before her friend folded twenty dollar bills covered with lipstick kisses and slipped them into my neighbor's boot.

 "It's just her birthday," the friend said while already I was pressing my lips to the last dollar I had in my purse.

 I'm thinking of the second birthday I spent sober, losing my bikini tan and late with the rent. Here is a girl who still plays with dolls and prefers to wake up at the exact time she entered the world: 10:31 a.m. By the time I arrive at Vaughn's, my hair curled and shiny as in my new driver's license photograph, I've gotten almost three hundred dollars pinned to my dress.

 "It's cheaper than buying you drinks," people joke.

 My friend tells me not to be disappointed if Corey Henry isn't playing and explains that Vaughn's isn't the way it used to be, that I'm thirty-three and we were twenty-six when we stayed out all night dancing, but I refuse to believe her. It's my birthday, after all, and everyone reminds me of this by adding to my stash.

 "Don't be disappointed," my friend warns as I pay everyone's way in before refastening the pin.

 I hear the trombone before I see him; I'm thirty-three years old and even Corey Henry knows it's my birthday, and months later, as I stand at a gas station watching dreams die under the I-10 ramp, I am reminded of the ten thousand safety pins my grandmother, who didn't know of this tradition but always sang on my answering machine, left me as I say goodbye.

Famille Vve. Paris neé Marie Laveau

by Barbara Trevigne

I come to visit you again as friends do. I walk the path of this cemetery; feel the air; and smell distinct, sweet, and pungent aromas. I know I am in a different place and time. Why are all these people here? You do not know them. Neither do I. But they come because they are curious. They have read or heard that you were this great Vodou Queen of New Orleans with mystical powers.

You are dead, of course. They do not understand that you are a spirit or that your spirit is not in this tomb with your fossilized bones. People want to touch you, leave an offering for you, and tell you the innermost secrets they would not tell a priest. The innermost secrets they would not tell God. You do not know them, neither do I. But I sit, watch, and observe. You hover above or sit next to me. We both hear them. They see neither of us. I strain to hear whispers of conversations, not the loud, lamenting cries that would emanate deep from the soul. Are they scared or embarrassed to express humility? Are they afraid to call out their woes? When they stand on the inscription tablet of your son, Archange, rotting food covering his name, the cement stained by ink marks and the oils of candles, do they consider you? Your children? The loved ones buried with you? Do they respect your ancestors? You were a mother, a wife, a grandmother, and somebody's daughter.

Yours is the most visited cemetery in New Orleans, the St. Louis One. And yours is the most visited tomb in that cemetery, the tomb of the Famille Vve. Paris neé Marie Laveau (Family of the Widow Paris, born Marie Laveau). Each year, thousands visit you. They genuflect at your three-tiered tomb and are reminded of the marriage between the rites of Catholicism and the spirituality of Vodou. From the fissures in your tomb, they continue to leave pictures of saints and handwritten notes. Mardi Gras beads, rosary beads, Attraction Oil, candles, religious medals, flowers, and coins as votive offerings are placed upon the marble in-ground tablet of your son, Archange Glapion, as a sign of gratitude or sometimes in discharge of a vow or promise.

And so we wait. We watch. We receive these gifts of anointment. People seek magic and power in times of despair. They do not visit you when they are happy. Some seek you for revenge. Most are strangers we will never see again. Others are friends who truly care. They are the ones who will preserve your tomb and chastise those who mar your name.

Blessed are those who honor and respect the spirit of their ancestors.

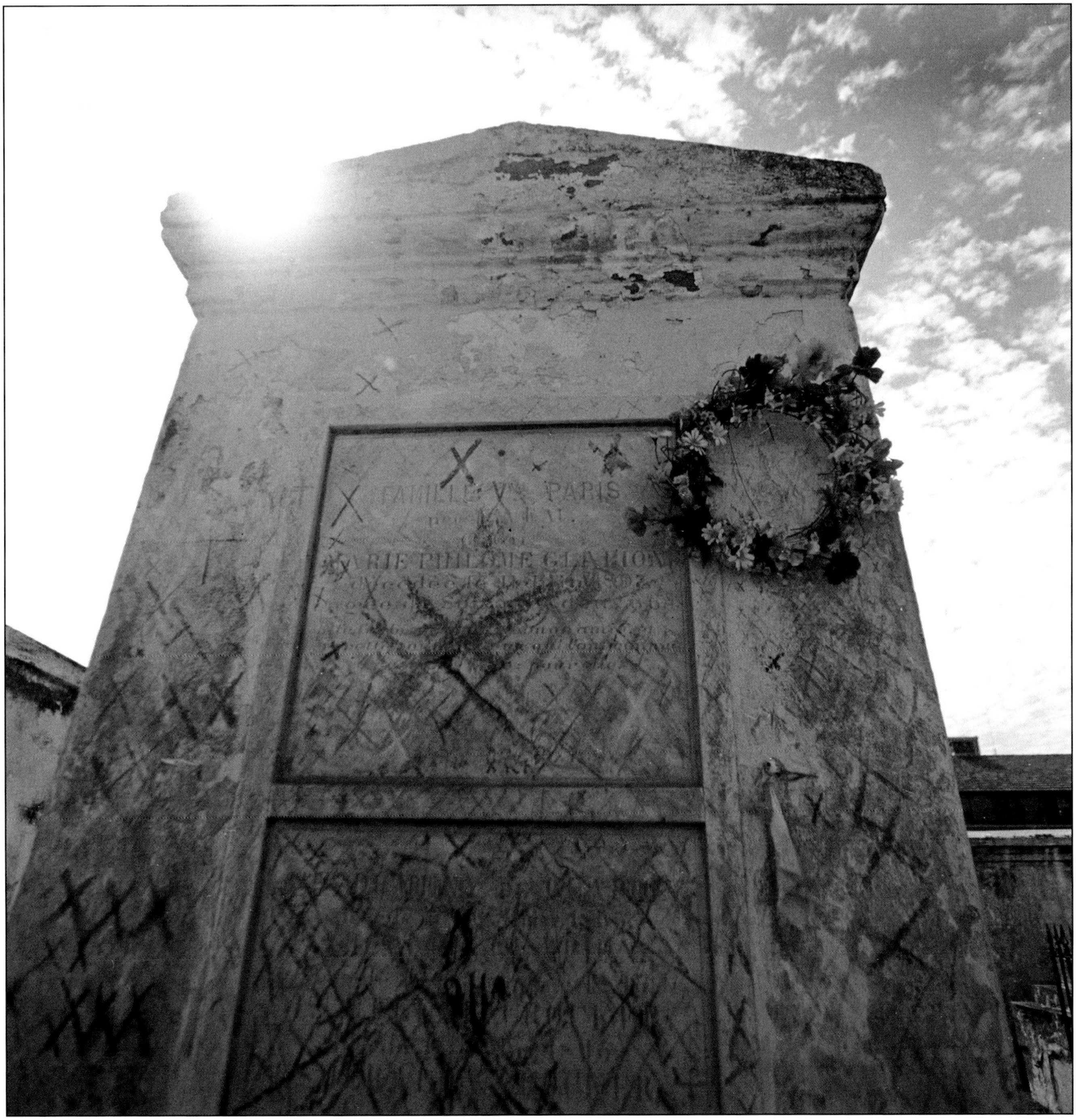
PARIS

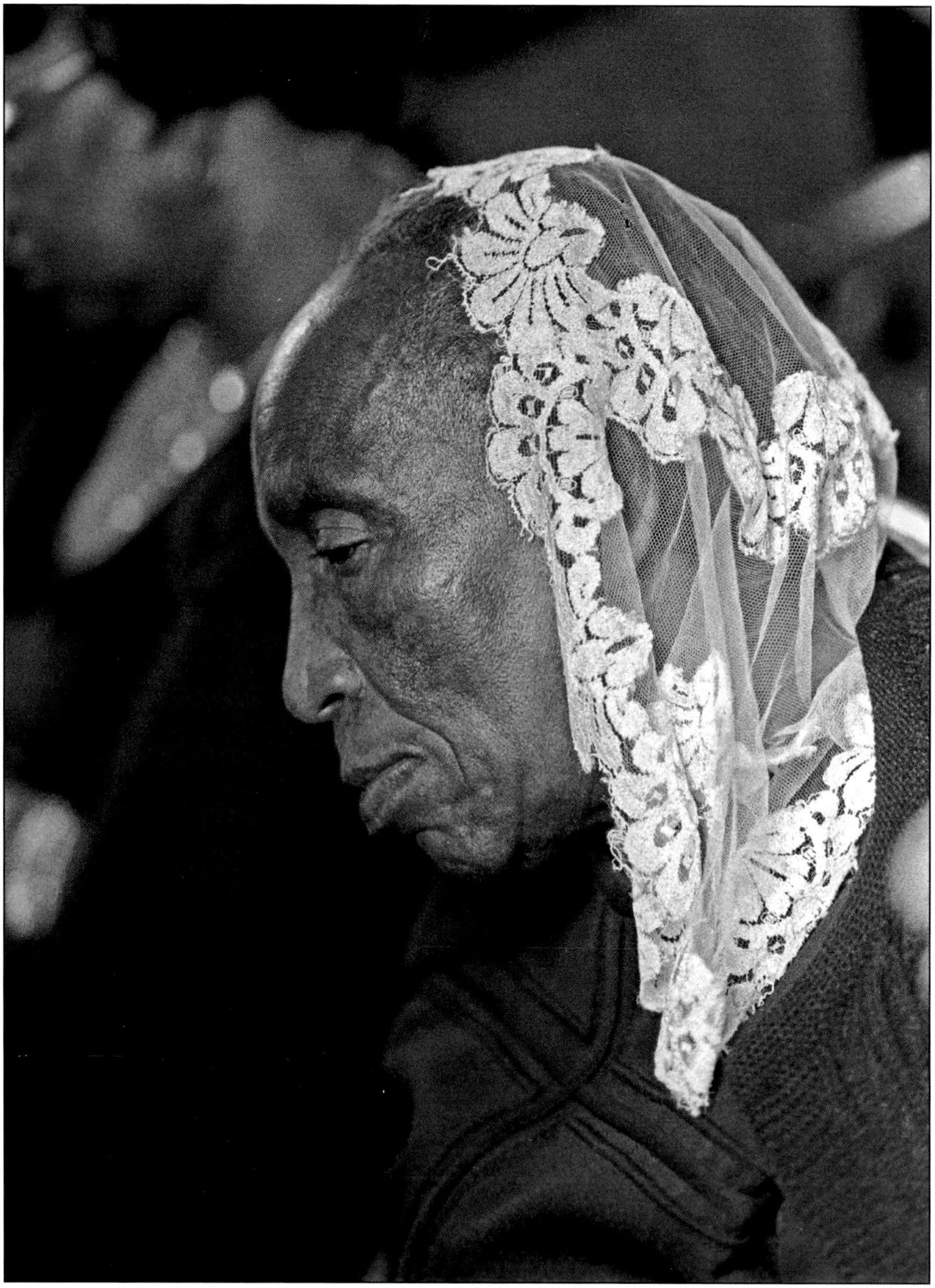

Unexpected

by Louis Maistros

Her life is not the expected poem, as comically human as your own.

Your fantasy of her was the last bit of magic that you owned; a molecule of forbidden possibility, empowering your imagination in a way that felt like sin or liberty; or something worse, or something better. Today you find her only just as you, and no more, but also no less. Yet you bandy about words like "fraud" and "scam" and "superstition."

Though you judge her she will not judge you; she understands the reasons behind the misconception; she has lived it; she has long since forgiven it; she loves you all the more for it because that's what she does, and that's who she is. Who are you?

You beg her for fortunes unearned—though you see she lives in poverty.

You seek from her cures for your ill—though you see she is withered and in pain.

You wish her to bring you love—though you see she is alone.

You ask for unfair advantage in the courtroom—though you judge her with extreme prejudice.

You ask her to facilitate revenge—without wondering why she doesn't seek same against those who come to her house armed with nickels, dimes, and disrespect.

She understands your contempt as a projection of your own self-doubt, and so she worries about your ability to find happiness within yourself. She will help you, God willing. And your nickels are not her motivation.

It's been said she is in league with the devil, but there are no devils in her faith. No blame, no spiritual scapegoat. There is only a desire to heal. The devil is yours alone to battle. He does not exist in her world, at all.

This desire of yours, to believe things untrue about her, is not a process of faith, but a process of spiritual despair. She knows this, she has been there, and so she does not fault you.

You ask her the big question, the one she is asked daily, sometimes hourly:

Does voodoo really work?

You ask her this as a child asks about the existence of angels, with wide-eyed wonder, hoping beyond hope that there are things in this world that transcend the flesh-and-blood realities of hunger and loneliness; collateral damage and bad credit.

If she were cruel she might put it to you like this:

Do the prayers of your own faith "really work"? Why must her faith "really work," while yours is allowed divine mystery?

Her only prayer is this: that you may find your own magic, in your own heart, in your own faith, in your own God-given ability to love others and to be loved, and that you may allow these things into your soul without question or regret.

Let's ask it again, and spell it right this time: Does Vodou really work?

Yes, it does. But not because of any hocus pocus stuff. It works because faith has healing properties, and because the unconditional love that she has shown you today has made an impression on you. And this is a thing that *your own God*, the one who lives in your heart, will not let you forget.

Salted Earth

by John Biguenet

A friend in dusty northern Texas tells me gardeners there have a saying: "If it's dying, it's a flower." In lush, subtropical New Orleans, we have had the opposite problem: how to keep things from growing.

With the help of the U.S. Army Corps of Engineers, though, that problem has abated. Thanks to the collapse of defective levees the Corps designed and built, most of New Orleans was flooded with up to twelve feet of saltwater in 2005. Because the Corps was unprepared for such a catastrophic failure, that water was allowed to stagnate in place for weeks as it grew more and more heavily contaminated by the gasoline and oil and mercury leaching out of the hundreds of thousands of vehicles submerged in the flood, by the household chemicals and cleaning agents stored under the sinks and in the garages of the tens of thousands of inundated homes, by the industrial solvents and other compounds in the flooded service stations and factories and warehouses of the city, and by the raw sewage that overflowed into the fetid lake that had been New Orleans.

So when my family returned home on a sweltering October morning more than a month later, our garden looked as it had after an extraordinarily rare snowfall the Christmas before. With so much destruction to absorb, I did not grasp what I was seeing until the white crust crunched under my rubber boots. Salt, I realized.

The evaporating water had left behind salted earth. The bleached grass that bordered our garden was yellow with rot. The hearty rosebushes of August had withered into brambles of thorns. Hibiscus and camellia bushes were brittle as kindling. All that was left of eight-foot-tall Japanese magnolias as old as our grown children were brown stalks jutting from dead earth. And everything stunk of death. I hacked down what was still standing.

With a house to gut, we could not tend our garden. Nearly a year later, we moved back into the part of the house that had been made habitable. But even a year after that, almost two years after the levee collapse, we still had not hung a single painting on its walls nor had we been able to bring ourselves to plant a new garden.

And so, while we were away for a month that summer, a friend took it upon herself to give us flowers. Enlisting another friend, she brought in fresh earth, planted perennials, trimmed the wild lantana that had floated in on the flood and rooted, set a satsuma tree in the center of the garden, and mulched everything with pine needles, a memento of the pine trees the neighborhood had lost to the saltwater.

Returning at the beginning of August, we were as surprised by the blooming garden as we had been two years earlier by the salted plot of withered plants that had welcomed us home.

We have cared for the garden we were given out of love, and it has flourished. But we still haven't hung a painting on the new walls of our house.

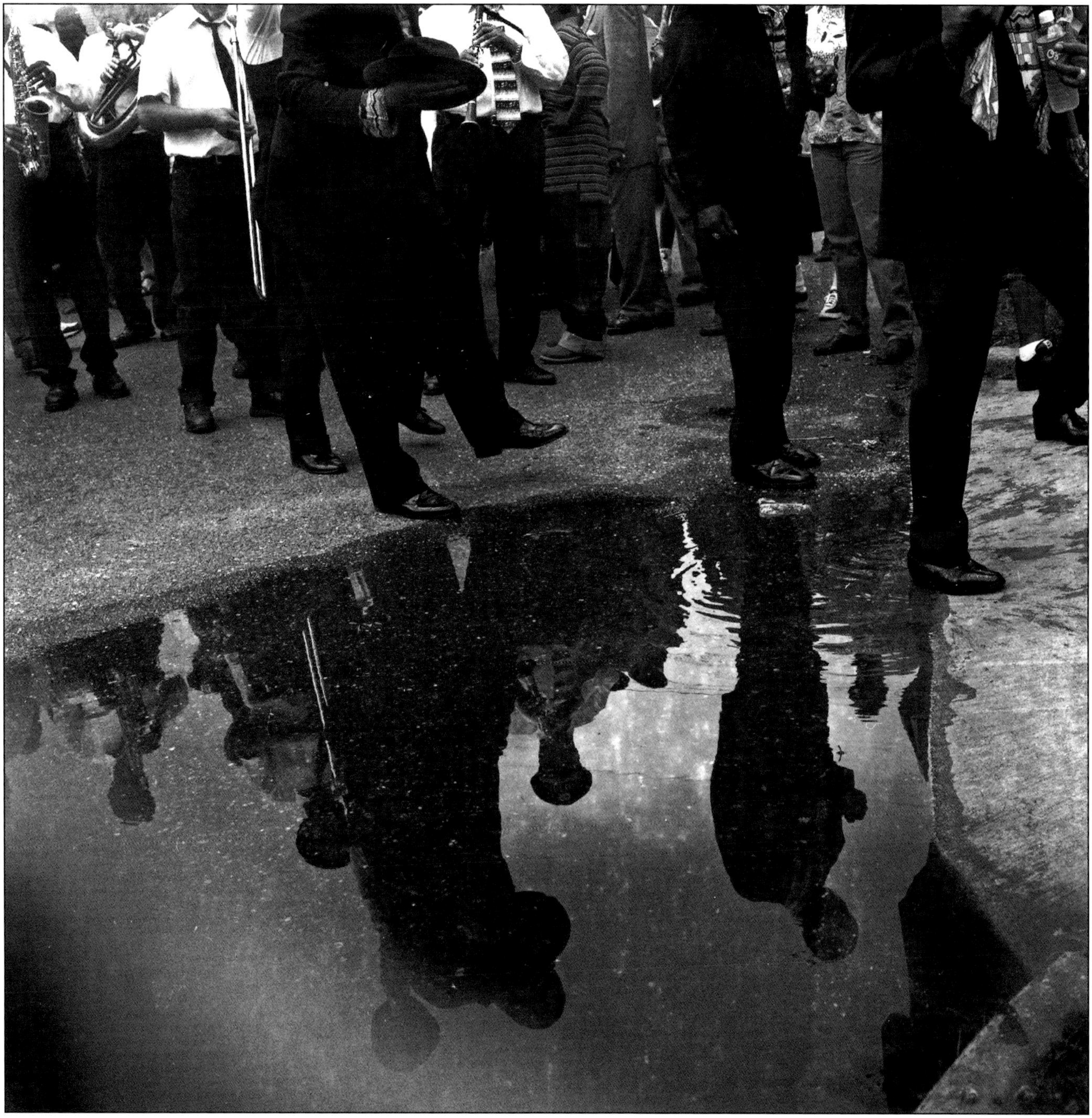

Dat 9th Ward

by Page 1NE

Cross da canal, Dat Lower 9,
9th Ward Step'rz, Have'n 2nd line,
Forstall Park, Play'n football,
Heineken, Crawfish, Hole in da Wall,
Desire and Florida, Both projectz,
Gold teeth in da mouth, Platinum chainz on neck,
Chir'n play'n to see who'z da fastest,
Future gymnast, Flip'n on mattress,
Hot sunny dayz, In da fire hydrant,
Block party, Barbecue chicken fry'n,
Loud rap machine, Real loud, Turn'd up,
Hair get braid'd on da porch, Frozen cups,
Marshall Faulk, Came out Dat 9,
Lawless, Carver, Nicholls, School time,
Da boyz club, Hang'n on da corner,
Play'n on da neutral ground, Just cause we wanna,
Got Luv fa my set, An Page 1NE Luv Hard,
Dat 9th Ward, Dat 9th Ward,
Dat 9th Ward, Dat 9th Ward

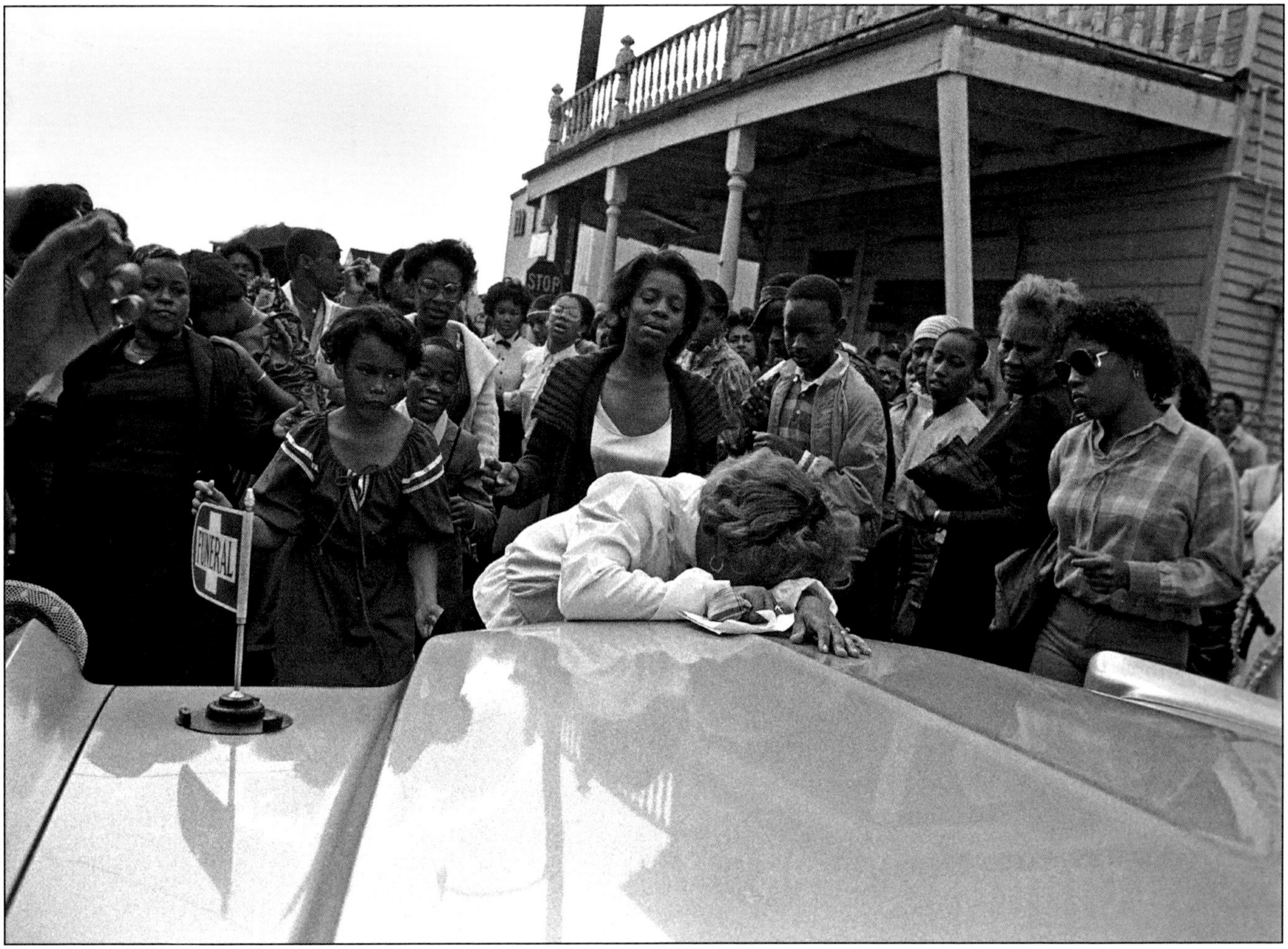
STOP
FUNERAL

What to Do with Your Goat in a Drowning World

by Andrei Codrescu

Hear the helicopters come over the roof
Water's up to my attic windows
And I'm stuck here with my goat
I can see my neighbor in the hole on his roof
He's got two dachsies and a tomcat
Just across the rushing river is his sister
She's cradling her baby and a rooster
Circling helicopters circling helicopters
Will take me but not my goat
Will lift me up from muck and flood
But they won't take my neighbor's dogs or cat
Or his sister's baby's rooster
Helicopters overhead nation to the rescue
Take the people damn their friends
I'm not going without my goat
He's not going without his pets
Baby won't leave without her rooster
Lord oh lord why don't we have an ark
That's the helicopters leaving
That's the nation to the rescue
Leaving us here in the dark

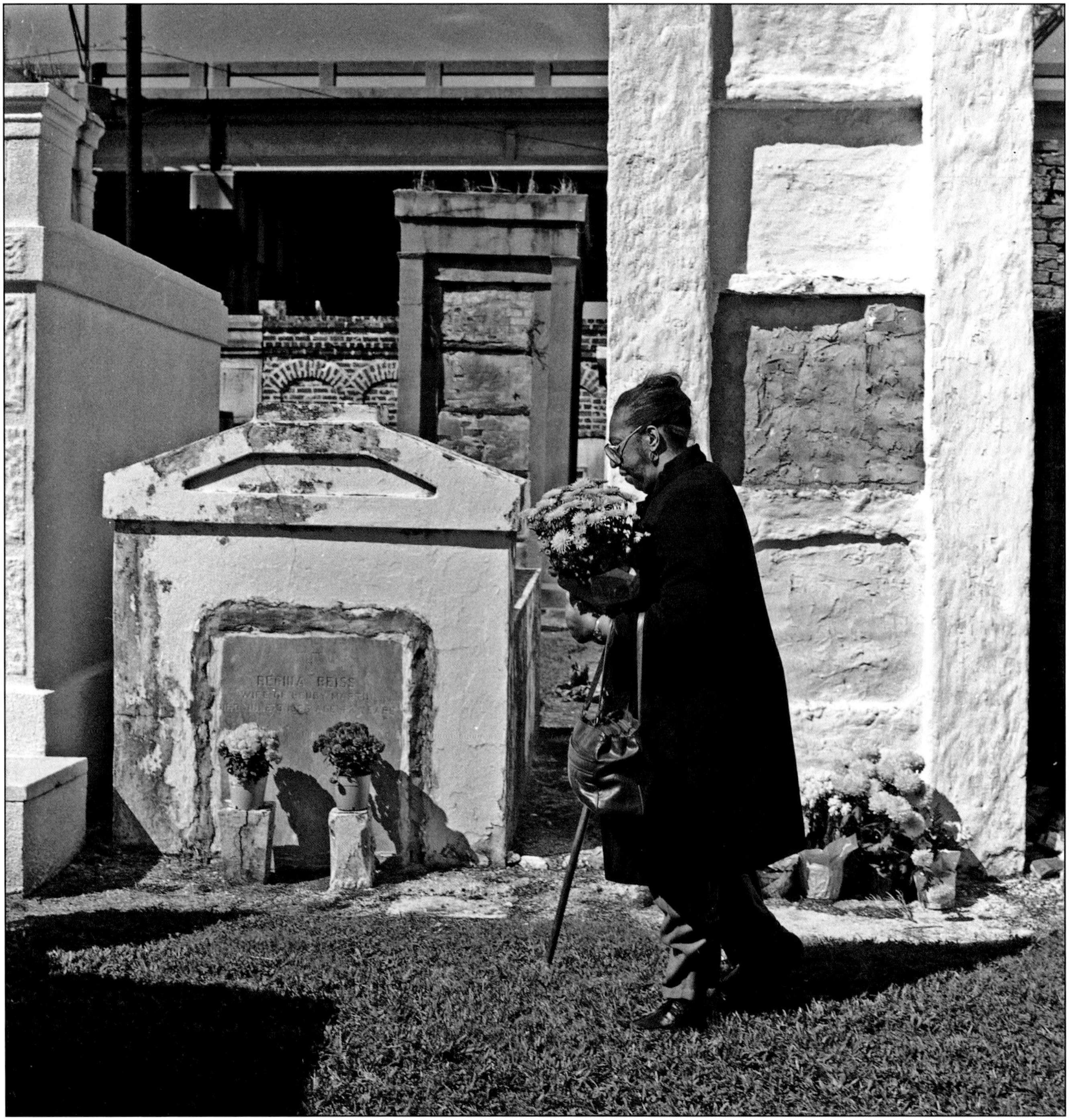

Anti-requiem

by Louis Maistros

In New Orleans, a cemetery is a place where life is welcome.

Here lives music and art and wild mystery, a place where children may remain children and puritanical rituals of gloom are run off on a rail. Here a stand is made against the passing of time, where rare splendors partner-up with dust and ash, where sadness cuts to the bone but is banished before long—and a first line of defense is drawn against the inevitable gone-too-soon.

In New Orleans there exists a delicate truce with all preconception of mortality and hereafter; be they scriptured, scripted, believed, doubted, lied-about or wildly-guessed. It is a truce renegotiated every hour of every day over chicory and smoke and liquor and sometimes something stronger but always with love and always with respect.

Here is where life's brevity is acute, where the dead share altitude with the living, where the waters rise too soon, too fast; taking, taking; but sometimes to give back, to guide the sorrow-blind and ghostly to and beneath the short and chopping waves that surround, to a place of mysterious finality called *Spiritworld*, where grand reunions are awaited, where ancient and bittersweet prayers are at long last addressed in no uncertain terms.

The divine is made human in this juncture of beauty and decay, and so the heavy brows of Catholic saints are aligned and have sameness with African *Iwas*, their holy burdens shared and lightened like the music that connects them, standing together as one, with upright backs and shoulders broad enough to carry us through the rain and into the sun-crazed light of day.

The grieving who enter this yard of plain brick and stone, humble and holy, on hands and knees; these ones will give themselves over. Caught up as they are, helpless and trembling as children, they will let go. There is no way for them but to surrender in sound and spirit, to fall backwards into the arms of un-provable faiths, to allow their souls the momentary luxury of deathly plummet; through to the hollow bounce of rock bottom, to suffer ecstasies unreal shot out through the business end of a trumpet, soaring ever skyward to the waiting arms of life, of love, of having survived the unthinkable a hundred times over, and now once more.

And still yet again.

In New Orleans to run from death is to leave life behind. They are intertwined, these things. We know this, we accept this, and this is who we are.

In New Orleans everything that has gone to ash only serves to inspire and invigorate the living. In death, we weave our souls into the fabric of the collective memory. In death we invent life anew.

Katrina:
Death and Rebirth of a New Orleans Life

by Dr. Michael White

Nearly six weeks after Hurricane Katrina's aftermath devastated New Orleans, I returned home with the feeling that life as I had known it was gone forever. After maneuvering through miles of lifeless debris-filled streets, I arrived at my flood-ravaged home. Beneath the wet, moldy wreckage lay rooms of books, recordings, photographs, sheet music, interviews, and research that represented decades of my life's work in jazz.

Unearthing random pieces of lifeless, swollen, rusty, moldy clarinets from my vintage collection was like finding my own discombobulated corpse.

As devastating as the loss of my home and collection were, the next couple of years proved to be even more difficult. A host of post-Katrina problems, the slow recovery process, and the effects of posttraumatic stress were coming close to draining the last vestiges of life out of me. Just as all seemed lost, God and music came to my rescue.

In December 2007 a "recovery residency" at local artist retreat facility, A Studio in the Woods, brought much needed rest and a chance to connect with God and nature. I soon found renewed joy in living and was able to open up to a spiritually charged creative state, during which I composed three-dozen songs and further developed a new stylistic approach to traditional New Orleans jazz. While some of the original music reflects the sadness of the Katrina tragedy, most of the songs are upbeat and joyous. I had subconsciously internalized and adopted the philosophy of our traditional jazz funerals: Celebrate the sadness of death, but also optimistically transition into a new existence.

Then came the revelation that despite the devastating losses and continuous hardship brought on by Katrina, I was still very fortunate and blessed with things that could never be lost or washed away: my rich life as a musician and the strength, knowledge, and wisdom passed down to me by dozens of elderly musicians who had mentored my early career.

Nearly four years after Hurricane Katrina I find myself in the early stage of a new life. Though recovery remains a slow and ongoing challenge, I have been very productive—performing, teaching, writing, and composing. I feel myself growing as a musician and have ventured into very different musical styles for the first time. My recently released recording, *Blue Crescent*, contains a dozen original, traditional jazz compositions with a fresh and personal perspective on tradition.

Another major loss came in April 2009 with the death of my mother after a long struggle with Katrina-related illness. She had been my best friend and confidante for many years. Yet I am comfortable in knowing that my mother—like my elder musical mentors—is not gone, but very much alive inside of me. They are all now a part of my soul and the spirit which fuels every breath that sings through my clarinet. With the grace of God and the wisdom of the elders, I look forward to many more years of growth and productivity. It is exciting to be where I am today. My old life is gone, for sure, but the new one is full of potential and optimism for the many songs to be written, youth to inspire, and concerts to be played around the world—bringing the spiritual ecstasy of New Orleans music around the world.

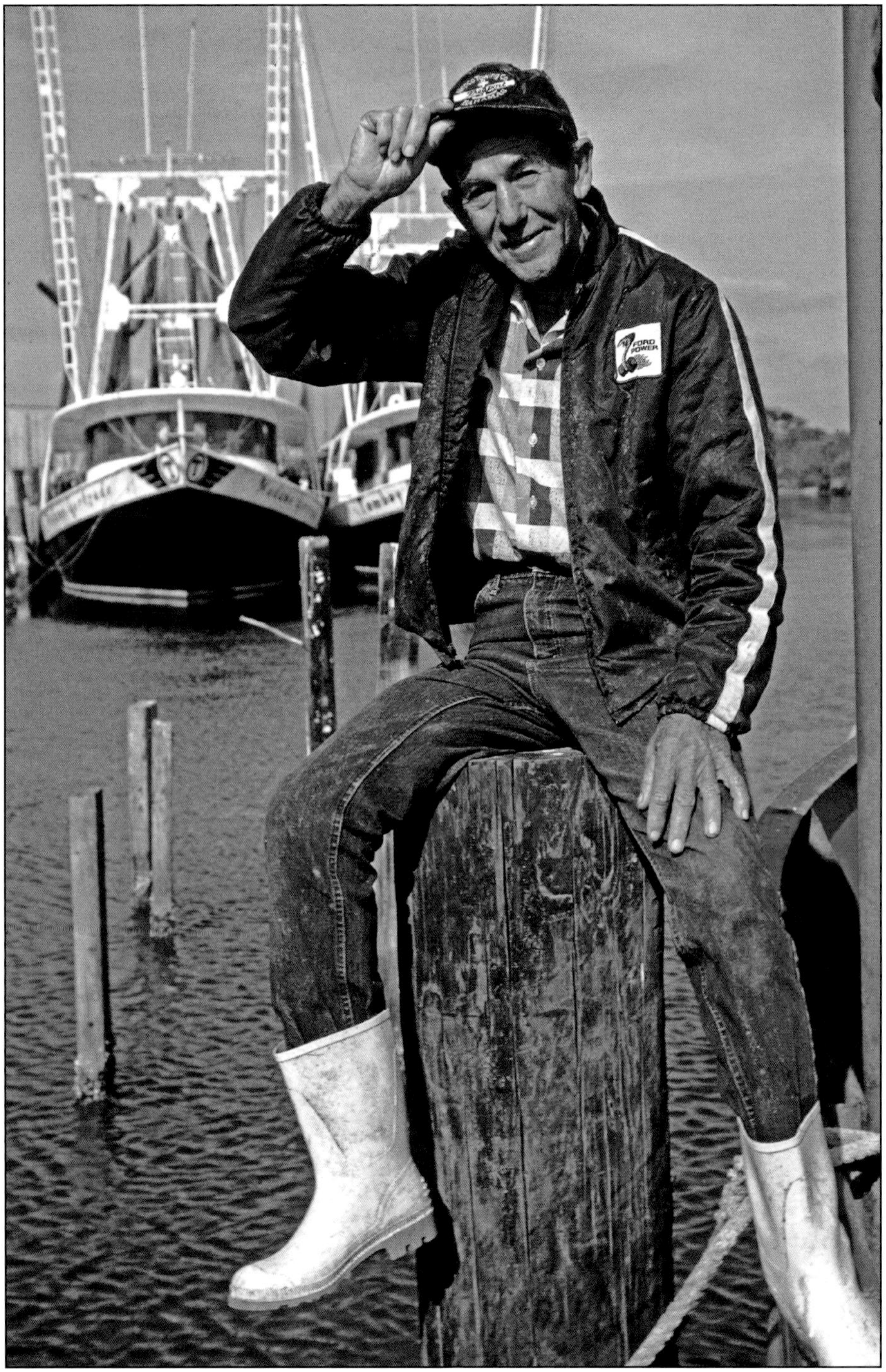
FORD POWER

End of the World

by Joshua Clark

The last thing I heard sitting in my boarded-up, trembling New Orleans apartment before the power went off at dawn on August 29, 2005, was that Katrina was about to make landfall seventy miles south in Plaquemines Parish. Sadly, it was the last thing many people would ever hear about the parish.

On each anniversary of Katrina, we must revisit New Orleans, yes, but it is the regions south of the city that hold the key to its survival, as well as the economic and ecological well-being of the whole country. None are perhaps so vital as Plaquemines Parish, the county that begins five miles down the Mississippi River from the city and runs into the Gulf of Mexico. Just as Plaquemines was ground zero for Katrina, it is too for wetlands erosion. It is the fastest-disappearing landmass on the face of the earth, a national crisis that America can avoid.

Louisiana's coast is unique. There are almost no beaches, only 3.4 million acres of marsh and swamp between New Orleans and the Gulf. These wetlands have always buffered Louisiana from hurricanes, because storms fueled by warm water die when they hit land. But largely because the wetlands that might have absorbed Katrina's storm surge had been eroded, New Orleans flooded. And if we let the Gulf creep up next to the edge of New Orleans, it will take one storm to wipe the city away.

I saw such a tragedy foreshadowed in Plaquemines. When the flooding receded, it left hardly a shadow because there was nothing left to make one. For its size, the parish is one of the richest places on Earth. Oil rigs blotch its horizons; refineries light its nights like science-fiction cities; and giant shrimp, oyster, and fishing boats troll its water. While it supplies the country with seafood, fuel, and immense federal tax revenues, it faces obliteration as a consequence.

Thousands of miles of channels have been dredged for oil pipelines and navigation, funneling saltwater from the Gulf into freshwater marshes, killing vegetation that holds them together. Ironically, these very channels kill the pipelines' main defense against storms—the wetlands. And so, damage caused by Katrina and Rita shut down 90 percent of crude oil production in the Gulf, and gasoline prices soared because Louisiana provides over one-fifth of all domestic oil and gas.

Disregarding Plaquemines' unique culture, or its massive habitat for endangered species, or that Louisiana's wetlands are the largest coastal ecosystem in North America, a good percentage of the things you use everyday probably came through Plaquemines' waterways, part of the world's largest port system.

But in reaping the benefits of this region, America sows the seeds of its destruction. Most of Katrina's damage to Louisiana was man-made, because in seventy-five years we have undone 2,500 years of wetlands growth.

Unlike earthquakes, wildfires, or terrorist attacks—after which no one questions rebuilding the affected areas—wetlands erosion is preventable through river diversion and hydrological restoration projects. The science and engineering is here, now. But the policy is not. That must change.

Katrina's damage is far from healed. And yet, the storm is fading from the news. When the president spoke on Jackson Square during Katrina's aftermath, I huddled with others around a radio two blocks away. He said, "There is no way to imagine America without New Orleans." And we cheered at his words, because for two weeks we had all witnessed New Orleans without America. Please, don't abandon us again. None of us can afford it.

Ooh Poo Pah Doo

by Ned Sublette

You have asked me: what can't be lost?

For convenience, and because it sounds better when we sing it, let's call it Ooh Poo Pah Doo.

By which I mean the cultural continuity of New Orleans. Which is to say, the memory of the struggle.

I want to tell you about Ooh Poo Pah Doo.

The Indians, the Social and Pleasure Clubs, the Baby Dolls, the Skeletons. Tambourines and fans. Battle dances and brass bands. The manly art of sewing. $300 green shoes. Bonnets and bottles, skull and bones.

I want to tell you about Ooh Poo Pah Doo.

The collective knowledge released when the crowd shouts *hey!* on the three-*and* after the brasses play *da-dat-dweeeeeeee-dat* on a Sunday afternoon second line.

I want to tell you about Ooh Poo Pah Doo.

St. Louis Cemetery #1, where those wrought-iron Kongo crosses on the tombs cross not at the chest but at the center, showing us the kalunga line that separates the living from the land of the dead on the other side of the water.

I want to tell you about Ooh Poo Pah Doo.

Holt Cemetery, where Buddy Bolden's bones are buried though no one knows the exact location of his grave, and where Jessie Hill's final resting place is marked with a stone that says, "Ooh Poo Pah Doo."

I want to tell you about Ooh Poo Pah Doo.

The memory of the struggle of a black island town with the sea at its ass and a hostile white state on the other side of the bridges.

The struggle for the civil right to dance down the street, free from fear of thug or cop.

The struggle to remember what you saw, heard, and lived, when even your shoebox of pictures is gone.

The struggle to tear down the symbol of disrespect that is I-10 over Claiborne.

The struggle to bring services to the poor.

The struggle to survive but at the end of the day you have your food, your drink, your family, your community, your place in the densest, most original musical territory of the United States.

I want to tell you about Ooh Poo Pah Doo.

The link to the revolutionary territory of Cuba, embargoed by the United States in an embargo that is also an embargo of New Orleans.

I want to tell you about Ooh Poo Pah Doo.

The link to the revolutionary territory of Haiti, never more obvious than when disaster strikes and the United States government's first act is not to help, but to contain.

I want to tell you about Ooh Poo Pah Doo.

The knowledge that we make each other possible, we gods and humans. Gods can crush humans, but they too will die if humans fail to remember them. The gods don't dare take all the humans out, because that would be suicidal on their part.

Ooh Poo Pah Doo can't be lost, because Ooh Poo Pah Doo is indestructible. But there are unquiet spirits hovering in the air.

That's why we need so many sousaphones.

The dead are dancing with us.

I want to tell you about Ooh Poo Pah Doo.

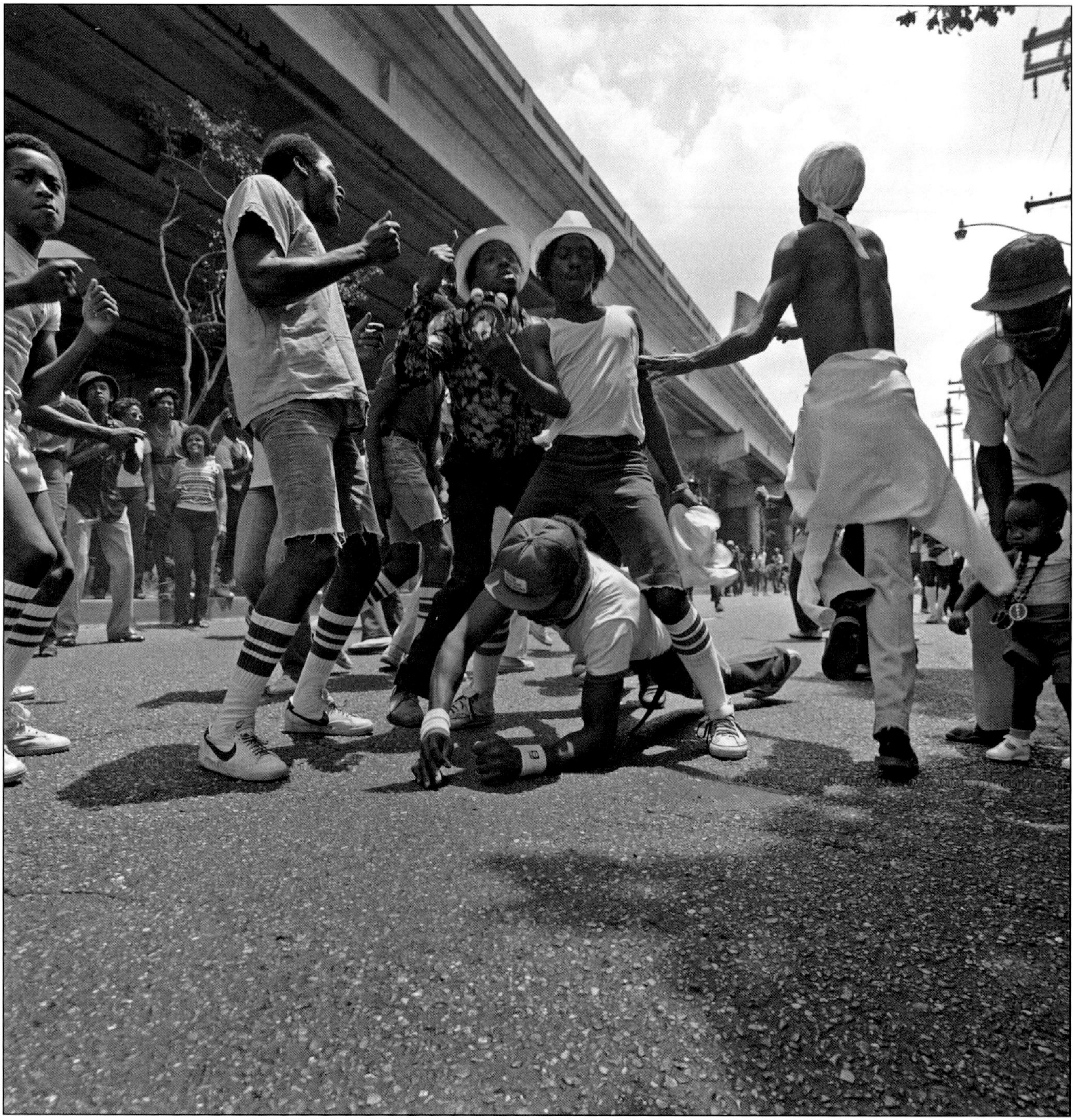

What the Water Can't Wash Away

by Jorin "Jahn Be" Ostroska

Now that so much has changed—it's easier to know what's important in your life, what keeps you alive, keeps you going for another week or another day. Now that so much of what we had has been washed away, layers of cultural strata cleanly swept into various corners of this country, at least we still have something that can bring us joy . . . at least we still have the Second Line. I cling to it like a lifeboat—like a jagged floating board that buoys my spirit, gives me hope, or at least a temporary peace of mind. My name is Jahn Be and I only exist because of the Second Line—and each week a new golden chalice of a Sunday awaits my thirsty lips and hungry feet yearning for dance and euphoria. I live to be submerged into the fluid glory of this fantastic African street parade. Of course, without the brass bands we are nothing, we would be just another boring procession—but no, thankfully, the brass, the Rebirth, the Hot 8, the Free Agents, is still here. Urgent, heavy, real as ever. It's so easy to feel the depth of that groove, the deep jagged crack that syncopates the Second Line music. The Tuba that cushions the embattled concrete, which heaves drunkenly underneath this brown moving sea of people. The electrifying horns that spark the fire in my feet, making it impossible to stay still. I buck and sway like the river: fluid, changing, and always on time. These streets list like heavy seas, concrete topples, and pavement crashes. This lifeboat of humanity exhilarating on white-water rapids of funk. Dying and becoming, moment-to-moment, under the thick, green, treacherous arms of our live oaks . . . rolling past skeletons of the Magnolia. Ashes of the Lafitte. Broken lives in heaps, tears dried up in the shock of rubble piled high about the St. Bernard and Calliope. This parade of men, this social aid and pleasure . . . it's now only a Band-Aid to hide the complexity of the wound within us all. But we dance in spite of it, or because of it—we feel the fountain of the dance well within us expressing everything that we cannot talk about. And those of us, the survivors, the fools, the hangers-on, we drink a Heineken and smile big at one another 'cause we're all in the same lifeboat and it's sustaining us, keeping us afloat for one more day. And though I am a card-carrying member of the Revolution and the Keepin-It-Real Social and Pleasure Clubs where twice a year I bask in the spotlight of my own parade, I truly exalt on the sidelines where the real dancers shine. On the sidelines we do it for love. Without the finery of ostrich plumes and deep-crushed velvet, without the pomp and circumstance of 1500 dollar handmade Alligator shoes. Here is where the soul alights and tree stumps, garbage-can lids, manhole covers, old Buicks, and shattered bus stops become stages for the ascension of our spirits. In these transcendent moments we are the shining stars of this unique city and nothing, not even all that water, can take this away.

Part Three:

Big Chief Got a Golden Crown

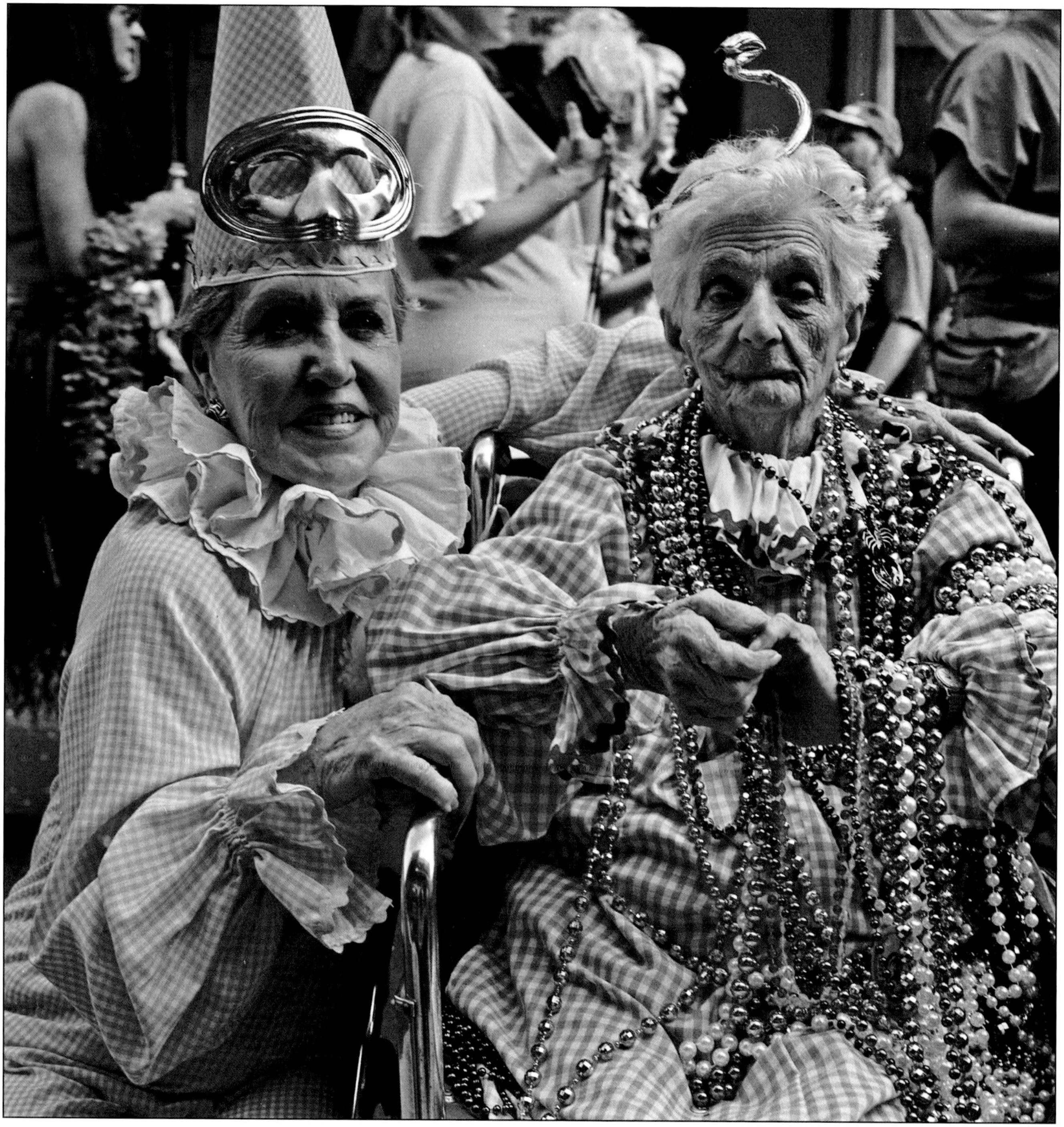

Mardi Gras

by Christian Champagne

One Mardi Gras when I was a young boy just drifting from childhood into adolescence, my Uncle Sidney, the patriarch of my family, tagged along to the Hermes parade. He wanted to see one more Mardi Gras parade before he died. In my paradigm of the psychological landscape of masculinity, the fact that my hard-drinking longshoreman great-uncle wanted anything to do with something as ethereal as Mardi Gras seemed odd.

There is no doubt that on Mardi Gras Day, New Orleans communion consists of cold fried chicken and beer, that women do indeed show their breasts for beads, and that college kids get too drunk. But all of us who have grown up in this magnificent, flawed American masterpiece of place first met Mardi Gras as children. To a child Mardi Gras is a fairyland, a Christmas morning that lasts for weeks, an endless piñata. And with variations on a theme, it remains so for those of us who love it in all its magical incarnations.

On the first Mardi Gras after Katrina I walked Uptown along the parade route and shared the beautiful weather and company of many other Orleanians, many just back for Mardi Gras from their Diaspora. It was a tribal hug.

Explaining Mardi Gras to someone who has not experienced it is like trying to describe the taste of chocolate. It's toddlers dancing to brass bands. It's teenagers partying in a human sea including children and adults. It's those same adults worrying about all the things that adults worry about in the modern world, yet still able to dress up like a devil or, that post-storm year's topical choice, a stinking refrigerator.

Mardi Gras is a cultural snowflake that dances differently in every soul. A celebration tailored for every crazy member of the human family. The memory of my Uncle Sidney huddled against the damp cold watching the floats pass by that long ago night illuminated by flambeaux reminds me of the eternal human fun both winking and bowing to mortality that is an essential element of Mardi Gras. It makes my muse both cry and revel in the fact that we, the citizens of this mischievous American treasure, have spun the human condition into a portrait that sings in opposition to the inevitable.

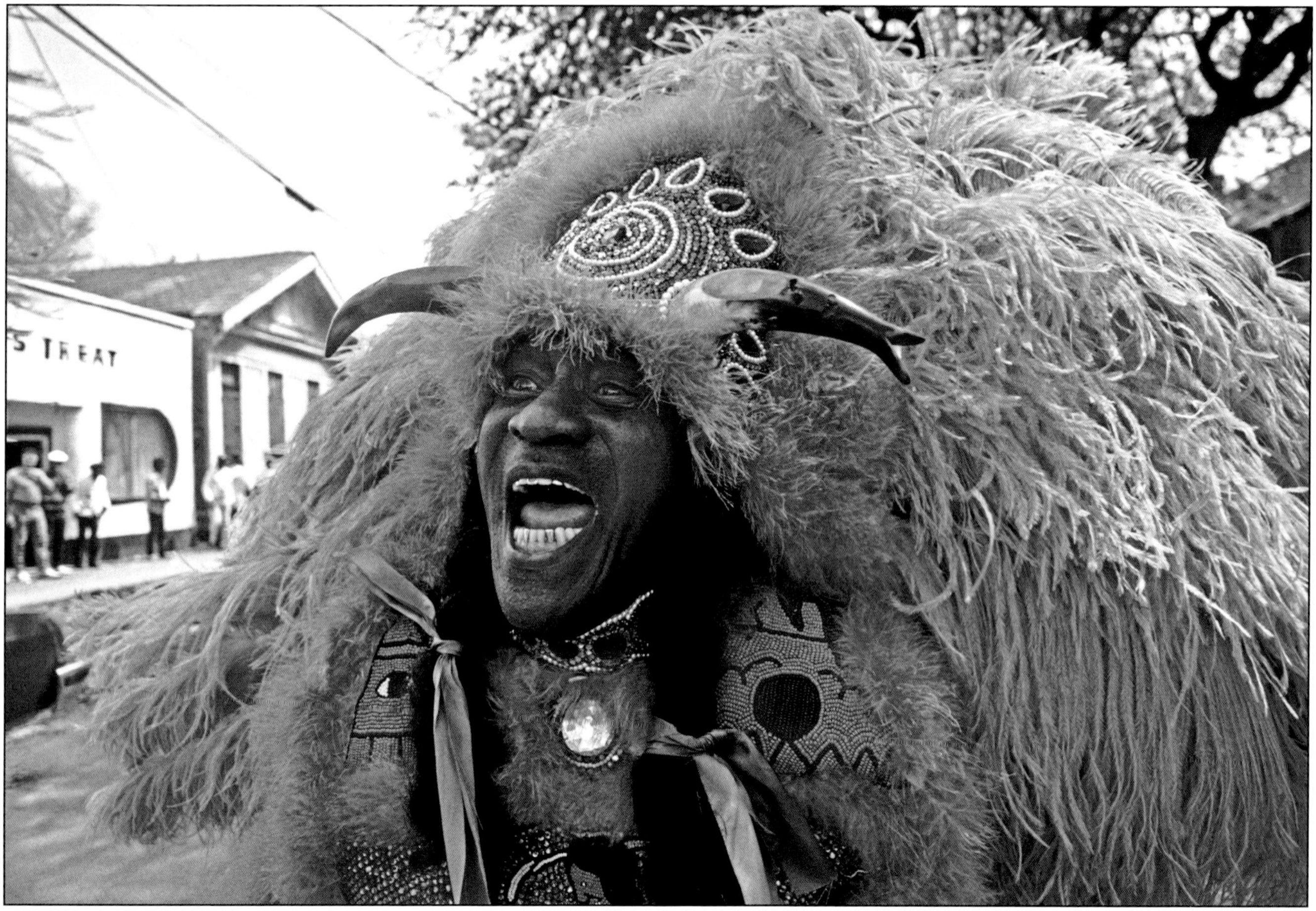
S TREAT

New Orleans: Black Indians at Mardi Gras

by Dr. Mona Lisa Saloy

Over one hundred years ago, Black men in New Orleans began to mask in homage to the bravery and indomitable spirit of the Native peoples of America, combined with the traditional masking in Africa and the Caribbean, the Black Mardi Gras Indians process in all their glory for everyone to see.

Amid the canals and downtown streets of New Orleans, between the boulevards and uptown neutral grounds, kicking up the dust, rambling in rhythms, spread eagle in the streets, chanting, humming, and hollering to cowbells, tambourines and drums, clapping and singing, dancing to African calls and responses felt in the gut delivered in the best Rhythm & Blues bravado, tinted soulfully with Gospel riffs, bent low in Blues notes, these Black Indians on Mardi Gras or St. Joseph's Day make kids break their necks to see.

Our manhood, these Black men emerge into the streets, processing like the personalities of God himself, some in fire engine red fury peacock feathers and beads, some in cloud soft white plumes and headdress, angelic, dancing down the streets, parting the gathering crowds hungry for a glance at their glorious display. Each tribe, each year, the Indians make new "suits" choosing different colors all at their expense. These carpenters, metal latherers, plumbers, mailmen, bartenders, chefs, daddies, husbands, brothers dancing with grace, chanting, sing their hearts out from early in the day to past dusk just for us, the folks on the block and in the neighborhoods. The Spy Boy scouts ahead of the entire tribe, making way for the Big Chief and his crew. An expert lookout, the Spy Boy is first, adorned in splashes of yellow one year, as a feather on his flag spear, then maybe red the next. Next, enter The Wild Man. The Wild Man is scary, the sheer energy of his cries, the frantic waving of his arms and spear. Sometimes, his "suit" is laden heavy with Ju Ju, big medicine, his entire face a mask, his headgear spouting two large pointy horns. His "suit" will tell the tale he shouts this year, his heritage from Houma braves to Black Kings in the Mother/Father Land, Africa. His medicine is melody and healing, protection of the ancestral spirits for the entire gang and tribe.

Then no one outdoes the Big Chief, since he is always the prettiest, with the most elaborate plumes, the most bold and big feathers spread across the sky, the most enchanting beading telling his story for the season, all on a Mardi Gras Day.

The sight of Black Indians is shocking, exciting, and we dance long before the Big Chief arrives; and when he does, we embrace thrills of joy. This is our Mardi Gras Day. These Black men with the history of their race on their faces, the rhythmic essence of our culture in their moves; thousands of beads painting a cultural story in their 170 to 200 pound "suits," their pride glowing with each passerby who watches and joins the dancing. This is our Mardi Gras Day, only in New Orleans.

A Lifetime Addiction

by Council Chief Ronald W. Lewis

I used to work at a little neighborhood grocery in the mid-1960s called Money Savers. Ricky Gettridge came by the store one day and said, "Well, Ronald, I'm masking. Come by my house." He lived on Tennessee Street near the St. Claude Bridge in the Lower Ninth Ward. We went to middle school together. I went over not knowing that I was going to end up with a lifetime addiction to the thread and needle.

Ricky's daddy, Merlin Gettridge, masked with Allison "Tootie" Montana, the Big Chief of the Yellow Pocahontas (YPH). The YPH were from the hub of the Seventh Ward, where there were lots of craftsmen who worked with their hands—bricklayers, cement finishers, ironworkers, latherers like Tootie, and plasterers like Ricky's daddy, Spyboy Hoppy. They transferred those skills of their labor to their costumes.

The design of Ricky's suit was a fighting kite, and he gave me this flower design to sew. As a Yellow Pocahontas, he used sequins and beads. They were the hardest things in the world to pick up. You got to pick up the sequins first, and then you pick up the bead, then you loop over and go back under with the thread. It becomes repetitious, and you're talking about thousands and thousands of these itty-bitty things. That one design took me as long to sew as it took the family to put together a whole suit!

From my start with middle school, the urge just heightened about the Mardi Gras Indian culture. It has mystique to it. Curiosity.

Over the years, I got to know some of the greatest Mardi Gras Indians who ever wore a suit, and not just the YPH family, but other Mardi Gras Indians, too, like Walter Cook, Sr., who had the greatest stories about making these suits and creating an identity. He had such a simple way of telling you about masking. He'd tell us, "Do your best and then when that day comes, wear your suit and don't worry about what you didn't get done." He talked more about the people who were the chiefs of certain gangs, and how proud the men were. I was like a child in a candy store, just absorbing everything that he offered.

I started seeking out people that said they were masking. I helped people sew. From sewing, you learn how to decorate, you learn how to design, and after a while you become an integral part of the society. It's a family. When you're sewing, everybody gets on the same page. You're sharing in those old war stories, and there's a ritual of having refreshment: beans cooked and hot dogs. It becomes an event in itself.

As you get older and get more experience in making the suits, you pick up a visionary thing about the beads. You can almost count how many beads go in a certain spot. It's like an artist with a brush who gets his stroke and flow into his painting. You get the feel in your hands, in your eyes, and your juices just flow. In the year of making a suit, you may go through numerous hardships and distractions. The sewing become a meditation. Your focus is only on what you working on. It's therapy, really.

St. Joseph's Day

by Katheryn Krotzer Laborde

Before you enter the coffee shop, stop for a paper. Go inside, order some joe, but skip breakfast. Open the paper—you'll find the notices announcing the locations of St. Joseph altars all over the town. Conjure a mental map and plan your pilgrimage.

The first altar you hit is in a church hall. One stark white wall, smudged from years of meetings and weddings, is hidden by the tiers of the parish's St. Joseph altar. The tiers— boxy, linen draped—are stacked to the ceiling. Move closer, fold into the crowd as it snakes past the candles and candies. Framed images of deceased parishioners shadow the cakes that bear their earthly names. Statues of saints elbow bottles of wine. Glossy breads—shaped like sandals and shepherds' staffs and wounded hearts, like crosses and crowns and martyrs' eyes—cover every possible inch.

Everywhere there is the smell of candle wax and breadcrumbs, stuffed artichokes and fried eggplant, red snapper and antipasto. Fill your plate and buy a glass of Chianti. Claim a space at a table. Let the sounds of Louis Prima distract you from the conversations of neighbors.

Put some money on the table and steal a dried fava bean for your pocket. Another dollar will buy you a crocheted cross that hangs from a silken cord. This you hang from your rearview mirror as you make your way to the next altar. Zipping through a yellow light, you should pause to think about the Sicilian immigrants who brought this tradition to New Orleans, and appreciate the weeks of work that go into the ritualistic feast that thanks St. Joseph for the gift of not going hungry. But, you don't. The day stretches before you, beautiful and lazy. Munching anise cookies, you drift from altar to altar, each one a little different, each one quietly the same.

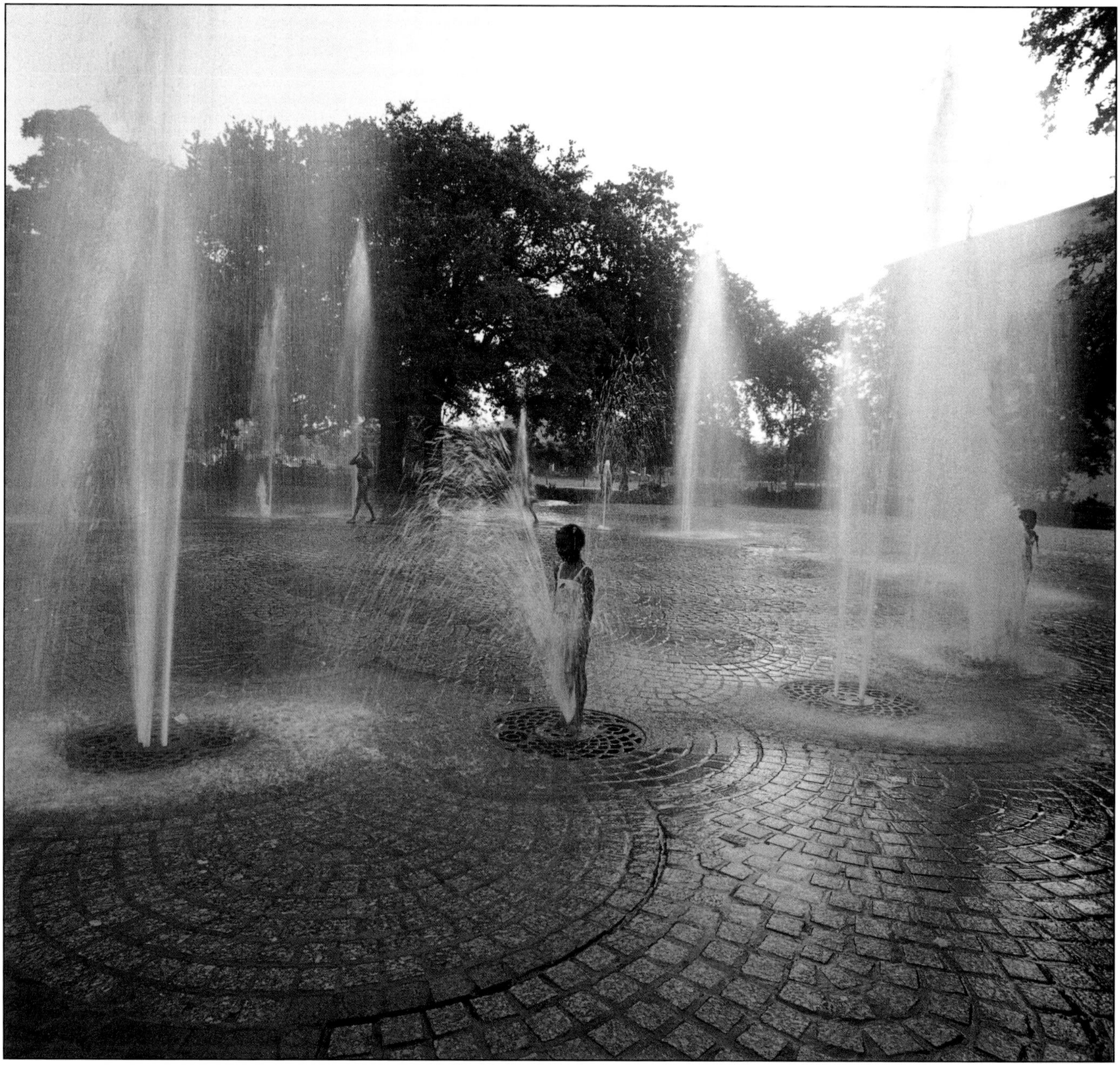

Congo Square

by Luther Gray

New Orleans is a magical and historic place. The city exists on many different levels. There is a spirit about the place. And if you want to find the epicenter of that spirit, visit Congo Square located within Armstrong Park.

Congo Square is in the "vicinity" of a spot which Houma Indians used before the arrival of the French for celebrating their annual corn harvest and was considered Sacred Ground. The gathering of enslaved African vendors in Congo Square originated as early as the late 1740s during Louisiana's French colonial period and continued during the Spanish colonial era as one of the city's public markets.

By 1803, Congo Square had become famous for the gatherings of enslaved Africans and free people of color who drummed, danced, sang, and traded on Sunday afternoons. By 1819, their gatherings numbered as many as 600 people every Sunday.

Among the most famous were the Bamboula, the Congo, and the Calinda.

The dance known as "Bamboula" may have had its origins in the Congo where the word means spirit. In Congo Square, the Bamboula was known as a dance of love danced sensuously by a man and woman who start dancing slowly then dance faster and faster until their movements climax and then a new couple takes their place, and the dance begins again. The rhythm played for the Bamboula dance has evolved over centuries to be known today as the rhythm of the second-line. The Calinda dance has its roots in Haiti, where it was done as a beautiful dance done by women in long skirts that flow hypnotically as the women move in circles.

These African and Caribbean dance, music, vocal expressions, and many others have influenced Mardi Gras Indian traditions, the second-line, New Orleans jazz, gospel, rhythm and blues, and funk.

The tradition of gathering in Congo Square continues to this very day. Drummers still gather in Congo Square on Sundays. Concerts and community events continually occur on this Sacred Ground. People go there to reconnect to their ancestral memory, meditate, and pray. Young and old are introduced to the historic events that have occurred and the history that is to be made. Many of the largest commemorations in the aftermath of Hurricane Katrina have taken place in Congo Square. Thousands gathered in Congo Square to drum and celebrate the spirit of the people of New Orleans during the one-year observances of Hurricane Katrina on August 27 and 29, 2006.

In January 2009, Armstrong Park and the Mahalia Jackson Theater of the Performing Arts reopened after major renovations were done due to damage from Hurricane Katrina. Congo Square is now being utilized more often for festivals, ancestral rituals, peace rallies, children's celebrations, drum circles, and daily walking tours.

Congo Square will continue to spiritually enrich those who visit and participate in the drumming, dancing, and cultural events that occur regularly. No visit to New Orleans is complete without a visit to Congo Square. While there, say a prayer of thanks to God and all those who have come before us and paved the way for us to have a better life. It is our responsibility to carry on the rich traditions of Congo Square and teach them to our children!

We Cry at Birth and Rejoice at Death

by Morgan Clevenger and Fred J. Johnson, Jr.

New Orleans, October 2005, Post-K

If Death is the true "freedom," a Jazz Funeral is the ultimate freedom celebration. For Africans and African Americans in colonial and contemporary New Orleans, life has been full of hardship and oppression. Death is often seen as the release, a going on to a better place. A Jazz Funeral is both a personal and community celebration of the life of the deceased and a public/private mourning that provides closure to the family and eternal remembrance of the departed.

New Orleans' unique community death rituals evolved from West African community and tribal practices. The belief systems of the Senegambian people, ancestors of many New Orleanians, are still essential in New Orleans culture today. Music is sacred, freedom rituals expressed as parades heal the village, funeral processions ensure the memory and souls of the deceased are not lost, and community alliances are the key to survival. As early as the 1780s, Mutual Aid and Benevolent Societies were formed by free and enslaved blacks of New Orleans. These social organizations were crucial for African American survival in the New World. Denied access to any form of medical or burial insurance by whites, members relied on each other for assistance through hard times and illness and ensured proper burials at death. These social groups also continued the expression of African forms of ceremony, dance, music, and celebration that evolved from the practices and rituals of Congo Square, the only place in America where free and enslaved people of color were allowed to openly express their culture.

Every element of a traditional Jazz Funeral is imbued with deep spirituality and symbolism. First, the physical body of the deceased is solemnly carried out of the Church or Funeral Home. As the casket is put in the carriage or hearse, a Brass Band plays a spiritual dirge or hymn. The procession leaves with the hearse leading, followed by the family. Next, a Grand Marshal, male or female, will lead the way; sometimes there are multiple Grand Marshals. If the deceased was a musician, club member, or Mardi Gras Indian, a delegation of his or her counterparts will form a processional division to represent the deceased's affiliations in life. The Band follows playing religious hymns and spirituals. The hearse, family, Grand Marshal, Brass Band, and processional divisions are the First Line, and the rear is brought up by the Second Line: friends, acquaintances, and strangers who have come to honor the spirit of the departed.

The procession goes through the neighborhoods and places the deceased frequented, giving a final "ramble" to the deceased and an opportunity for the living to pay tribute and preserve the deceased's life in the form of remembrances and stories. At a determined point, the procession will "cut the body loose" with the band forming an "alley" in the street for the hearse to drive through as family and friends touch the hearse to say their last goodbyes. Traditionally, the Band and procession would go to the burial site for this ritual, but today the site is often very far. In both cases, once the body is "cut loose" the tempo of the music changes from solemn to joyous, and the mood of the mourners transitions from sadness to celebration.

Every Jazz Funeral honors the spirit of the deceased and the spirits of the ancestors who have come before; in this way the spirituality and history of the people is constantly renewed, affirmed, and passed on.

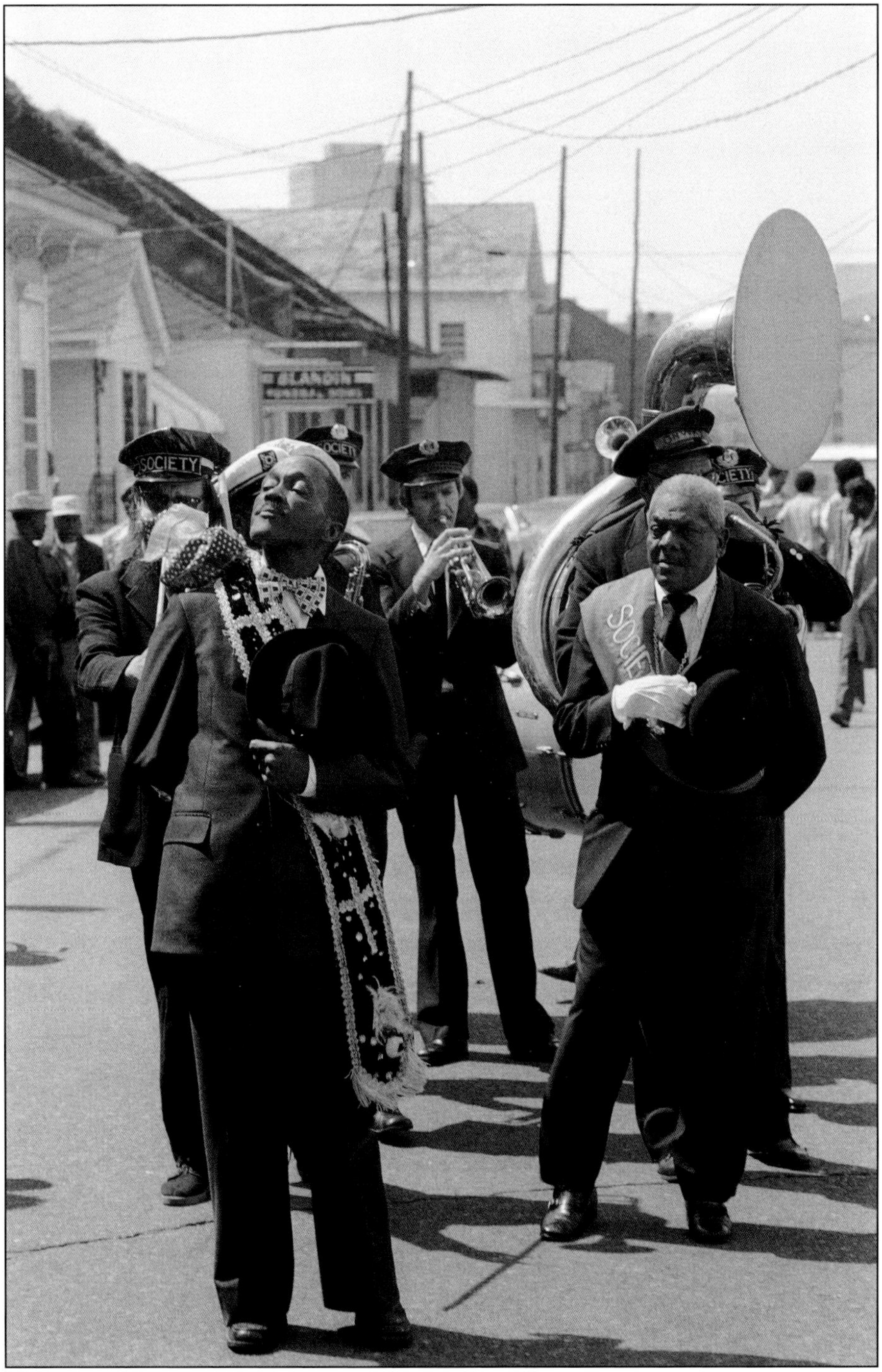
SOCIETY
SOCIETY
SOCIETY

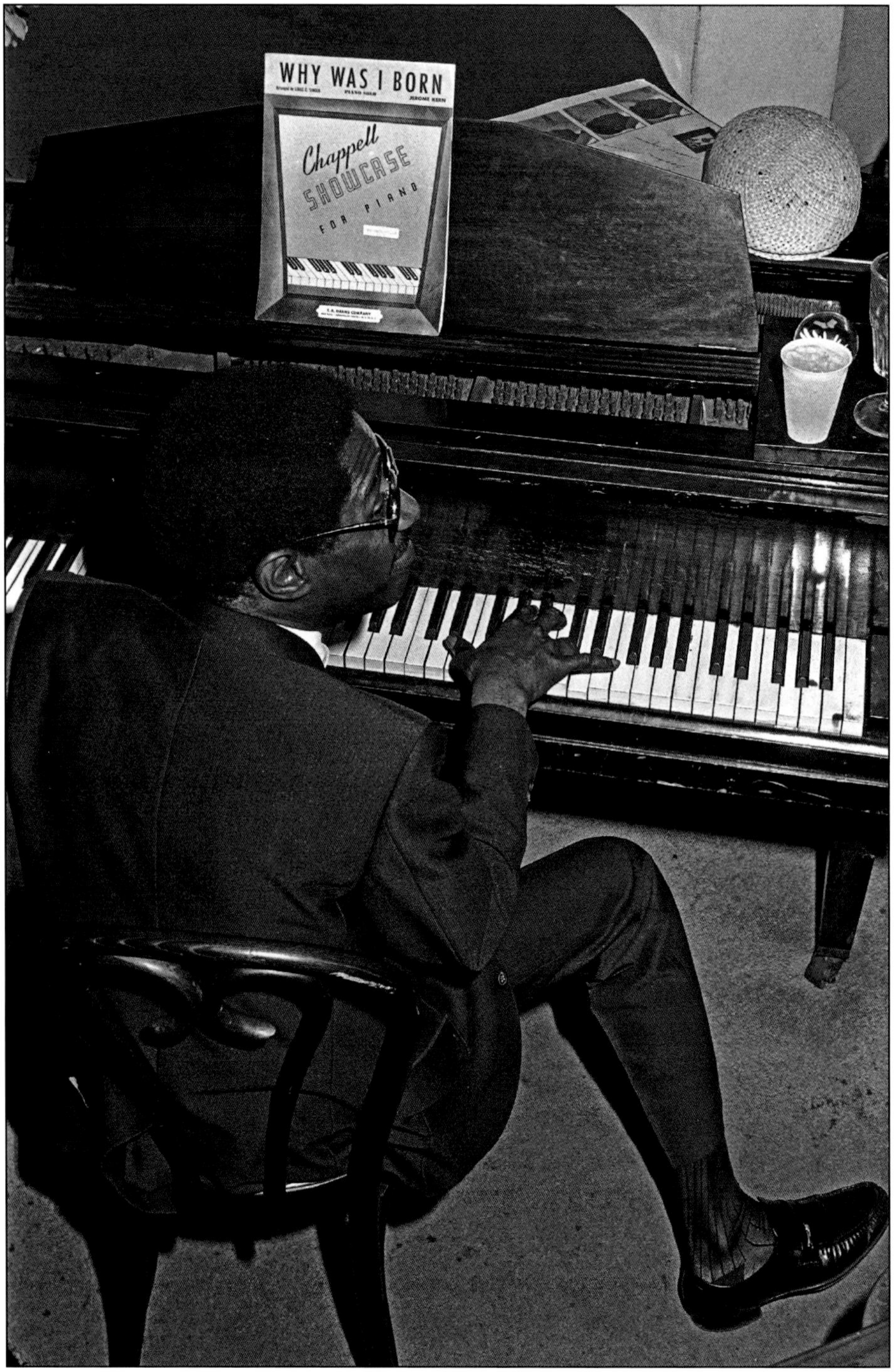
WHY WAS I BORN
PIANO SOLO
JEROME KERN
Chappell
SHOWCASE
FOR PIANO

Sound

by Tom Piazza

If New Orleans music were just jazz and no more it would still loom larger than any other art produced by Americans in the twentieth century. American music would be unrecognizable without Louis Armstrong, King Oliver, Jelly Roll Morton, and all the other artists who invented and developed jazz. But the story doesn't stop there.

Ray Charles and Little Richard both made their best early recordings in New Orleans, accompanied by New Orleans musicians. On Ray Charles' "Mess Around," in fact, you can hear Ray play a piano figure that Jelly Roll Morton played years before on his "New Orleans Blues." Fats Domino was one of the archetypal rock-and-rollers, and all of his recordings (most of which were arranged and orchestrated by the Crescent City's Dave Bartholomew) are suffused with the New Orleans spirit.

But probably no one had a more profound influence on musicians, especially pianists, than pianist and singer Henry Roeland Byrd, also known as Professor Longhair, who exported the Spanish tinge spoken of by Jelly Roll Morton, a kind of left-hand rhumba beat, and placed boogie-woogie and blues figures on top of it in the right hand. His songs, like "Tipitina" and "Go to the Mardi Gras," are perennial classics, and all you have to do is hear a few notes to know who you are listening to.

And how could you leave out Percy Mayfield, Lloyd Price, James Booker, Ernie "Mother-In-Law" K-Doe, Lee Dorsey, Huey "Piano" Smith and the Clowns, the Meters and the Neville Brothers and Dr. John . . . . And others unknown outside of New Orleans except by dyed-in-the-wool music freaks, people like Smiley Lewis and Big Boy Myles and Eddie Bo and Sugar Boy Crawford, who did the original version of "Iko-Iko" (he called it "Jock-a-Mo"), later made famous by another New Orleans group, the Dixie Cups. Today you can still hear local giants like guitarist and singer Deacon John, horn players Kermit Ruffins, Irvin Mayfield, and family members James, Troy, and Glen Andrews, pianists Ellis Marsalis, Tom McDermott, and David Boeddinghaus, and so many others, more than you could fit on this page or in this book. New Orleans is its music, and there is never any end to it.

My Heart, My Soul, My 'Hood

by Kami Patterson

New Orleans is a city of neighborhoods. While the total number and exact demarcations vary according to whether one consults city planners, historic commissions, or the residents themselves, nobody disputes the fact that an amazing variety of formal and informal subdistricts has emerged since the city's founding in 1718, each with a distinct ambiance.

Jane Jacobs, in her classic book *The Death and Life of Great American Cities*, espouses recreating exactly the kinds of diverse neighborhoods still enjoyed here, which were torn out of many urban centers in the 1950s and 1960s. Because the city clings tenaciously to her old-world, old-school character, we enjoy some of the most organically-grown neighborhoods in the country.

New Orleans is possessed of that most rare, satisfying combination: while saturated with sophisticated big-city delights, it manages to retain the intimate aura of a small town. The constraints of water on all sides create a natural sprawl deterrent. Neighborhood business and service clusters bring people out of their cars and onto the sidewalks. Within walking distance of my house are a coffee shop, sno-ball stand, bookstore, hardware, dentist, eye doctor, dry cleaner, grocery, several restaurants and bars, a library, police station, and shoe repair. This is what makes New Orleans so fundamentally different from the sterile, isolated, car-centric swathes that mar other cities, where houses seem separated by invisible moats. Having so many locally-owned services within quick reach changes not only the scale, but the pace. Life is relaxed and convivial here.

Each neighborhood has its own traditions and unique offerings. On a given Saturday one can sample local coffee and fresh produce at the Farmer's Market in the CBD, find handmade jewelry at the Freret Market, catch a crawfish boil in Mid-City, then a painting party and gallery tour in the Bywater, dinner near the Fair Grounds and drinks in the French Quarter or one of a myriad neighborhood bars. Hidden gems and treasures nestle in every neighborhood: soul food restaurants, po-boy shops, independent clothing and record stores, seafood sellers, and the still-ubiquitous mom-and-pop corner groceries. Many areas still boast street-side fruit stands or ring with the singsong cry of the traveling produce purveyor's truck: "I have peaches, I have plums!"

Despite her wild reputation, New Orleans is a city of good neighbors as well. Life is lived on sidewalks and verandas. We wave and stop to chat during afternoon strolls, know each other and our dogs by name. We can be found on each other's porches having a Friday night beer or cheering the Saints. There are annual block parties and community clean-ups. When the elderly lady down the street doesn't appear daily, someone checks in on her. Sometimes, yes, we even get in each other's business—the spirit of the classic nosey Irish Channel door-popping lady lives on. We know our children, characters, heroes, villains, leaders, and ne'er do wells. New arrivals are welcomed and old-timers, some from families who have lived here for generations, are revered. New Orleans' lifeblood is in the neighborhoods that coalesce to create a city culture even greater than the sum of its interwoven parts.

Bouncing with Jubilee

by Garnette Cadogan

It's a Sunday night in May 2007, and almost 2,000 people crowd in to hear the aptly-titled DJ Jubilee—the city's most popular D. J. who has been at it for twenty-five years—at The Venue, a warehouse/nightclub ten minutes' drive uptown from the French Quarter. "Walk with it," he chants, "Now walk with it!" Bodies swerve side to side as knees shoot up; the crowd resembles a band of disorderly drum majors. "Now dip with it!" Backs incline forward and knees rise again. "And dip with it!"

This weekly indoor block party began shortly after Club Sam's, New Orleans' main hotspot for bounce music, was shut down the previous summer due to violence. Succumbing to the city's rhythm rather than its rage, people flocked to the new location. "When people came back home they wanted their music," says Jubilee, "The King of Bounce" (who happens to be a special-education high school teacher by day). He describes the sound that dominates local nightclubs, block parties, high school dances, and drive-by loudspeakers as "dance party-type music that represents everybody."

Everybody in New Orleans, that is. Though bounce has been a local craze since the early 90s, and has been the musical soundtrack of New Orleans since then, it hasn't enjoyed much mainstream acceptance beyond its catchphrases: "wobble wobble," "back that thang up," and so on. And no wonder: Like most New Orleans cultural traditions—Mardi Gras Indians, Social Aid and Pleasure Clubs, Second Lines, you name it—bounce is intensely local. Bounce D. J.s and rappers regularly pay homage to the city's housing projects, neighborhoods, blocks, and even community dance groups. "I'm down with the Ninth Ward" is just as common as "I'm down with P&C," the corner of Philip and Claire Streets in the Third Ward. At his gig at The Venue, DJ Jubilee plays song after song with the same rattling beat, often supplying the vocals himself. "Magnolia"—the famed Third Ward housing project, shuttered since Katrina—"is in the building," he singsongs. "They say that," the crowd refrains. "Calliope"—another Third Ward housing project, also depopulated now—"is in the building!" And everyone responds in Fat Albert imitation: "Hey, hey, hey." "St. Thomas"—the project where Jubilee grew up, long ago demolished—"is in the building." And the sweaty, ebullient crowd agrees: "You already know!"

These chant-propelled call-and-response songs, tied to the omnipresent stuttering, sampled beat known as the Triggerman, have a pattern and aesthetic that recalls Jamaican dancehall reggae as much as American hip-hop. For outsiders (not only to the city, but also to the music, for bounce has many detractors in its hometown) it all sounds the same. For locals attuned to its vernacular, though, bounce has sharp distinctions. There's "old-school bounce," with its raunchy raps over samples of Derek B's "Rock the Beat" and The Showboys' "Drag Rap." Then there's "sissy bounce," with its frenetic rhythm overlaid with the sexual boasts of transvestite rapper Katey Red or gay MC Big Freedia. Currently, the fashion is playing R&B hits over the Triggerman—"remix bounce," as Jubilee calls it. Whether a listener can tease these subgenres apart or not—and whether that listener likes them or not (and, I must admit, the raunch is not to my taste)—one thing is undeniable: the music is exuberant and jubilant—infectious even. To stand still is to stand against festivity (a crime in New Orleans, as any local will inform you). It's no surprise, then, that Jubilee promises me, "Once you catch on to that craze, you can't get rid of it."

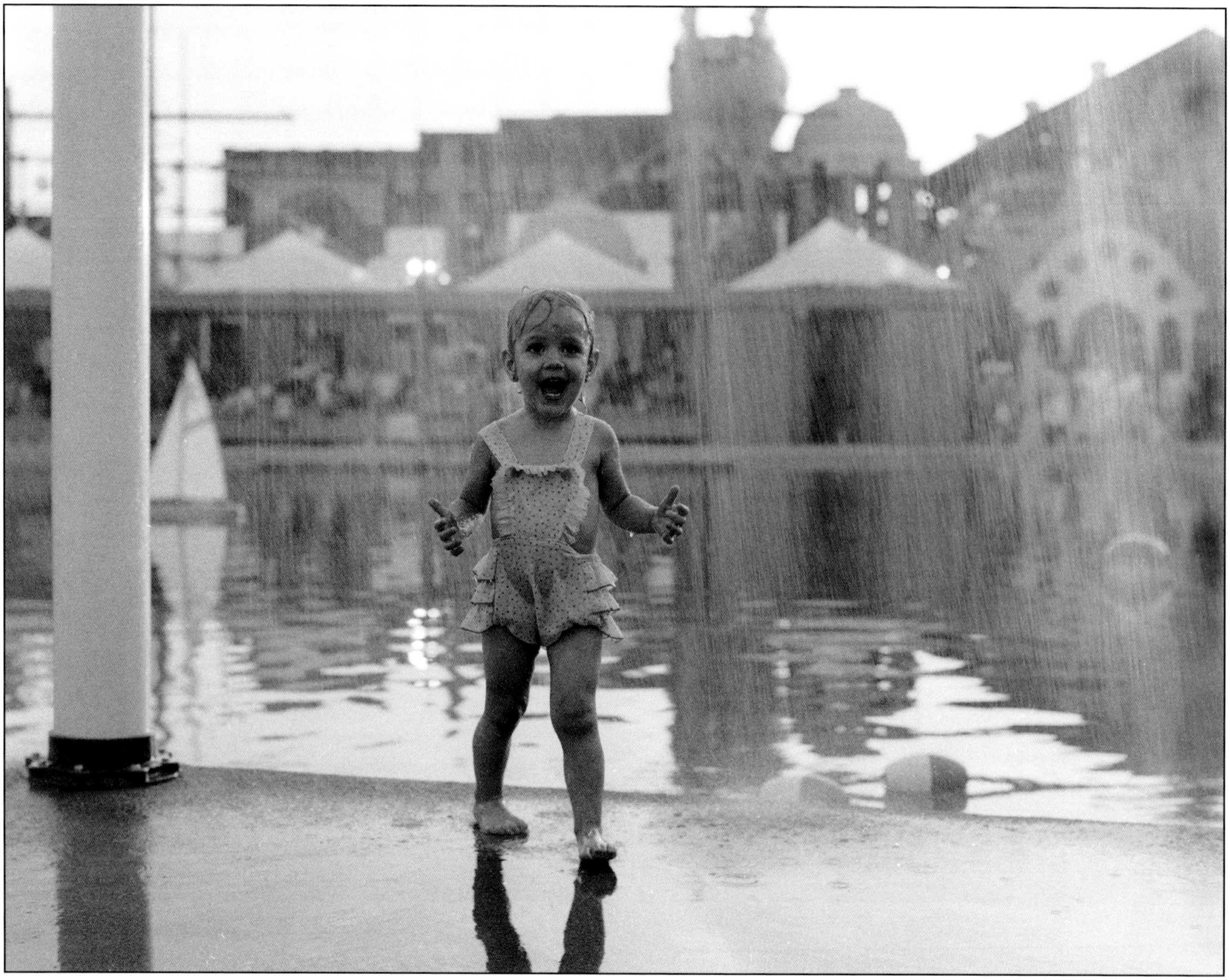

Have You Met Miss New Orleans?

by Kelly Wilson

She owns the complicated eyes of Walker Percy, the smirk of Truman Capote, and the delicious curves of Zora Neale Hurston. Her skin textured by Kate Chopin and her breast shadowed by Tennessee Williams.

Mark Twain, Walt Whitman, and Richard Ford give her long legs, graceful arms, and a backbone.

Miss New Orleans' voice has the depth of William Faulkner, the bite of Lillian Hellman, the raw whisper of Robert Olen Butler. In the kaleidoscope of her hair, I see George Washington Cable's Creoles and John Kennedy Toole's loveable fools. Sherwood Anderson, O. Henry, and Grace King send blood through her muscles, while Lyle Saxon and Robert Penn Warren give her a living past.

On a Sunday afternoon, the lady takes me on a stroll through her city. We meander by Faulkner House on Pirate's Alley. Promenade down Chopin's Esplanade Avenue. Wander past 632 St. Peter and hear Williams tapping at his typewriter, S-T-E-L-L-A. We stop for a ride at Carousel Bar, where we have a chat with Eudora Welty. Walk toward the Sherwood Anderson Apartments and bump into Carl Sandburg and Katherine Ann Porter along the way. We follow Walker Percy's Moviegoer to the theatre and shop with Ignatius J. Reilly on Canal.

At the Maple Leaf Bar, while poets sing over the clanking of bottles, Miss New Orleans and I lounge. I'm tired by the day until a voice cuts into the noise and silence falls over the room. A poet speaks—beauty and truth and city.

I turn to Miss New Orleans and introduce her to the next brush stroke. "Charmed, I'm sure," the lady replies.

Master strokes swirl to create an impression of the lady. Always an impression, incomplete and illuminating. But not one master has captured the lady fully, while each has given his or her New Orleans a heart and given America its literary riches.

The Queen of Canal and Broad

by Maria Montoya

Saturday, February 25, 2006

Canal Street costumer Helen Koenig isn't responsible for ALL that glitters at Carnival. But plenty of kings, queens, and Mardi Gras Indians believe the greatest free show on Earth couldn't go on without her.

Neither the shop nor the shop owner goes by one's proper name. But that's just the way things work in New Orleans. If you're looking for costume supplies you don't say you're going to Broadway Bound.

No, you're more likely to say you're going to see Mrs. Helen. Folks, they'll instantly know that you're speaking of Helen Koenig.

She is after all the Queen of Canal and Broad, the Goddess of Glitter, and Madam of Marabou.

Her shop, Broadway Bound, is where the who's who of Carnival gather in search of mass quantities of glitter, plumes, feathers, and detailing used to bejewel oneself for Mardi Gras.

Though she's never worn a crown, headdress, or gown herself, Mrs. Helen is Carnival.

On Fat Tuesday, the prettiest Indian Chiefs march through New Orleans' oldest neighborhoods flaunting the finest of feathers because Koenig herself has inspected each plume for the proper color. Long before any rhinestones are sewn on by a modiste, the eighty-four-year-old must deem them worthy of an Uptown debutante or even downtown drag queen. But her expertise is not limited to Carnival's royalty.

Koenig loves to help the costume novice. If the petite New Orleans native isn't behind the counter sorting mountains of marabou, she can be heard reassuring costume creators that their creations will be fantastic.

Before Hurricane Katrina washed everything away, snapshots of New Orleans famous and infamous kings and queens, chiefs, flag boys, and captains in their finery lined all of Mrs. Helen's walls. More than twenty years worth of nostalgia, yards of her finest lace, and even all of her best glitter were washed away in the flood. However, Katrina couldn't rob Mrs. Helen of her grace.

Her love for her city, her costumers, and all things Carnival will never die.

"God willing, as long as there's a New Orleans I'll be here," says Mrs. Helen, as she awaits new walls on which she plans to hang many more memories. "And as long as there's a New Orleans, there'll be a Mardi Gras because that's who we are. We are Carnival."

You're Gonna Need Some Hot Sauce with That

by Joel Dinerstein

In the midst of my first Mardi Gras season as a resident of New Orleans, I spotted an impossible notice on the blackboard of Le Bon Temps Roulé, my favorite Uptown dive: The Wild Magnolias, Sunday morning, eleven a.m. The Bon Temps is open twenty-four hours on weekends and of an early Sunday morning, it still feels like Friday night. "It always sounds like the bar on the *Titanic* in there," a friend once said. The Wild Magnolias are a legendary funk band—rarely seen Uptown—whose songs are built upon the quasi-sacred drum-rhythms of the Mardi Gras Indians, while Chief Bo Dollis hoarsely declaims over the groove. *On a Sunday morning?* Doubtful . . . but I made a mental note.

Then the logic of the gig dawned on me: Sunday morning before Fat Tuesday is the Krewe of Thoth parade. Thirty floats start rolling down from Audubon Park at eleven a.m. and *very, very* slowly make their way down Magazine Street before heading down to the Quarter. It takes four hours or so.

I awoke with a nasty hangover at ten-forty Sunday morning—threw myself out of bed, trudged the seven blocks to the bar. No music came from the back room, but in the front room the culinary angels sang. On the pool table stood a mound of fried chicken, piled a foot high. Jutting out from each corner pocket was a sheet-box of doughnuts. *I've never had fried chicken and doughnuts for breakfast,* I considered. *Until now.* I ordered up a Bloody Mary, balanced a drumstick and a doughnut on a napkin.

New Orleans music shows often come with free food. Kermit Ruffins still brings a pot of red beans & rice, the city's staple dish, to his Thursday night gigs at Vaughan's. Louis Armstrong signed all his letters, "Red beans and ricely yours, Louis." (Thus: "red beans and rice" = "love.") I was feeling the city's greasy love as I sauntered towards the back room, where the band's instruments lay in waiting. A dozen folks wandered around dazed, either from the slanting daylight or their ongoing Saturday night. Inside me, the sweet, gooey glaze of the doughnuts mixed it up with the chicken's fried *jus.* The better nutrients came from the

Bloody Mary: with its pearl onions and green beans, olives and lemons, the local version is a knockout salad.

A man walked up, my age, a local, baseball cap and shorts. He pointed at the chicken: "You're gonna need some hot sauce with that." I nodded thanks; next bite, I realized how right he was. I walked over and he handed me the hot sauce without a word. Where else would a man simply go up to another man, a total stranger, to save him from the blandness of his free fried chicken?

At 11:30, Chief Bo Dollis came on shouting full throttle in a sateen motorcycle jacket. At noon, two Mardi Gras Indians burst through the side door in a whirl of pictographic beadwork and radiant white feathers, and we all whooped with joy. Kids jumped up and down in a variety of happy dances, and the masqued Indians bent low to high five them. Parents and tourists snapped too many photos, none of which would ever capture the room's communal joy. In the midst of the choogling crowd I bumped into my colleague John, and he handed me a beer. When the set ended, we walked out past the pool table where only shreds of chicken skin remained.

A block up Magazine, one of my grad students called my name from the lawn of a large Victorian home. She held up a plate of crawfish with corn on the cob, sausage, and salt potatoes. John and I tilted our heads like Laurel and Hardy, then entered the wrought-iron gate for our second brunch. And the first float was still an hour off . . .

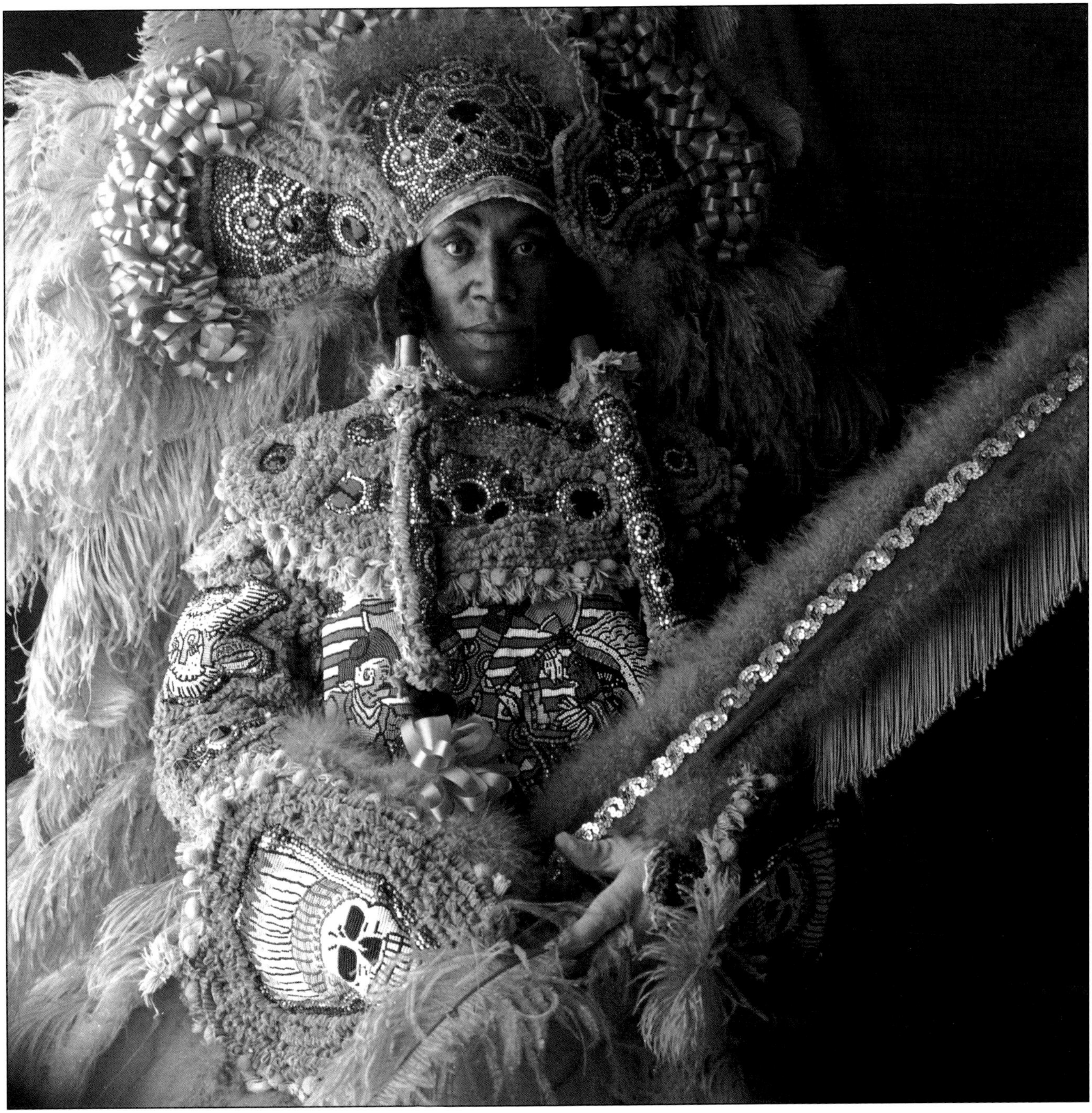

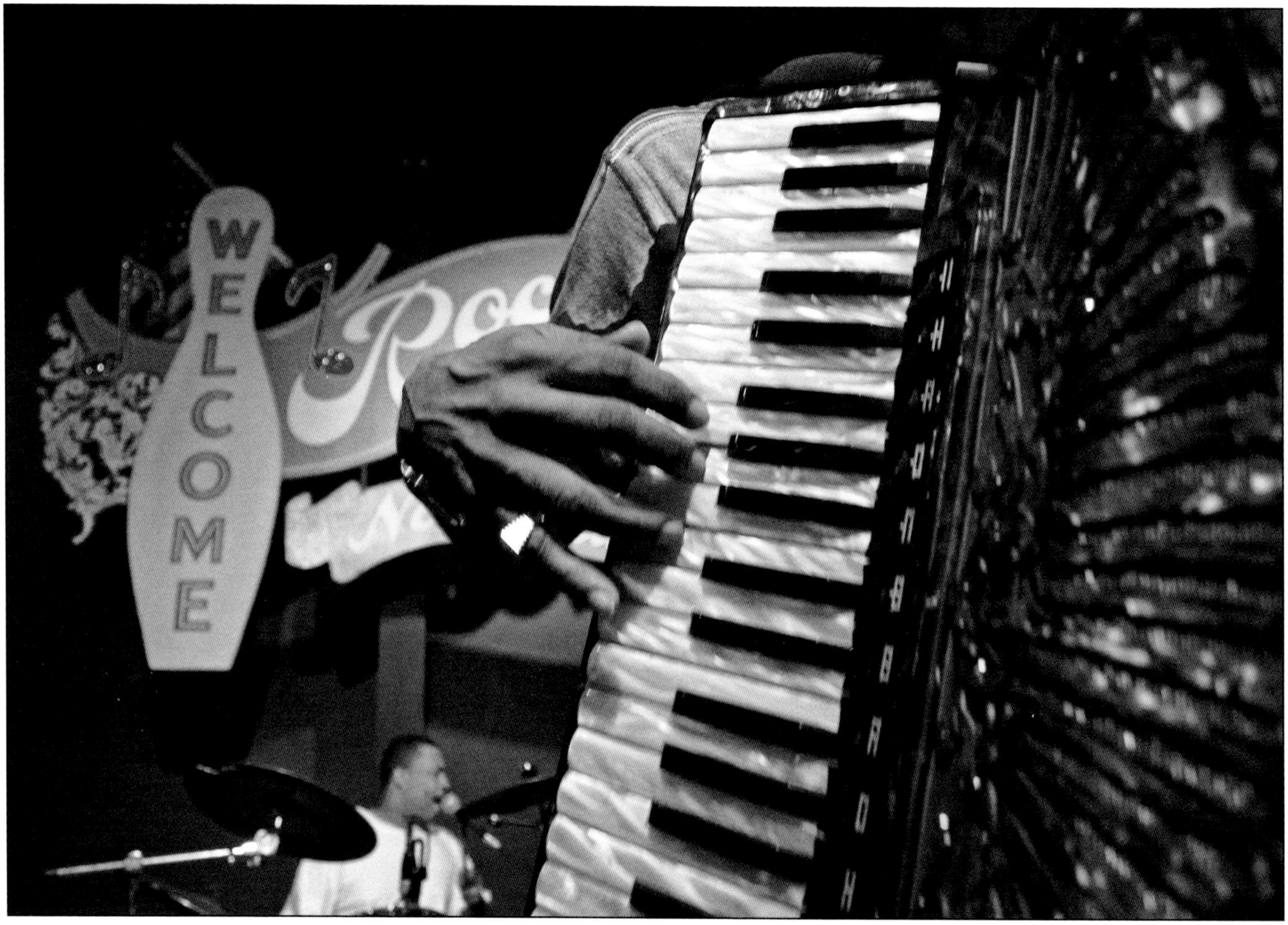
WELCOME

Mid-City Rock 'n' Bowl

by Patrice Melnick

I have always loved the bluesy wailing of the Zydeco accordion and the invigorating rub-board rhythms. Beau Jocque and the Zydeco Rollers were playing at Mid-City Rock 'n' Bowl on the Thursday night I went dancing, Zydeco night. I climbed the steps of the long, turquoise hallway and stepped through the archway that was graced by a faded print of the Virgin Mary. As I entered the club, I could feel the bass sounds beat deep in my chest as Beau Jocque's voice boomed. One side of the open room was filled with bowling lanes. Nestled at the far end of the room was the stage where the band played. Above the dance floor, a spinning disco ball scattered spots of light over the frenzied mass of dancers.

Wearing cowboy boots, some dancers stood apart, kicking forward, grabbing hands, and then spinning around. Others leaned into each other and swayed from side to side, knees between knees. Beyond the dance floor, people cradled blue-flecked bowling balls. Each of the bowlers would run, slide, release the ball, and then break into dance as the ball wobbled down the lopsided lanes toward the pins.

Over by the bar, smooth-faced barmaids clad in pleated turquoise and black bowling skirts poured drinks. A Heineken Beer sign with a neon-lit orange and green accordion-playing alligator hung on a wall. I felt the floor tremble beneath the pummel of the heavy-heeled dancers.

I danced with a handsome, pecan brown man called Bogart. As he turned me gently, I scanned the strands of green, purple, and gold Mardi Gras Christmas lights that ran the length of the room.

I felt my body lean back with the drawn-out call of the accordion.

"*Eh toi!*" Bogart called out as he spun me around on the last notes of the song.

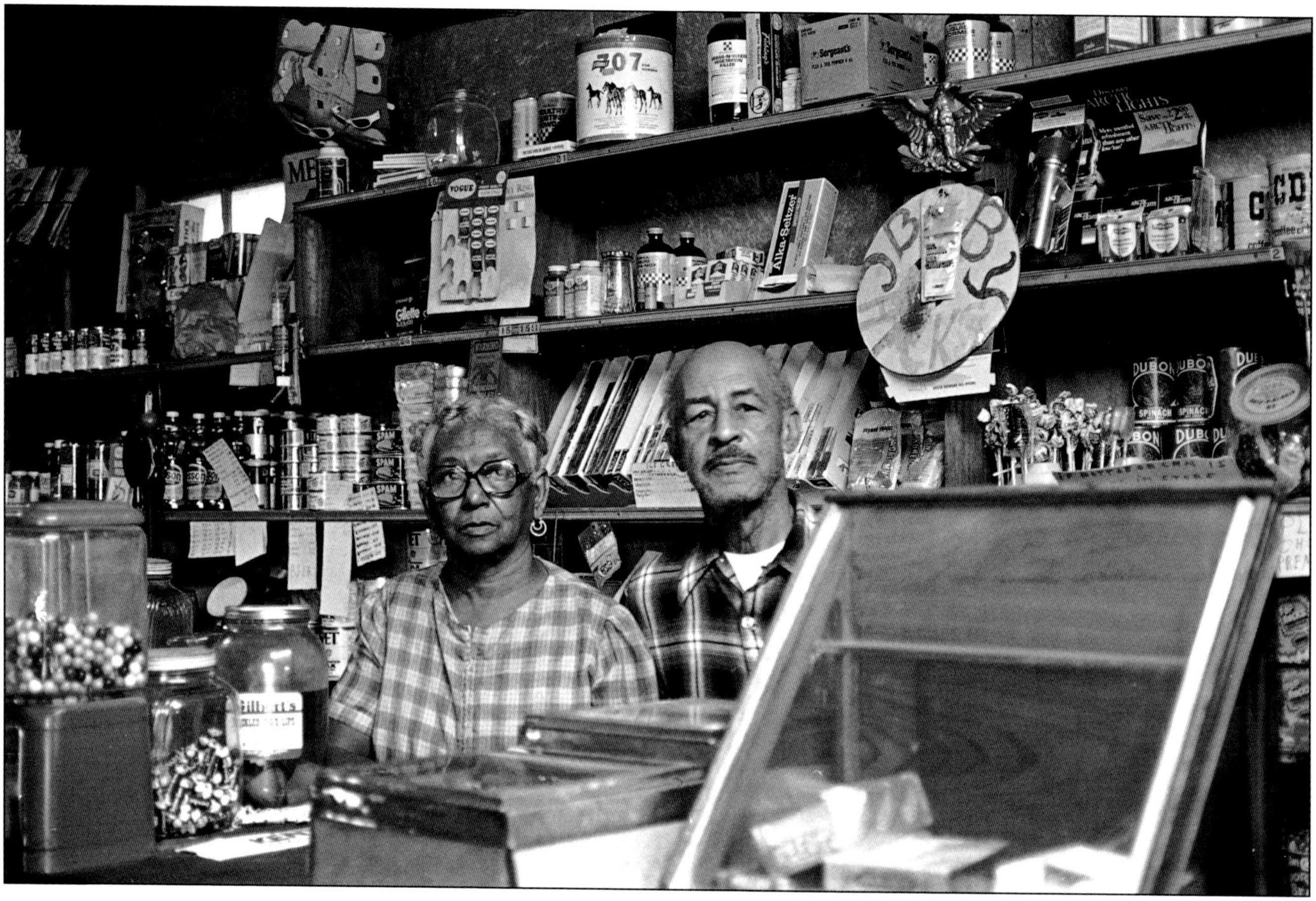
307
Alka-Seltzer
SPAM
SPINACH
Gillette

Making Groceries

by Marci Davis

New Orleans is a state of mind where proletariat pride is so substantial that the iconic culinary invention—a signature sandwich barely contained between the slits of crusty French bread—is called the Po'Boy.

"Making Groceries" is a classic New Orleans expression that comes from the French "faire le marché." "Faire" may be translated "to do" or "to make." It literally means to hit the market. Its other meaning is to procure the wherewithal to do so; to gather enough green to buy the greens.

"Making groceries" in the latter sense bespeaks a knowledge rooted in immigrant and slave cultures—an intimate understanding, on a visceral or "gut" level, of living well despite poverty. For these people, and for their descendents, hard work—as well as lean times—was not unknown. And yet in spite of constraints on money, food, and time, despite the upcoming rent—baby needs new shoes—nothing is going to get in the way of the enjoyment of life. *Laissez les bons temps rouler*, Baby. "Let the good times roll."

"Making groceries" acknowledges that there isn't going to be a fancy restaurant meal, but it bespeaks a modest optimism. The rent has been paid, the instrument sprung from hock, the lights kept on, and now it's time to take care of the lighter things. Like eating.

A hardscrabble life, and yet not without a certain *esprit de corps*, a can-do competence, the ability to take the simplest things—beans, rice, prawns, greens—and create a cuisine that has become renowned the world over.

"Making groceries." And perhaps a lagniappe, a little something extra: a smoke, a drink, a tip for the band. And with God's good grace, ya get up tomorrow and do it again.

Banks Street: Mid-City

by Gabriel Gomez

My tenant Mike sits with his pint glass of box wine on the porch. The miniature Weber sits between our double. The smoke lingers through the scrollwork on the railing before lifting towards the ceiling that will eventually be painted baby blue in lieu of chromatically fearful spiders. This essential idea based partly on incredulously ill-challenged lore is symptomatic of life in New Orleans: a candy necklace designed to enliven our tiny narratives, integral as humidity to life in NOLA; they are its quark.

It's Sunday and we are here again on the porch with the grill, the drinks, and the promise to venture beyond the A-1-addled sale steak from Sav-A-Center. Finn McCool's across the street is bursting with soccer mayhem, Mona's has got the church crowd pawing the musabaha, and the Honduran family is laughing in biblical unison across the street. Calls for incurable dogs abound.

Hell-bent kids are riding miniature motorbikes down the street in shirtless abandon; our crazy-old-man neighbor archetype who enjoys washing the street with a garden hose, spilling small articles of trash on the neutral ground and spraying dogs and their owners with Raid when they walk past his house, which coincidentally, has an AstroTurf-lined porch kept spotless like spontaneous pop art, is yelling at passing cars again.

Banks Street is dyed-in-the-wool as they say. The coals ash to temperature. The meat and vegetables are placed gingerly on the grill. Our neighbors pass. Our drinks refreshed. We sit among the temperate oak as we wait to eat.

Beneath Its Hanging Stars

by Jennifer Odell and Alison Fensterstock

Spectacular hair coiffed in a crown-like puff above a tumble of shiny black waves, New Orleans R&B legend Ernie K-Doe was once a regular part of the scene at his club, The Mother-in-Law Lounge. On many evenings, he wrapped his long fingernails around a mic and sang in tandem with his own voice as one of his hits drifted out of the jukebox, and his wife, Antoinette, popped open some cold ones for their guests. K-Doe might have donned a cape, or perhaps the night was right for a hot pink tux. But for the self-proclaimed Emperor of the Universe, Mr. Mother-in-Law himself, glittering fabulousness was de rigueur. And he shared it with everyone who came into his lounge of hanging stars, the Mother-in-Law. Years after his death, he still does.

A friend made a life-sized mannequin of K-Doe after his death in 2000, and Antoinette dressed it in her late husband's spangled suits and wigs, yielding a fine companion for her various music-industry appointments and events.

After the storms of '05 left Antoinette's moatless castle five feet full of water, the Mother-in-Law's rebuilding became a community effort. Regular patron Daniel Fuselier painted the busts of Antoinette, K-Doe, and his mother-in-law on the club's outer wall so they could keep watch over the neighborhood, along with dozens of the K-Doe's friends and supporters. It's a testament to the K-Doe's reach that no single friend—not even one of those painted on the wall—can identify all of those honored.

Alas, in the early hours of Mardi Gras Day, 2009, Antoinette K-Doe clutched her chest and dropped to the rubber mat behind the bar. By eight o'clock Mardi Gras morning, the word was out that the Empress had gone home to the Emperor.

Revelers still flocked to the bar for Carnival Day and shuffled through Antoinette's garden, shell-shocked, weepy, and dazed. Friends scrambled to serve beer. The Black Eagles Mardi Gras Indians sang a mournful "Indian Red."

On a sunny day in early spring, Al "Carnival Time" Johnson, Mr. Quintron, Lefty

163

Parker, and other friends carried the Empress up Claiborne Avenue from St. Augustine's Catholic Church. For the journey, each musician wore a white cotton glove emblazoned with an image of Antoinette, a white camellia pinned behind her ear.

Photographers climbed up the I-10 on-ramp to snap pictures of the second line as it rolled hundreds strong through Tremé. The K-Doe statue followed the hearse, in a carriage drawn by white horses wearing black plumes. At the door to the lounge, the pallbearers hefted her casket in the air three times to rounds of cheers, then brought her through the vivid doors once more, where she lay in state in a silver gown, clutching a single red rose.

Antoinette's daughter from her first marriage, Betty, moved back to New Orleans from Memphis to take over the bar in March 2009, bringing her own daughters to help. The Mother-in-Law's extended family now keeps both the spirit of apprenticeship and the importance of paying homage alive—at a Quintron CD release party one night and a birthday party for Al "Carnival Time" Johnson the next.

Ernie and Antoinette taught their friends well, by example: create magic. Be famous. Be kind. When the sun is down and the nightshifts come on, a family of friends, regulars, musicians, artists, and neighbors pays attention to one another, and to the club that draws them together.

It is important: the magic is theirs and our responsibility now. The Emperor and Empress may be dead, but like the flowers with which Antoinette filled her vacant lot off Claiborne Avenue, a culture continues to bloom in the place where their roots remain.

"What's Going on Like That?": Real New Orleans Coffee Culture

by Dennis Formento

Bob Borsodi's Uptown coffeehouses left an indelible mark on the city's coffee culture. From 1976 to 2003, Bob ran three successive establishments near Tulane University. Bob ended his own life in 2003, driven by the pain of inoperable bone cancer, but Borsodi's Coffeehouse had played host to hundreds of poets, actors, and their audiences, with brightly decoupaged tables and poster-littered walls.

On the first anniversary of his death, one hundred people paid tribute in the tiny gallery above Mid-City's Fair Grinds coffeehouse. Nobody got maudlin. Robert and Elizabeth Thompson, Fair Grinds' owners, later continued Bob's New Year's Day party, the "Day of a Thousand Croissants." From Bob's last outpost, Breezy's, the Thompsons had collected twenty hand-painted chairs and one of the decoupaged tables. The next year, Katrina poured two feet of water into Fair Grinds, but Robert and Elizabeth saved the table and chairs. In the months following, if you were rebuilding that desecrated neighborhood, you could walk to Fair Grinds for free coffee. Regulars aided the cause by dropping off a pound of fresh-ground now and then. The Thompsons have since gotten back into business, with a new kitchen and a giant brass chandelier that looks like a UFO from planet Kafenion.

True Brew Coffeehouse, which urban archaeologists say occupied the Fair Grinds site in the 1990s, also gave this Creolized neighborhood of musicians, writers, and their extended families a magnetic center. Before that, in the 1970s, it was a biker bar.

The community feeling birthed by Borsodi's extends to the Bywater-Marigny. Smoke sticks to the walls in Flora's coffeehouse, presided over by a dulcimer player named Ali. A sign above the pastry case greets customers perplexingly, with "What's going on like that?" Those walls have often pulsed with conga rhythms, the flow of hip-hop poetry, and the sighs of acoustic guitars. The place fairly simmers with coffee and nicotine, a Jim Jarmusch take on café society.

Around the corner from Flora's on Chartres Street is spacious Sound Café, owned by Baty Landis. Customers spread themselves out in Baty's place. During the day, high schoolers from New Orleans Center for the Creative Arts set up their laptops. On Wednesday evenings, there are brass band jams. In response to the social problems since the storm, the café regularly hosts community meetings to "Silence the Violence." Sound Café sells books by local writers, thus carrying on a tradition of great used book stores in the Bohemian haunts of the Crescent City. And so the circle is unbroken: Borsodi veteran, Harvey Stern, recently had a photo show in Sound Café, featuring eighty-eight framed 3 x 5s, from a decade of Third World travel. It was an exhibit that the city's art mavens didn't see, in the DIY style that this café society radiates. Bob Borsodi, gone to the spirit world, lives on in New Orleans.

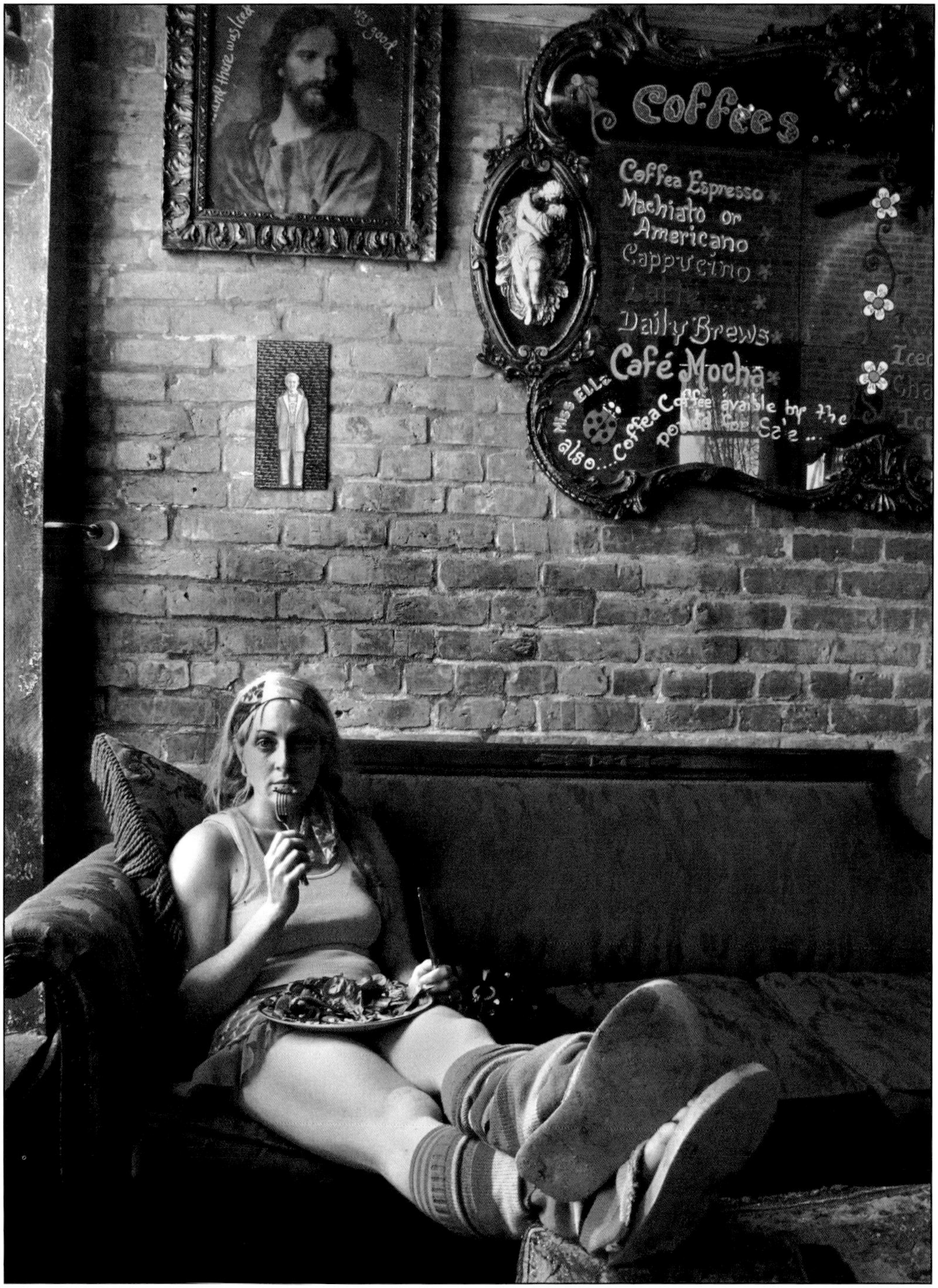
Coffees
Coffea Espresso
Machiato or
Americano
Cappuccino
Daily Brews
Café Mocha

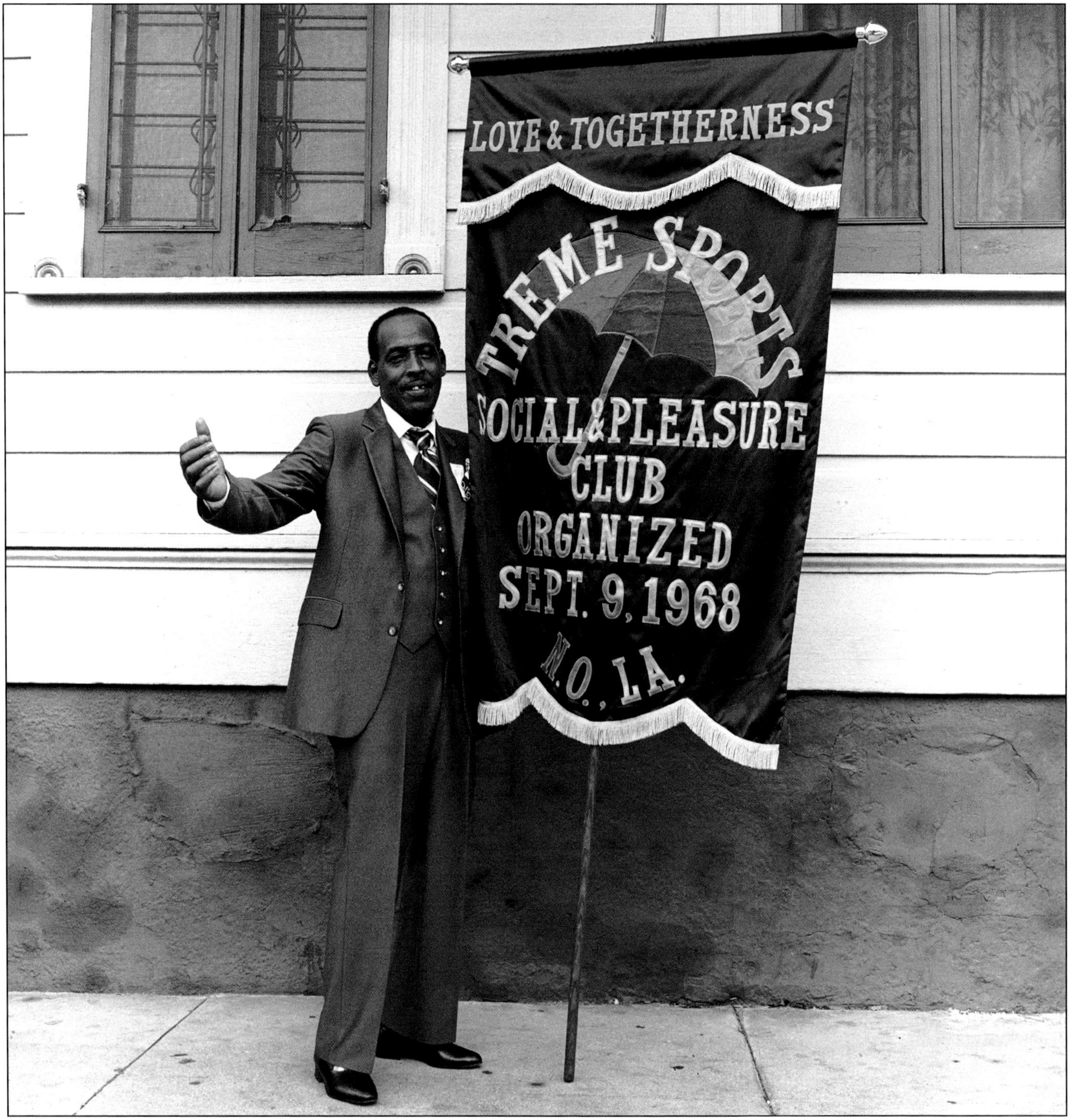
LOVE & TOGETHERNESS
TREME SPORTS
SOCIAL & PLEASURE
CLUB
ORGANIZED
SEPT. 9, 1968
N.O., LA.

Faubourg Tremé

by Lolis Eric Elie

Much has been made of our music.

New Orleans jazz has its roots in Congo Square, that Faubourg Tremé gathering space where during slavery black people, slave and free, played West African music, danced West African dances, and maintained a link to an otherwise distant shore.

But less has been made of the fact that in Faubourg Tremé, this music remains viable even as more modern, more popular forms compete for the attention of our youth. In this community the music is maintained for the joy of it, no lectures or museums necessary.

Much has been made of our second line parades.

When the social aid and pleasure clubs hit the streets with their wildly inventive dance steps, the volume of their matching colors, the audacity of their wide-brimmed skys and two-tone kicks whip photographers into lusty frenzies. The film all but exposes itself. Almost all of the downtown parades pass through Faubourg Tremé.

But less has been made of the fact that our street parades bring together all ages of New Orleanians. The generation gaps fade in these parades as the old and young dance together in a way that hardly happens in America anymore.

Much has been made of our food.

In those centuries when American food was known for being not worth knowing, New Orleans food stood out for its flavor.

But less has been made of the archaeological implications of our delicacies. The Afro-Euro-Indo combinations on our plates tell a forgotten story of how peace was made in our pots even as the lash flew freely and we mocked our own national ideals. That food, like our music, was nurtured during slavery time in the Sunday market place of Congo Square.

Much has been made of our architecture.

To cross the threshold of a Faubourg Tremé Creole cottage is to briefly travel to old Havana or Port au Prince. To analyze our shotgun doubles, with their Victorian flourishes and sturdy old-time construction is to witness how, in the days before we discovered cheap construction, our buildings were built with quality, even if their lot in life was nothing more than to provide housing for people too poor to afford mansions.

Less has been made of the ways in which Faubourg Tremé's old architecture enables our old culture. Our houses are close to the street, easily able to hear a passing parade even from the rearest of rooms. We can sit on our porches and comfortably converse with our neighbors across the street or in the house next door.

And when we paint our houses, our palette is the whole rainbow, not just the polite colors on either end.

Much has been made of our bravado, but so little is said of its roots in the Generation of 1860. Those men and women led the precursor to the Civil Rights Movement. In the 1860s and 1870s, Paul Trevigne and Dr. Louis Charles Roudanez founded *La Tribune de la Nouvelle Orléans*, the nation's first black daily newspaper. Their associates rewrote the state's constitution, desegregated the city's streetcars, and planned and executed the civil disobedience that culminated in the Supreme Court's *Plessy v. Ferguson* decision.

Little has been made of our flora.

But in those weeks immediately after the failure of the federal levees the night blooming jasmine were our sentries.

We had been invaded by the putrid smell of rotting food, abandoned refrigerators, dead animals, and hopelessness.

The jasmine stepped up, blooming loudly, fighting mightily to cover those other smells with the scent of their flowers.

These flowers announced our determination to return and rebuild even before we ourselves could articulate the words.

The Contessa Entellina Society: More Than Just a Momentary Connection

by Gina Ferrara

Our Lady of the Rosary church fills with men in dapper suits on a Sunday in September. Their buffed leather shoes catch the lights—both votives and overhead—as they file into the church. They gather in the back and greet each other with hearty handshakes and hugs. Their well-heeled wives and daughters find seats in the reserved section. As the organist begins the opening notes of *Ave Maria*, the men form two single lines. They are led in procession by a man holding an orange pennant embossed with a jeweled image of the Blessed Mother. The words "Contessa Entellina Society" appear in velvet indigo letters stitched with gold thread. The banner is placed on the altar as the men succinctly fill the first six pews of the church on both sides of the aisle.

Located on Esplanade Avenue, Our Lady of the Rosary is not a massive cathedral filled with beams and spires—though it shares with many of the old New Orleans churches an array of alabaster statues and vibrant stained-glass windows. Its magnificent stained-glass rotunda and ornate altar give the church the appearance of being an Old World treasure. The ceiling above the altar has vast frescoes filled with depictions of cherubim, angels bearing trumpets, and the image of the Blessed Mother offering a long, azure rosary to an adoring St. Dominic. Nothing is modern in this church, and on this day, the interior of the church is particularly well suited for the celebration. The priest greets everyone in Italian. Parts of the mass are said in Latin, and many of the older men who were in the Contessa Entellina procession do not hesitate when it comes time to say their response in Latin.

The priest gives a brief history of the society during the homily. The banner shimmers on the altar and moves slightly next to the ivory pulpit. All of the members are male. They are direct descendants from the village of Contessa Entellina which is located south of Palermo in Sicily. The village was settled by the Arbreshe who originally came from Albania, crossing the Ionian and Adriatic Seas, nearly four centuries ago to settle in Sicily. At the end of the nineteenth century, many of the Arbreshe starting leaving Sicily to establish themselves in New Orleans where they quickly went into business and soon formed this society to help other Arbreshe immigrants with medical and dental costs. The society embodies the *bella figura*, which is the Italian ideal of behaving with decorum and presenting oneself well. The men are devoted to the Blessed Mother, and they have this mass in her honor as well as to celebrate their own unique heritage.

As the Contessa Entellinians in dark and tailored suits turn to offer each other a handshake of peace, I think of my great-grandfather Alphonse who immigrated here from Santo Stefano and raised a family of eleven children. He lived to be ninety-four and had a shock of white hair which he washed daily with octagon soap. According to his papers, he had a job working in a brick factory with his brother. Always impeccably dressed, he ate his main meal at noon while slowly sipping red wine. He loved mortadella and Caruso. With his pocketknife, he would halve an orange into hemispheres which he readily shared. After his meal, he would light his pipe and blow wavering rings of smoke into the air. His laughter stirred through the house like a breeze from Sicily's coast. No doubt my great-grandfather arrived in the city at the same time as the men coming from Contessa Entellina—all of them with more than just a momentary connection to New Orleans.

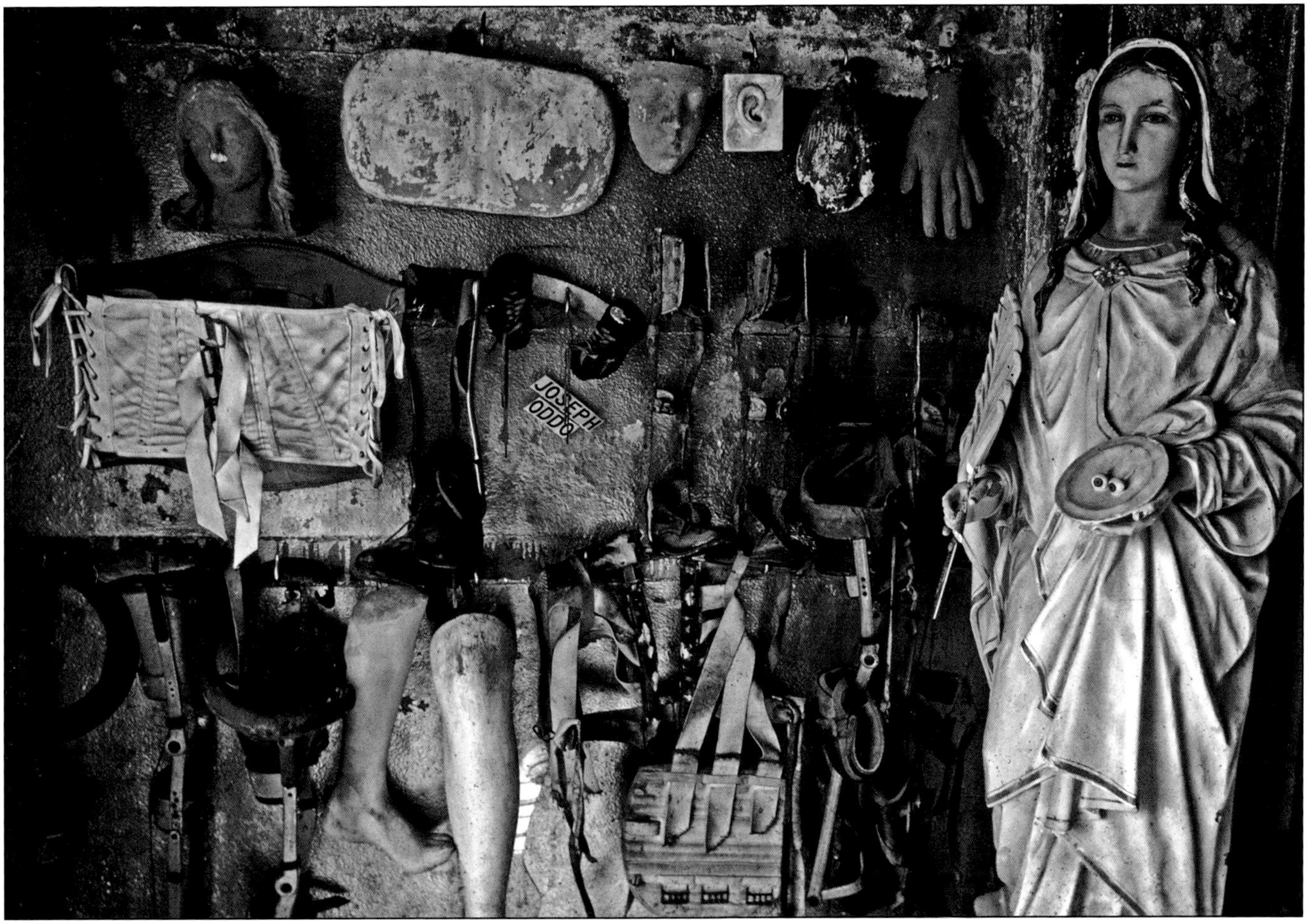
JOSEPH
ODDO

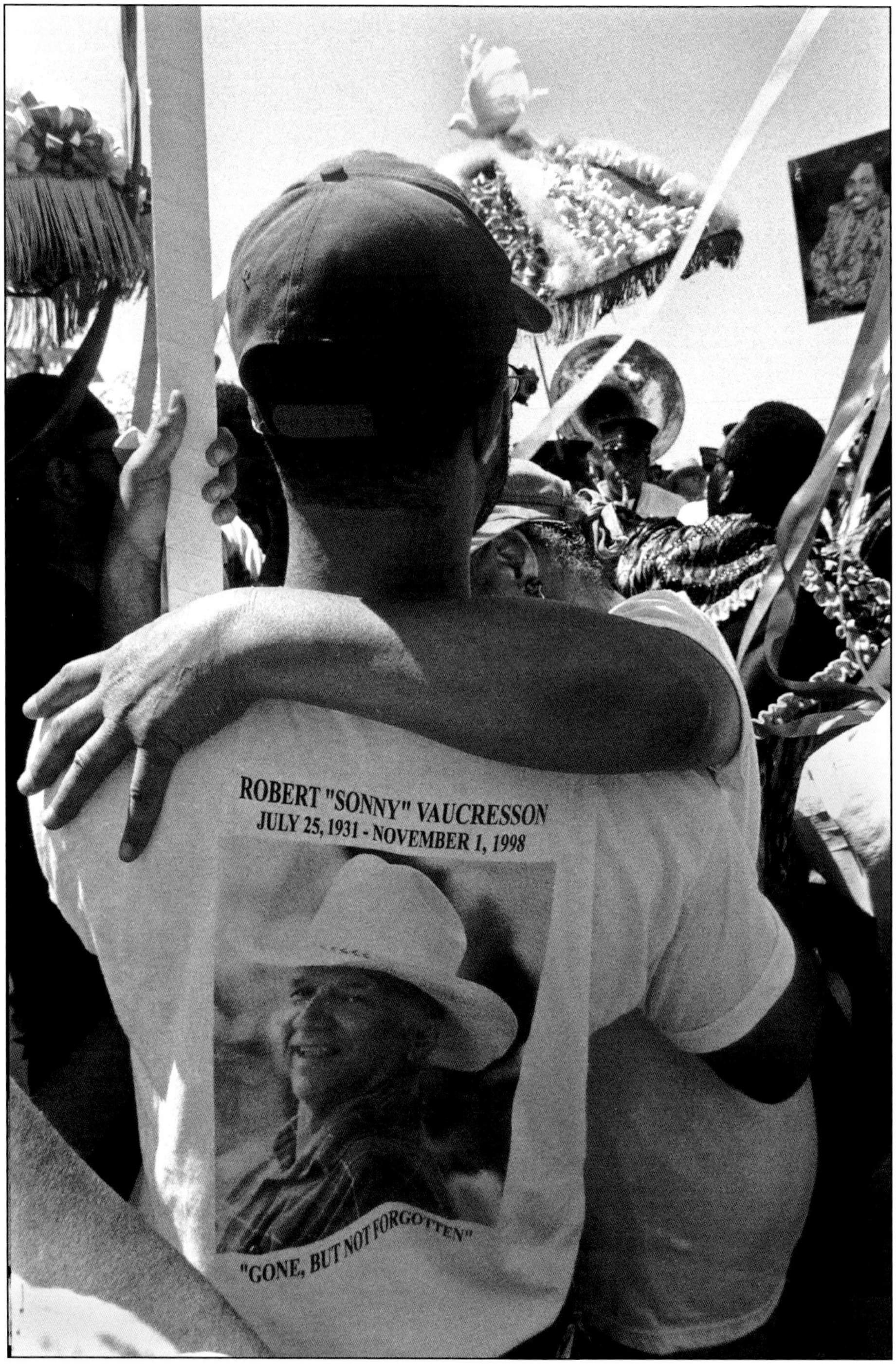

ROBERT "SONNY" VAUCRESSON
JULY 25, 1931 - NOVEMBER 1, 1998
"GONE, BUT NOT FORGOTTEN"

You Can't Get Hot Sausage in Baton Rouge

by Wayne M. Baquet, Sr.

What does food mean to New Orleanians? What is the "Soul" food of New Orleans? There is a general misconception by visitors to our city that the unique food of the city is Cajun. Natives of this great city know otherwise; it is emphatically Creole. Whether it is Creole Soul, Creole Italian, Creole Cajun, or Creole French, the Creole influence is evident. The resources of the area are unique, and the rich history of the settlement of the city by Africans, French, Spanish, Italian, and Native Americans, etc., living and working together has influenced the flavor of our cuisine.

Since reopening my restaurant, Lil Dizzy's Café on Esplanade Avenue and Robertson Street, a few months back, I've met hundreds of my customers, family, and friends dying for a taste of home. They craved the gumbo, seafood, poboys, fried chicken, bread pudding, etc. These are our comfort foods, and comfort is greatly needed.

Evacuees who were most astonished were the ones who evacuated closer to home, Baton Rouge. More than once I was told, "You can't get hot sausage in Baton Rouge." Everyone missed being able to get pickled pork, raw seasoning ham, local brands of smoked sausage and Italian sausage, French bread, coffee and chicory, and so on.

These are things we miss. These are the things that draw us back to New Orleans. Forget the crime. We pray for better policing and a better justice system. Forget the politics. We are in desperate need of good leadership. Forget the potholes. We have bigger things to worry about. Our foods and our traditions keep us drawn to this great city.

It will be a long time before things are back to normal for those of us who are returning to rebuild. Hopefully, Lil Dizzy's can be an oasis and momentary escape from this difficult process, where there are shrimp omelets and grits, coffee and chicory, hot sausage poboys, and hugs and kisses for those familiar faces we greet for the first time after the storm.

St. Augustine Marching 100

by Dr. Michael White

For more than fifty years the St. Augustine High School Marching Band has been an important and influential cultural institution. Known as the "Marching 100," the band has been featured at numerous local and national events, including appearances before the Pope, U. S. Presidents, major televised parades, and professional sports contests. The Marching 100 has won many awards, is frequently profiled by the national media, and has appeared in several movies and documentaries.

Shortly after the black, Catholic, male high school opened in 1951, recent music graduate Edwin Hampton started a band program. Paralleling the school's mission of promoting strength, leadership, and excellence in academics, Hampton adopted a policy of strict discipline, precision marching drills, and musical excellence. Each year under a blazing August sun, band camp is held—leading to final selection of members and training for football half-time shows and Mardi Gras parades.

For decades St. Aug football games have drawn record crowds who come as much to see the Marching 100's spectacular halftime shows as they do to watch the game. Hampton never failed to unleash an arsenal of musical and visual staples and surprises: from signature drum cadences and a fancy high-stepping marching style to the band's powerful sound and unique musical blend. Though the Marching 100 was the first local band to perform current radio hits, its repertoire of challenging marches—like *March Grandioso*—is equally as popular among fans.

For several years the band was a symbol of progress in the black community when it was featured in the Zulu Parade on Mardi Gras day. In 1967 the Marching 100 achieved legendary status when it became the first black band to integrate a major white Carnival parade when it marched in Rex. Despite racial taunts and physical attacks along the parade route, band members maintained rank. They responded with thunderous music and defiantly marched on with the attitude of a conquering army heralding change.

Since then, black school bands have been regular features of all Carnival season parades.

Many Marching 100 alumni have been inspired by Hampton's guidance, leadership, and cool persona. Several have moved into lifelong careers as teachers and musicians. Among the internationally renowned St. Aug graduates are jazz musicians Terrence Blanchard, Victor Goines, Leroy Jones, John Longo, and Dr. Michael White.

When Hurricane Katrina arrived in August 2005, Edwin Hampton was semiretired but still active with the band. Flood waters destroyed much of the school, including the band room, uniforms, and other musical equipment. In 2006, St. Aug band members marched on Carnival Day as part of a ninety-member combined group from three area schools. Donations coupled with an undying determination helped St. Augustine to return to its campus, rebuild the band room, and purchase new instruments. Virgil Tiller, a Marching 100 alumnus, became the new band director with a group that was half of its all-time high of 170 members.

By the 2007–2008 school year, the Marching 100 was near full strength and returned to its usual roster of performances. As the band boldly marched down New Orleans streets during the 2008 Mardi Gras season, it once again moved beyond its role as a high school group to become a metaphor for the resilience of all New Orleans in its post-Katrina return.

In a city where music and parades are a way of life, the St. Augustine Marching 100 stands out as a highly admired, influential, and emulated institution. It has often transcended its status as a high school band to become a source of community pride and leadership; a Civil Rights trailblazer; an incubator for music educators and professional musicians; and recently, a symbol of the city's strength, survival, and return post-Hurricane Katrina. Whatever the future of New Orleans music holds, the St. Augustine Marching 100 will be an important contributor—with its sonorous high-stepping legions proudly marching into the future. Go mighty Purple Knights!

Spiritual Awakening

by Herreast J. Harrison

My family and I have deep roots in the Upper Ninth Ward of New Orleans. These roots began to grow in 1965 when my husband selected the house on North Johnson and Independence streets as the family home. From that residence, he recommitted himself to a tradition he loved as much as he loved his family. The tradition I'm referring to has been carried on exclusively in the African American neighborhoods in New Orleans since the late 1800s. The tradition began being defined in the 1980s as the "Mardi Gras Indian" masquerade tradition. Originally, the tradition was practiced primarily by males of African descent who resisted being denied participation in the larger Eurocentric celebratory party on Mardi Gras day. This resistance resulted in the men masking as indigenous people of the Western Hemisphere while maintaining/retaining the African elements of drumming, dancing, and singing.

There are many aspects of the tradition that will never be known by the general public or, in some cases, even by the wives of the participants. My late husband did not inform me of all the complex roles, rules, and meanings of flags, signals, and songs. Upon realizing the complexities of what existed in the City of New Orleans and even in my own home through the perpetuation of this phenomenal culture, I knew I had to preserve, document, and promote an awareness of the laws after Hurricane Katrina. As a result of the flooding that occurred, many members of the tradition were dispersed to cities throughout the United States.

Before my husband's death, he was active in sharing information about the tradition with school children, adults, and anyone who showed an interest. His willingness to share information often created opportunities for him to travel, accompanied by his family and others, throughout the United States and abroad. He founded the Guardians of the Flame group in 1988. His personal mission and primary focus for the group was to show respect and reverence for the elders who came before him and to exhibit an enthusiastic spirit for nurturing the younger men that would come after him. He gave his newly formed group the name

Guardians of the Flame and charged his family with also guarding the flame with dignity.

I became acutely aware of the cultural significance of the ritualized aspect of the tradition on Washington Avenue on Mardi Gras day in 1990. My husband's group was meeting another group called the Black Eagles. I lost sight of my only son, Donald Harrison, Jr., who was masking with his father. As I searched for Donald, Jr., I was informed by the legendary Big Chief, Lawrence Fletcher, that he was in the large mass of people that was drumming, singing, and dancing. Determined to find him, I pushed my way through the mass. Donald, Jr., and a member of the Black Eagles were in the center of the huge circle. They were concluding their ritualized performance when I instantly realized that I was in a transformed state of being. I felt a heightened sense of self, a connection to something larger and more magnificent than I had ever known. That experience convinced me that I must continue to positively share what I've learned from my husband. I am now permanently reconnected to my ancestral roots.

In my husband's absence, guarding the flame now means that I am no longer to play my normal role as a behind the scenes person. Instead, I will be in the forefront of bringing awareness of culture and art to the community and that I must continue to contribute in some way.

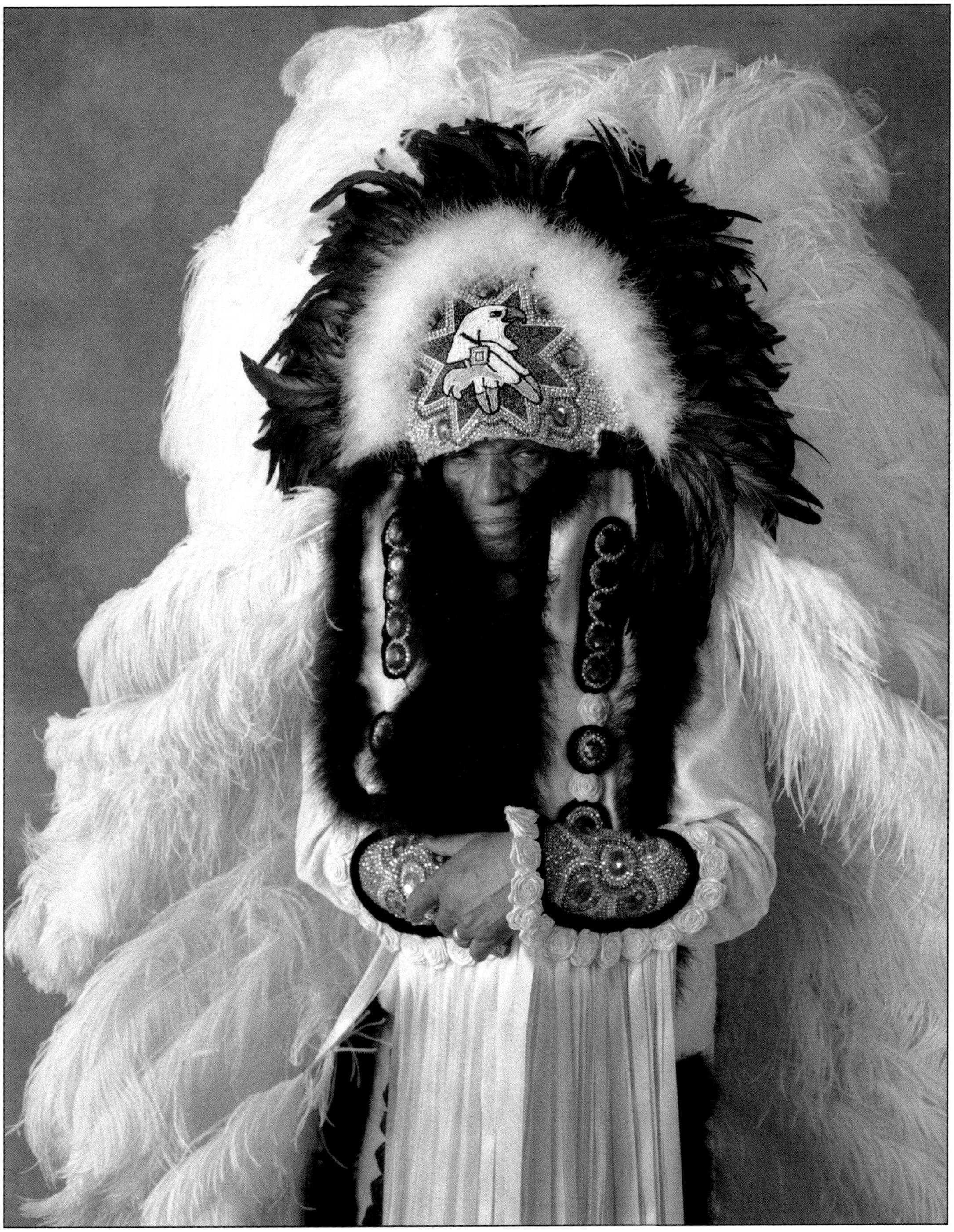

Part Four:

Didn't He Ramble

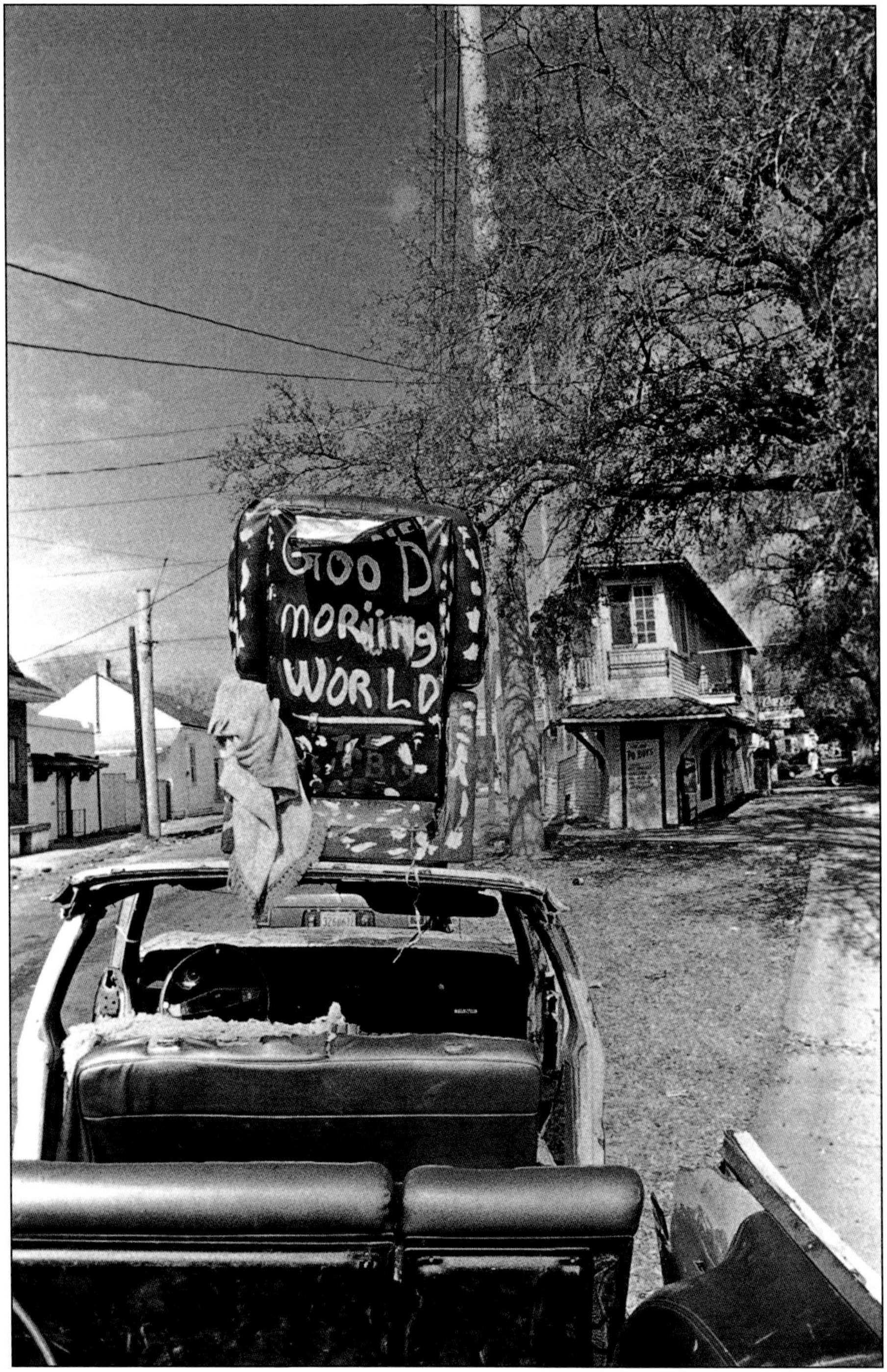
GOO D
moriing
WORLD

Offerings

by Simonette Berry

Every few days, the owners would put up a new message. Sometimes it was an advertisement, but most of the time it was a Bible verse or a cautionary phrase. I looked forward to that dingy little sign every day on the drive home, knowing it would appear as I came off of the I-10 overpass onto Claiborne Avenue. On an overcast afternoon in the spring of 2000, the sign read, "Free Marriages Performed for the Purchase of 1000 pieces of Chicken." It stopped me in my tracks; it was the best one they'd done all year. I decided I wasn't going to let this one get away. I pulled over under the "You Can't Beat Wagner's Meat" sign and started taking photos. This was the first time I stopped to devote my full attention to one of these ephemeral New Orleans facades, and I've chased them ever since. I am afraid to let them escape, these little mysteries of our salvation.

Performance is a part of daily life here. The famous costuming tradition is translated into a different ceremony through the decoration of homes and businesses. Like some gypsy tribe finally come to rest, many New Orleanians announce themselves by gilding the outside of their homes with Mardi Gras beads, LSU and Saints regalia, found junk, toys, mannequins, metallic fringe, large colored "tacky lights," Virgin Mary lawn statues, rainbow banners, handwritten signs, and rococo tableaus of lit-up figurines. Each facade creates a little altar honoring something vital.

The store front of the Edward's Shoe Repair shop on Magazine Street is meticulously adorned with discarded pumps, handbags, and hand-painted signs that advertise everything from used luggage to attorney-at-law services. One reads, "I will heel you. I will save your sole. I will EVEN DYE for you." The orchestration of objects is intricate; whoever put them up did so with a serious eye, no matter how worn the objects themselves might appear.

For a taste of something different, drive by the LSU house on a quiet residential corner in Metairie. It is festooned with purple and yellow team banners, flags, and bright bolts of cloth draped in between starched bows. Tiger-striped pinwheels spin furiously in the grass leading down the driveway. The bumper stickers on the monster truck are a call to arms.

The porch of a large Uptown home is decorated by an old Vietnam veteran in honor of friends who have passed away; "RIP," reads the bicycle that hangs from the rafters above the door, swinging beside the profiles of a six-foot-tall inflated Santa and a gleaming Harley parked there for the winter season. These houses stand out like shining sunlit panes in a stained-glass window; they are the finest and most elusive element of New Orleans, legends in their own communities.

Outsiders ask: "Why did you stay in a sinking city and rebuild? Why do you still walk around after dark in a city with such a terrifying murder rate? Why do you parade down the street when someone dies or sing when you are sad?" My answer: I remember driving down St. Charles Avenue a few months after Katrina. A gigantic oak tree had fallen across the neutral ground. One day, a man began covering the tree in beautiful swirls of shining metallic colors. He knew it couldn't stay there forever. He painted it anyway, working under the hot sun for days, trying to give the few people who drove by a sense of hope, however fleeting it might be.

That tree was his redemption, his rise above the waterline. People do not ask why these things are done. They are unconscious offerings to the spirit of the city.

The Resurrection of Church's

by Louis Edwards

If you had been inspired, as I was, to take a trip through the Third Ward of New Orleans during the summer of 2008, you would have enjoyed the rather miraculous vision of the area's spiritual underpinnings in various stages of bountiful resurrection.

As Hurricane Katrina is so often referred to as a storm of biblical proportions, I found it interesting to scan this patch of post-K landscape through the prism of religion. (Isn't the refuge of the Bible really the refuge of story, metaphor, poetry?) The eyes of the enlightened are never really to be trusted, of course—even eyes as intensely skeptical as mine—but judging from the rebirth of temples, chapels, and sanctuaries I saw manifested along the mean streets of Central City, God Himself appears to be as charmed as lucky Lazarus. The principle at work seems to be this one: If you *re*build it, He will come.

In adherence to this creed, saints (self-proclaimed grand or modest) have been resurrected: Greater St. Stephen Full Gospel Baptist Church; Little Saint John Missionary Baptist Church.

Mountains have been moved back into meaningful service: Mt. Zion Lutheran Church; Second Mt. Bethel.

Everything old is new again: New Zion Baptist Church; New St. Mark Missionary Baptist Church; Greater Bright Morning Star Baptist Church New Sanctuary (under construction).

A perfectly pious blend of cognition and logic has been restored: Jerusalem COGIC (Church of God in Christ).

Luminosity beacons magically at the end of the tunnel: Guiding Light Baptist Church; Pure Light Baptist Church.

Hope is alive: Stronger Hope Baptist Church.

The people united will never be defeated: Peoples United Methodist Church; United House of Prayer for All People.

Seeing all these houses of God (and many, many others), which He presumably inhabits, at least occasionally, if only during hours of worship, as He is reportedly everywhere, left me gazing nostalgically at the plots of land where more literal housing stands or, in some cases, once stood. The Third Ward, pre-Katrina, featured the geographical equivalent of a holy trinity of uptown public housing projects—the Magnolia, the Melpomene, and the Calliope (officially the C. J. Peete Projects, the Guste Homes, the B. W. Cooper Apartments; colloquially—which is to say *reverentially*—the Mack, the Melph, and the Callio).

Hellishly troubled before that baptismal summer of 2005, these housing projects were home to crime, drugs, poverty, to be sure, and yet they were also home to masses of urban humanity.

Now, the Magnolia is gone, demolished by forces surely as powerful as any god—Time and Politics. The Calliope is halfway dismantled, a speckled ruin of toil and rubble; its Earhart Boulevard side is inhabited by a Pompeian cluster of dark-skinned idealists—part African-American, part anachronism. The residents of the new Melpomene, a seemingly more fortunate and futuristic breed, are ensconced in completely refurbished townhouses that, alas, appear to have indeed been transformed into a complex that more closely resembles the term "Guste Homes." What the masters of Time and Politics will do to them is anybody's guess. Their stories, like everyone else's, must be told before they are written. The devil may well be in the details, but he is also in the tales. Earthly *and* biblical.

But then thoughts of Hades gave way to the promise of heaven when, during my tour, I came to the intersection of North Claiborne Avenue and Martin Luther King Boulevard, and I found myself looking longingly up at an abandoned little cathedral of American ghetto sustenance: *Church's Chicken.*

Since the storm, I'd lamented its disrepair, this former haven for the hungry, who, at least during the more desolate hours of late-night need, had nowhere else to turn. I'd begun to resign myself to the idea that it wasn't coming back. I'd lost faith in the notion that it would ever return to life; the fast-food gods, it had seemed to me before today, must have forsaken us. (Persistent hunger makes heathens of us all.)

But the plethora of resurgent churches I'd just witnessed . . . the renewals, the rebirths, the resurrections. Too many to count! If it could happen for churches, then surely it could happen for Church's, too! As the New Orleans Saints, our gods of the gridiron, had shown us in 2006—Good Lord, you gotta believe! Church's—and its wings of desire, or at least the wings *I* desired—could rise again. It's impossible to be agnostic about fried chicken. Ah, the grace of grease! Yes! On that summer's day, face to face with faith, I felt the Dickinsonian creed light my spirit: Hope really *is* the thing with feathers.

New Orleans is My Spirit House

by Jerry W. Ward, Jr.

I yearned to live in New Orleans long before I took up permanent residence on Gentilly Boulevard in 2003.

As a young boy in the 1940s and 1950s, I made many trips by train from Washington, D.C., or Mississippi to the Crescent City. There my parents had met and married. I think they fell in love over bowls of gumbo. My mother had spent the most glorious days of her life in New Orleans enjoying Mardi Gras; her exceptionally large family of uncles, aunts, and cousins; and dancing to the best jazz on earth. I vowed I would one day have the magic of her city. My New Orleans relatives, whose musical speech put clipped accents and drawls to shame, treated me to breakfasts of warm French bread, café au lait, and Creole cream cheese, 3-D movies, rides on streetcars, sneaked sips of Dixie 45, and intriguing tales about my rainbow Catholic family. Mr. Dunwood's lunchroom on Delachaise Street made the best beef stew that a kitchen could produce; the highlight of a summer's night was getting Brown's Velvet ice cream on Louisiana Avenue, and I much preferred my godmother's exotic seasoning to my mother's subtle St. James Parish Creole flavoring. How well they cooked was one way of discriminating between the relatives I liked most from those I visited only as a matter of obligation. Krauss, Kress, Maison Blanche—shopping on Canal Street was special. I knew I belonged in this city. The people, the food, and the life-pulse of the city were ideal. As I gaze each morning at John Scott's remarkable "Spirit House" sculpture at Gentilly and St. Bernard and listen to the bells from St. Leo the Great, I know that my soul has found home.

Our Lady in the Kitchen, St. Michael by the Phone, St. Jude on the Bathroom Shelf

by Katheryn Krotzer Laborde

By the time you finish trimming the rosebush so you can see the Blessed Mother's face once more, chipped and worn and in need of a new paint job as it is, you realize that now is as good a time as any to remove that St. Joseph's statue, planted upside down in the yard last spring when you wanted to sell the house. Your wife changed her mind, and then she changed yours, but the St. Joseph stayed, forgotten until now.

Yeah, St. Joseph upside down in the soil near the azaleas, forgotten, much like that promise of twenty bucks in the poor box you made to St. Anthony earlier in the week when you lost your keys.

Your wife sticks her head out the door and, spying you by the fence, asks what you're doing. You tell her, and she tells you that there's spaghetti in the Crock-Pot when you want it. Sun glints off her hair, short now but still blonde as it was when you first met at a St. Francis Xavier CYO dance all those years ago, her skirt hiked way up. She told you her name was Barbara but everyone called her Anne, her middle name. A-N-N-E, she yelled in your ear. You had told her, shouting over the music, that your sister's middle name was Ann, with no "e."

Your daughter's middle name is Anne, like her mother's. And it occurs to you now that every girl you ever knew had the middle initial of A. A for Anne as in Anne, mother of the Blessed Mother. Ann as in St. Ann as in St. Ann Parish and St. Ann National Shrine and Rue St. Anne/St. Ann Street in the Quarter.

As in *St. Ann, St. Ann, Bring Me a Man.*

The earth-crusted statue isn't all that deep in the soil, and St. Joseph pops out like a carrot. It occurs to you that you should wash it off and put it on the mantle by the palm frond you got after Mass last Palm Sunday—a yellow and spiky thing it is now. Easter is coming soon: time to pick up your mom and Make the Nine. Besides birthdays and holidays, your mom only holds you to two commitments a year—whitewashing the family grave on All Saints Day and visiting nine churches on Good Friday. Back when she was young she used to walk the nine, it was easy to do—there were three churches in every direction from the house. But now churches are closing, or being closed. Your mom reads the *Clarion Herald* and picks her nine from churches she figures will be closing soon, turned into "missions" or sold to the highest bidder. This breaks her heart, she tells you, this woman who wears a medal blessed in Medjugorje and prays to The Little Flower.

Who fries fish every Friday and never misses her neighbor's Novenas.

Who gargles with holy water every winter to ward off the flu.

The back door swings, and Anne says she's running over to the Winn-Dixie for some things. No matter what she's going for, you know she will come home with other things, including a religious candle from Aisle Nine. These she puts all over the house, and during hurricane season you find them burning at all hours—Our Lady of Guadalupe in the kitchen, St. Michael by the phone, and St. Jude, Patron Saint of Impossible Causes, on the bathroom shelf. Next to these are Lucky Beans swiped from that year's St. Joseph's altars, and lottery tickets, and prayer cards fished from pockets after a funeral, and small mounds of little plastic rosaries. Some white, others blue—they seem to multiply over night.

A Lesson in Perseverance

by Sunday Angleton

If I were to write New Orleans a love letter, I would sign my name with a flourish to rival even Hancock's. At the bottom of my love letter, I'd scrawl Sunday Angleton. Sunday spelled like the day of the week and not like the ice cream. Angleton spelled like the CIA agent and not Angelton. Believe me, I'm not that sweet, and I don't have a halo. When I meet people, I tell them I'm a writer and a teacher. If it seems I am smiling a bit too enthusiastically when I say teacher, it's because I love my job. The job that I fought, the job that I swore I would never have, the job that many, if not most, English majors are expected to work, is now the job I love.

I first started teaching in 2005. I taught for one week before Hurricane Katrina ruined the school and the homes of most of my students. I taught at Nelson Elementary School in the seventh ward, and most of my students lived in the Saint Bernard housing project. When the school temporarily relocated uptown in January of 2006, I quickly realized my students' extraordinary ability. Every day I went to work, I watched kids smile and laugh, learn and share, sing and dance despite the uncertainty and chaos around them. Sure, you might be thinking, they smiled and laughed because they were unaware of what was going on around them—young children are like that. If that's what you think, there's something you should know.

My first eighth-grade class had four students fifteen or older, and one of my students already had a child of her own. The class clown of that class, the student who always made us laugh, was a kid whose momma would sneak him enough money on her payday to feed his little brothers and sisters. It was his responsibility to make the money last, to keep the babies full, and to protect the cash from the other members of the family who, desperately addicted to drugs, would regularly threaten to kill him. When he passed with a basic in English and an approaching basic in math, we both laughed while we cried. "Aww, Ms. Angletons," he always pronounced my name like I was somehow plural, "you know I be better with my money than I am with them words."

Watching my students, I've seen perseverance take so many forms. I saw perseverance every time Talysha did her homework because I knew she shared a single FEMA trailer with a mother who worked late and two little sisters. Talysha went on to be in the top of her class at Ben Franklin High School, and her baby sister was accepted into Lusher Arts High School. I saw perseverance every time Kelly handed in a new draft of a short story. Kelly was determined to first be the best writer in the Iberville, then the best writer in New Orleans, until finally he was the best writer in the country. "I can probably do it by the time I'm fifty. That's right, by the time I'm fifty, my name's gonna be on every book in the library! Ya heard me?" Kelly is my inspiration every time I sit down to revise a story. If he could write story after story despite his baby brother's constant crying, the loud noise and unusual hours of his neighbors, and his parent's divorce, I could find time to revise my own writing. The greatest gift the city of New Orleans has given me is a model of perseverance, and that model of perseverance is evident in her children.

If I were to write New Orleans a love letter, I would address it to her children. In that letter, I would say thank you. The children of New Orleans have taught me to smile when I thought it was impossible, and I'm still smiling today.

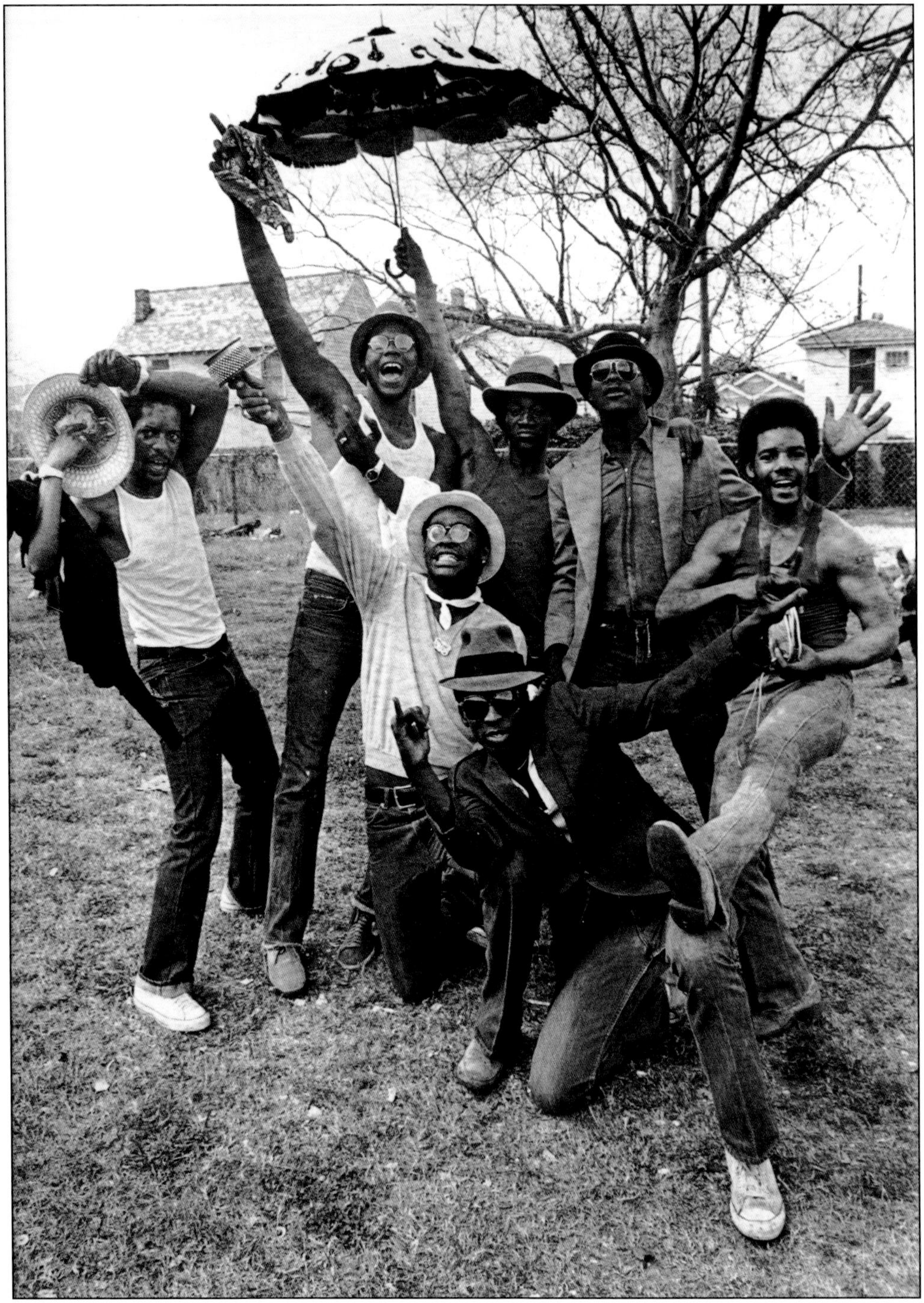

Forgive Us if We Make Lemonade and Refuse to Cry

by Lloyd Dennis

People who are back in New Orleans are definitely developing an attitude. It's called "make lemonade or die" and is simply the spirit of a people who have survived hurricanes, floods, foreign invaders (the Americans), yellow fever, fires, and the Confederacy. Sometimes we, who for months have stood in line for FEMA, furniture, ice, water, food, clothing, work, snow balls, or a cardboard tub of hot sausage, get an attitude when the newly returning act impatient or indignant about things being a mess.

It's actually funny when someone gets upset because service is slow in a restaurant, a sure sign that someone is a freshman in the rebuilding process. So many of us remember when there was no place to eat and how thrilled we were when we got our first piece of French bread wrapped around our favorite poor-boy ingredients. In the same way out-of-town relatives and friends are completely bewildered by our calm acceptance of our discomfort and inconvenience and how we can even think about partying and enjoying life when so much has to be done.

I guess we could pout and cry or stress out because there are not enough contractors to fix everybody's house at the same time, or we can figure out how to make gumbo or crawfish bisque on the propane stove in our trailer and have friends over and have a cocktail and laugh. There is a wisdom here born of more history than America and more tragedies than Greek theater. We care about our situation and we are working to make things better but that doesn't stop our lives, and our attitude is that we shouldn't stop enjoying life just because it isn't exactly what we want it to be, right now.

We also know that the people who yell at their contractors will get the slowest and worst work, and those who bring lemonade to the work site will get better quality and a shorter timeline. So we make lemonade. We had national publicity and the hotels and French Quarters were least damaged, most of the parade floats were already made, so we celebrated Mardi Gras, and some people wanted us to be sad, but you know this is the place where we will dance in the street after a good funeral.

Yesterday I ordered my Jazz Festival tickets and, no, my roof isn't fixed, my fence is still down, and I'm still arguing with insurance people and haven't filed my taxes yet, but hell there are only two weekends of Jazz Fest, and I can afford to actually pay for tickets with my higher post-Katrina income, so that's called lemonade, this week.

I am beginning to really appreciate the shake up in our lives caused by the lemons Katrina dropped as she passed, and I agree with the conversation around the table at Sweet Lorraine's last night (yes, we still have a drink with friends). The idea being that adversity doesn't really build character, but simply reveals it. The point was that people who can function in difficult times have character, even though if previously untested, they and those around them may not have realized the character they possessed.

So maybe that is why we can dance at funerals, and celebrate Mardi Gras and Jazz Fest with half our city still broke down and missing, because wasting a minute of joy must be a sin . . . because after all God is good . . . all the time.

Saint Anne Remembered

by Scott Garver with an Introduction by Henri Schindler

Every Mardi Gras morning since 1974 a band of revelers, masked and beautifully costumed, has marched in the often foggy morning from Bywater, up Royal Street to Canal, waiting to hail Rex, the King of Carnival. La Societé de Saint Anne began as a contingent of a few dozen friends arrayed in spectacular Babylonian costumes and bearing aloft a finely sculpted golden bull of papier-mâché. In each succeeding year the Saint Anne procession has grown to number several hundred, becoming one of the most anticipated events in the Vieux Carré. This armada of dreams, seemingly carried on waves of joy, has become an anticipated Carnival fixture, an institution. It is awkward if not impossible for magicians to discuss their magic: for thirty years it was my great pleasure to serve as Captain of the society, but the guiding spirit and genius of Saint Anne has always been Paul Poché. What follows is a memory of Saint Anne at its apogee, written by an acolyte who has become, in turn, a designer of the pageants of Hermes.

Henri Schindler

As a child growing up in New Orleans there was never a Mardi Gras—and by that I mean the day itself—when I was not in costume and mask. As a young adult, I was secure in the smug certainty that I KNEW what Mardi Gras was until 1988 when an invitation arrived: "La Societé de Saint Anne."

The great day arrived, and we left my friend's French Quarter courtyard apartment at ten a.m. and began to walk into the Faubourg Marigny. "Are we going to Chalmette?" I whined. "Mardi Gras is THAT way," I said. "No," my companions assured, "Mardi Gras is THIS way!"

We finally came to a charming Creole cottage. In front of this cottage, like undulating, gaudy jellyfish, stood two dozen or so hoops suspended from tall poles. Suspended from these hoops swayed lengths of ribbon in every color—gently, beautiful, and silent.

The home, I would later learn, was the home of Paul Poché who, with his friend

Henri Schindler, designed and created the Comus parades and founded this "party" almost two decades before. The rooms in which I found myself were an amalgam of Aladdin's Cave, Tutankhamen's Tomb, and Nero's Golden Palace conjured by Fellini and Buñuel on mescaline. The walls held a Rex's ransom of gorgeous, recondite ephemera—parade bulletins of Comus, Rex, and Proteus, a century old; ball invitations; tiaras. The great, gilded accoutrements of previous Comus pageants were propped and suspended everywhere—papier-mâché flowers and leaves, stars, dragonflies, crescents in abundance. I was INSIDE a Mardi Gras float.

The denizens of this sensual sty were appropriately arrayed for a Leveé at the Court of Versailles, an Eleusinian orgy, a Papal Coronation, and a Cecil B. DeMille biblical epic. The utter sumptuousness of the couture and the setting in which they were seen rendered me hopelessly enchanted and incredulous.

Then the Rites began. A jazz band entered. They played. And there, at ten a.m. on a Tuesday morning, we danced. The house literally vibrated with revelry and song. And, as we danced, SHE entered.

I saw, I touched the Great Whore of Babylon that morning when Comus still graced Mardi Gras, and the world was young. It was only the second of the three appearances She made in New Orleans. She held in her purple-gloved hands a bronze bowl out of which emanated clouds of frankincense. She wafted it about amidst the dancers. I watched the Great Whore speaking cheerfully to a Renaissance Pope in Triple Tiara, engulfed in clouds of it, as we became a procession. The band, marshaled by the Pope and perfumed by the Whore, led us in riotous parade—the only great Triumph which still graces the venerable facades of the Vieux Carré on Mardi Gras. This Triumph of Saint Anne, this Glorious, Other Worldly, Sensual, Decadent, Elaborate, and Benignly Erudite Triumph marched down Royal Street and, arriving at Canal Street, awaited His Majesty, Rex, King of Carnival.

This was, indeed, Mardi Gras.

I long for it, and for Comus, to return.

Because of the society's ever-growing number, the Rites at Paul Poché's home were discontinued long ago.

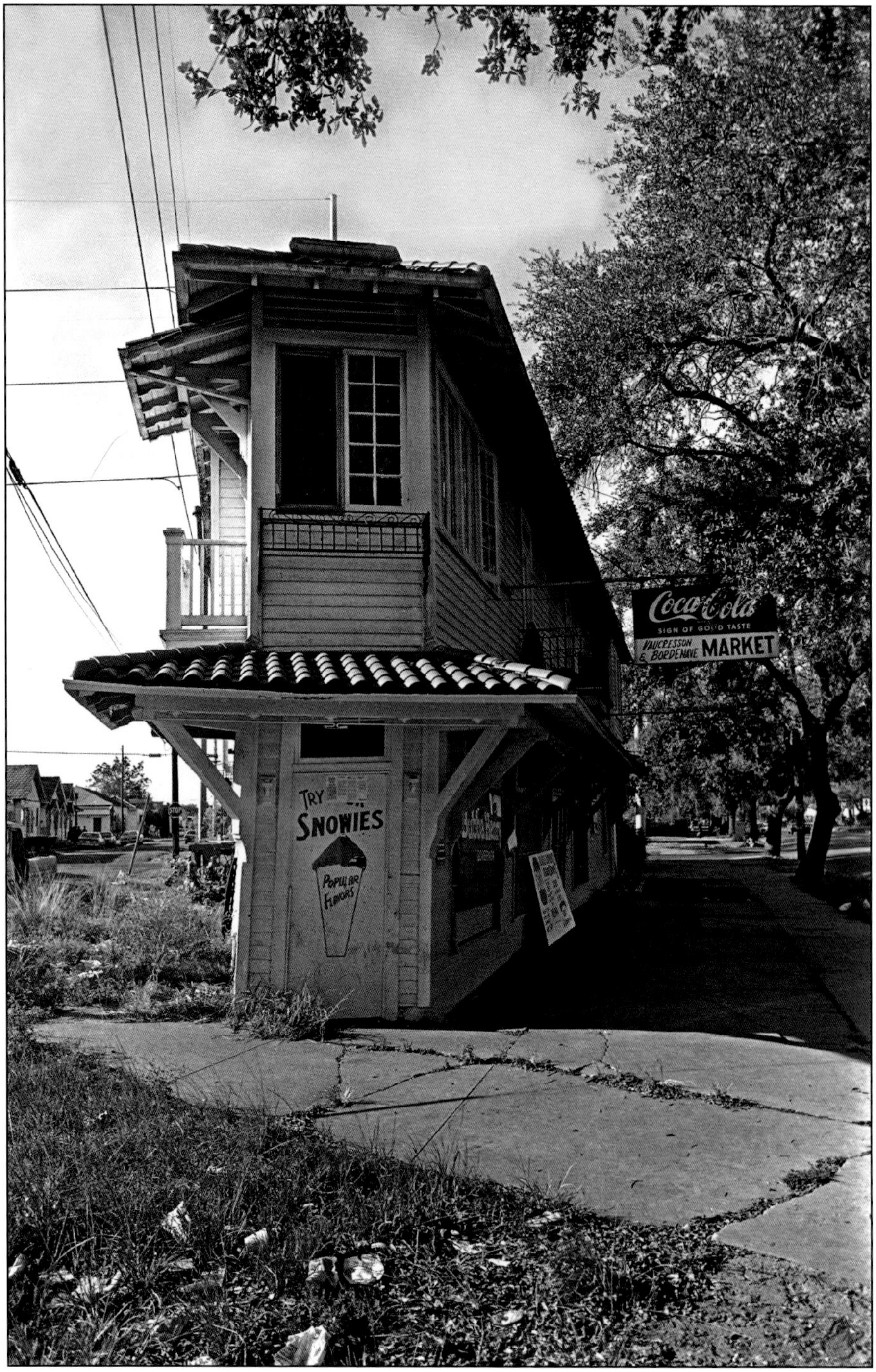
Coca-Cola
SIGN OF GOOD TASTE
VAUCRESSON & BORDENAVE MARKET
TRY
SNOWIES
POPULAR FLAVORS

Sno-Balls

by Kami Patterson

Summertime—there's no denying it's hot, sticky, and sweltering here. Blink an eye and you'll break a sweat. But tucked away in New Orleans neighborhoods like mini-oases, open only during summer's heat, sno-ball stands provide icy, gaudily colored indulgences that take the edge off the inferno.

Unlike its northern cousin, the more granular crushed-ice sno-cone, delicately shaved, fluffy ice is the key to a classic New Orleans sno-ball. When Ernest Hansen patented the Sno-Bliz machine in 1934, he revamped an ancient treat from Roman times into a unique local delicacy.

Folks line up patiently, exchange pleasantries and neighborhood news, make new acquaintances, and run into old friends. As for flavors, there are the basics—grape, cherry, lime—but they range far beyond the commonplace to coconut, iced coffee, nectar cream, wedding cake, Cajun red hot, orchid cream vanilla, bubble gum, tiger's blood, strawberry shortcake, Creole cream cheese, and even dill pickle. The list varies with the proprietor's imagination, and each neighborhood stand boasts its own collection of flavored syrups, in clear, cream style, and sugar-free, many completely homemade.

Some aficionados enjoy adding soft-serve ice cream (known as a stuffed sno-ball), chocolate syrup, condensed milk, or creating a personalized flavor mix. Served in cups, Chinese takeout boxes, or on paper plates, usually with a spoon AND a straw, the city hosts a multiplicity of options for frozen goodness—Hansen's Sno-Bliz on Tchoupitoulas, Plum Street Sno-Balls Uptown, Tee Eva's on Magazine, Pandora's in Mid-City, and Ro-Bear's on Jefferson Highway are just a few. Many New Orleanians are fiercely loyal to stands they've been frequenting since childhood. The digs range from historic wooden buildings to cinder-block boxes adorned with bright murals, to mobile trailers and carts, all offering overheated patrons a bit of "air conditioning for your insides."

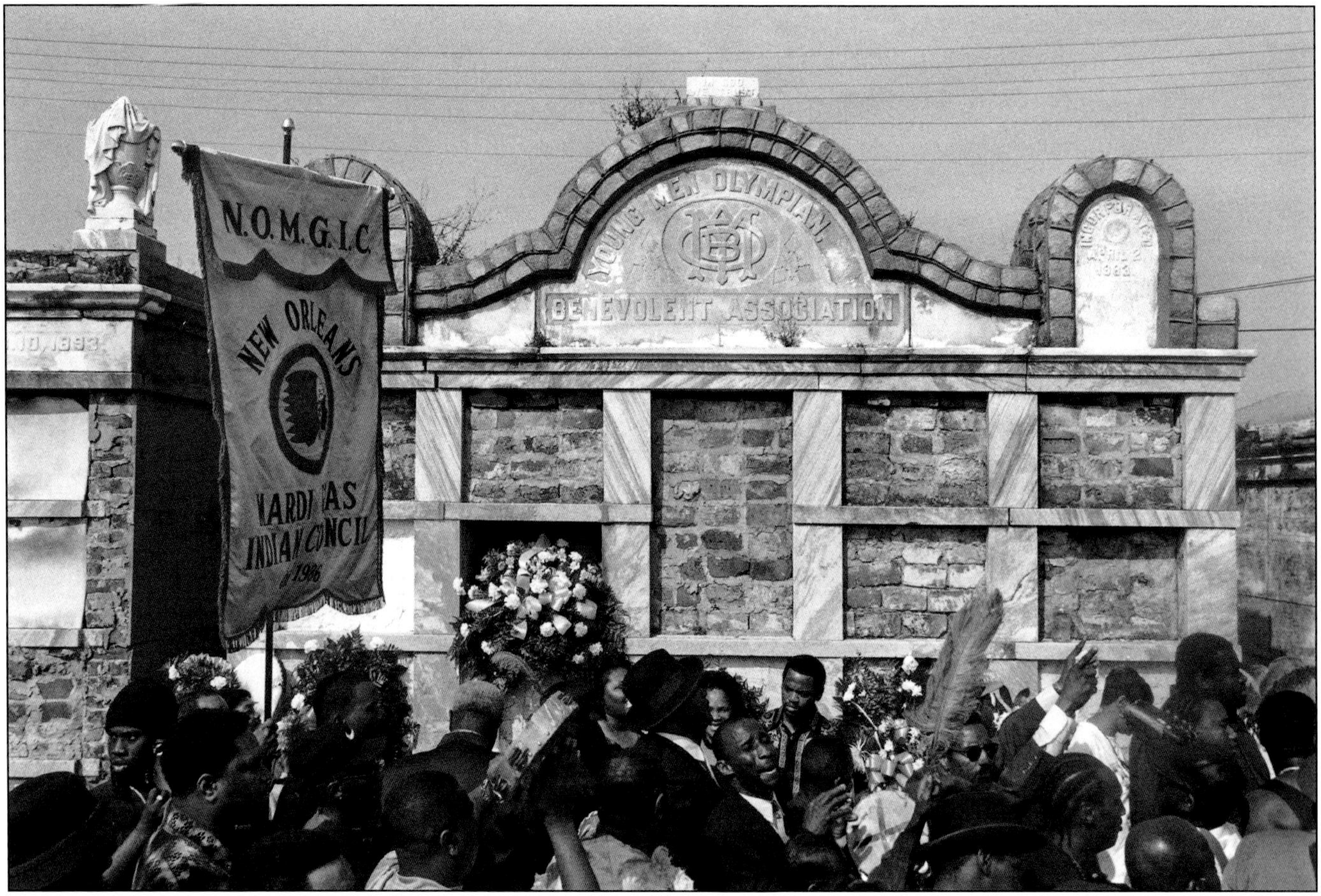
N.O.M.G.I.C.
NEW ORLEANS
YOUNG MEN OLYMPIAN
BENEVOLENT ASSOCIATION

The New Orleans of Possibility

by Michael Sartisky, PhD

Culturally speaking, today New Orleans stands virtually alone as the most genuine, vibrant, and unique of all American cities. In a Walmart nation, it is the French Market, coffee shop, snowball stand, po-boy shop, Lucky Dog cart, mule-driven taffy wagon, and most of all, the local club and dance hall. With our unique and unprecedented mélange of peoples of many nations, ethnicities, religions, and hues we foreshadowed America's own polyglot evolution as a nation: French colonists and refugees from Saint-Domingue; Acadians cast into diaspora by the British; Spanish administrators and soldiers; enslaved Africans and *gens de couleur libres*; indigenous tribes such as the Houma, Tunica, and Coushatta; Sephardic Jews; Sicilian and Lebanese vendors; and Irish laborers put to digging drainage canals in pestilential swamps because they were more expendable than slaves as they had no capital value. We were both multicultural and culturally sophisticated—with offerings from French opera and chamber groups to masked balls and bordellos rocking with barrelhouse pianos and ragtime—before most American cities were a gleam in a speculator's eye, before they were a hamlet or a crossroads, before they had a barbershop quartet.

New Orleans was, is, and will be—even more so if we perish—the shrine and seedbed of American culture. Our patron saints are Louis Moreau Gottschalk, Scott Joplin, Buddy Bolden, Jelly Roll Morton, Louis Armstrong, Louis Prima, Fats Domino, Professor Longhair, Dr. John, Irma Thomas, the Neville Brothers, Ellis and Wynton Marsalis, and Kermit Ruffins. Few American writers attained any stature who did not sup on the open oyster of New Orleans, whether Walt Whitman, George Washington Cable, Kate Chopin, Lafcadio Hearn, O. Henry, Tennessee Williams, Lillian Hellman, Ernest Gaines, Walker Percy, Anne Rice, Richard Ford, or William Faulkner.

But do not mistake New Orleans for some antiquarian artifact, no quaint anachronism frozen in time. New Orleans is a seething pool of assimilation and syncretism, of reinvention and recreation. It is a negotiation and a navigation between grace and dysfunction. It is a Creole place where cultural intermarriage is a badge of honor and affirmation of humanity. Situated precariously on the edge of the American continent, New Orleans' marginalization is a special vantage from which to see the mainstream of American culture, a certain slant of light which sees nuance and possibility better than normality.

The Purple Martins on the Causeway Bridge

by Julie Kane

The longest bridge in the world, the twenty-four-mile Causeway, spans Lake Pontchartrain north of New Orleans. Few outsiders know that the steel girders under the bridge provide a roost for up to 200,000 purple martins at a time migrating along the North American Flyway—making it the largest purple-martin sanctuary in North America. But every spring and summer evening just before sundown, dozens of New Orleanians, who will celebrate anything, gather under the Causeway's south end with lawn chairs and picnic coolers to watch the magnificent aerial ballet as the birds hunt insects and then settle into their perches for the night.

As the sun reddens and sinks in the west, thousands of the blue black swallows stream to the foot of the Causeway from their "day jobs" up to thirty miles away in all directions. Like an orchestra tuning up, their flight paths start out random and disorganized. Gradually, as if communicating with one mind, they begin to swoop and soar and turn and bank in squadrons and formations, feeding on mosquitoes and dragonflies, until the sky is filled with a visual symphony of synchronized loop-de-loops and barrel rolls and lazy eights. As the lake gulps the last of the sun, they begin making passes under the bridge, thousands at a time in a single wave, wave after wave, cooing and settling in, until the last bird is tucked in for the night, oblivious to the roar of commuter traffic overhead. When it is all over, the human audience bursts into applause.

Hurricane Katrina smashed into New Orleans in late August of 2005. With so many human beings dead, missing, or grieving their catastrophic losses, it seemed selfish to worry about the plight of those tiny, feathered residents who had also been cast into exile and homelessness by the storm. Yet, as the date of the spring migration neared in a city still lacking basic services in many areas, those of us who had seen the martins soaring in happier times formed a question: Would they return?

The answer was yes, and in numbers almost as great as before, though not even the martin experts seem to understand how the birds survived or why they returned. But then, there is nothing very rational about the attachment to one place on earth. Feather or flesh, we are connected to each other, and our spirits dance on the air as they near home.

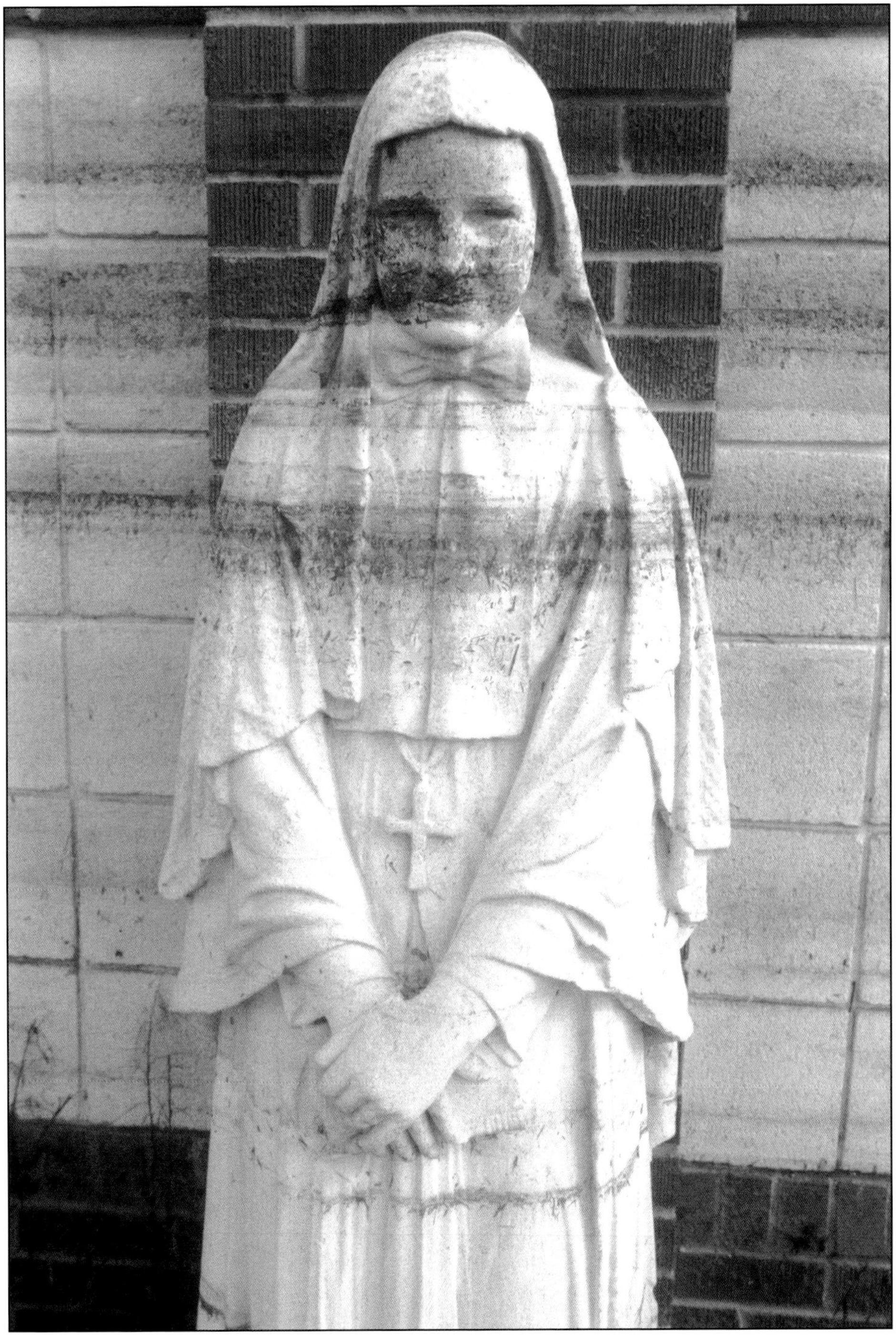

Thanksgiving Day

by Christian Champagne

Thanksgiving Day in most of the United States means family gatherings and turkey dinner with all the trimmings. But for a certain tribe of Orleanians going back generations, Thanksgiving means horse racing and corned beef and cabbage.

Thanksgiving Day is the traditional opening day at the Fair Grounds Race Course in New Orleans. Thanksgiving is easily one of the biggest days of the meet at the third-oldest thoroughbred racetrack in the country.

Every season, as soon as reservations were available they were snapped up the same day. When new management tried to institute a new procedure to streamline the reservations process in the track clubhouse dining area, it caused one of those only-in-New Orleans letter-to-the-editor assaults. Which speaks to the importance opening day holds in the hearts of many.

In some circles the anticipation of opening day at the track, while not quite approaching religious zeal, does renew a kind of Christmas-like anticipation in the hearts of seemingly jaded adults. It's akin to the opening of deer season or summer vacation.

Opening day at the track is also in the tradition of American Thanksgiving because it is a sort of family reunion. Old acquaintances forged in the crucible of chasing winners and more losers in post times past are rediscovered. For those who habituate the Fair Grounds there is an old-style camaraderie that is essential to the experience of horse racing. There is a propriety of the truly committed. More than once on opening day you will hear talk of how the place is a madhouse, but soon it will be reclaimed by the regulars.

However, there is no better way to take in the human pageantry of horse racing than to go on a busy day like Thanksgiving. The collegial gathering of every strata of a society can be seen commiserating honestly with each other in search of a winner.

The human stream passing before you between races is like a museum of people. Unlike a museum though, these people are alive.

The Fair Grounds is the oldest sports cathedral in New Orleans with a lineage going back to before the Civil War. The Fair Grounds has been at its present location since the first decade of the twentieth century and boasts many famous former participants, including General George Armstrong Custer, in its colorful past. On any given day though, there is always a new crop of characters to be seen.

I like to say that the Fair Grounds is as close as New Orleans comes to a Wrigley Field or Fenway Park. It's a place where champion racehorses are buried in the infield and more than a few patrons have had their ashes scattered. Many Orleanians remember fondly spending time with their grandfathers, fathers, and mothers, pursuing the passing parade and the sweet passion and spectacle of horse racing New Orleans style.

New Orleans may be one of the last places in the United States that not only keeps romance of a gone-by time alive but nurtures it as an endangered species or, in the case of the Fair Grounds, a beloved uncle of aunt. And most years it begins on Thanksgiving Day. Leave it to New Orleans to create a holiday on top of a holiday.

Jazz Fest

by Stanton Moore

As a professional drummer who travels the world for a living, I've played and attended many festivals around the globe, and yet nothing compares to the experience of the New Orleans Jazz and Heritage Festival—known to us locals as Jazz Fest. Nowhere else in the world is there such an eclectic mix of music, art, culture, and—ah, the food. Where else could you be listening to Bob Dylan in the distance while standing in line for a Crawfish Strudel and bump into Zigaboo Modeliste—the great drummer for legendary New Orleans band, The Meters—and then not be able to chat because you are drowned out by a passing gang of Mardi Gras Indians?

As a musician who spends way too much time traveling, it's quite a thrill to be able to walk out of my front door and be at the greatest festival in the world in just fifteen minutes. To hop on stage, play for 10-50,000 people (depending on our slot that year), and be home to chill in minutes after the gig.

Of all the festivals I've played, Jazz Fest has the most musically exciting line-up, year after year. Of course there are always great Jazz, Blues, Funk, Brass Band, and Mardi Gras Indian acts to catch. But there are also big-name, world-famous acts that invariably cause (foot) traffic jams all around the main stage. In recent years, Sting, Lenny Kravitz, Paul Simon, and Bruce Springsteen have all made appearances. To the hard-core Festers though, these acts are welcomed with open arms for they draw the crowds away from the rest of the Fest and make it easier to float between Economy Hall (the traditional Jazz tent), the WWOZ Jazz tent, and the Gospel Tent. And once you and your friends are comfortably in place inside one of the tents and out of the sun, you can send one of your small crew a few steps away to bring back a sampling of some of the many great culinary offerings. You can rest assured that if you say, ". . . just get me some of what you get," it will be good. Whether they bring back Crawfish Monica, a Cochon de Lait Po-Boy, or an Oyster Patty, you'll be happy.

The overall cumulative experience of Jazz Fest is unlike any in the world. The weather, the music, the food, constantly bumping into friends you haven't seen in a while as well as local heroes . . . it's all what keeps people coming down every year and what makes some locals want to move to Mid-City (the neighborhood that surrounds the Fair Grounds and is host to the Fest). It's our beloved Fest and it gives us, and all of our visitors, more to love about our magical hometown of New Orleans.

Julu and the Pussyfooters

by Rebecca Snedeker

I've always wondered about the women in high heels at second line parades, but last Saturday night I found myself dancing down Clio Street in gold stilettos, smiling ear to ear and surrounded by old friends and new, as we kept step with the Midnite Disturbers brass band. It felt just like Julu, the annual parade that many of us who were there that night roll with on Mardi Gras mornings, but the moon was high in the sky, and we were gussied up in formal wear instead of costumes. One stepper observed, "It's like Julu is having a prom!"

Our parade Julu is named after Zulu. Zulu began in 1909, when a group of African American men dressed in blackface and grass skirts and threw shaved-and-painted coconuts to onlookers. As one version of the story goes, they were spoofing Rex, the white Carnival organization who considers their leader to be King of Carnival. Julu began about eighty-four years after Zulu. In the early 1990s, a group of Jewish, gentile, and atheist musicians called the New Orleans Klezmer All-Stars started following Zulu's parade, and some of the Klezmers' friends followed the band. The tradition continued and somewhere along the years someone jokingly said Julu, and the name stuck.

But last Saturday was not Carnival but a wedding. Henry, our Grand Marshal, had just tied the knot, and we were strutting behind him and his bride, Larisa, from the Big Top toward the river. The end of Clio Street was barricaded, but by the time we reached St. Charles Avenue, someone had moved the barricade and was stepping out onto the avenue. No newcomers to stopping traffic, our pulsing parade crossed to the neutral ground. Larisa, the bride, was marching right up front along with Henry. Larisa is the Grand Marshal of the Pussyfooters. This all-female Carnival marching krewe dons leotards, tights, and pom-pom boots and struts down major parade routes performing hot choreographed dances. The Pussyfooters were in full swing with our Julu crowd, two krewes mixing in one big joy throb.

As we reached the neutral ground, a charging streetcar clanged its bell and rolled by. Passengers waved eagerly, and the tuba player bowed to them. Our dancing finally culminated on the steps of an old condominium building. I felt so happy, watching my friend Henry with his beautiful bride. He loves to dance like no one else I know. And together, this celebrating is what we all know how to do.

On the way back down Clio, a tall piano player danced on the hood of my sweetheart's parked car, and later back at the Big Top, the Klezmers played the hora, and the goy bride and groom were lifted high in chairs. Then the Pussyfooters did a fine line dance, and trays of petits fours were served. In one evening we'd felt the touch of so many rich parts of Henry and Larisa's lives, a beautiful reflection of this couple who have chosen to live their lives here and to lead us in parade.

Sometimes I wonder about what it would be like to live in another place. But last Saturday I felt the sense of home here that makes it hard to imagine living anywhere else. For all the questions I have about New Orleans, I don't want to go anywhere else. The feeling of belonging is so strong. That night I earned the worst blisters I've had in years, and the dead skin is only now peeling off. My feet are scarred from all that joy.

Fun for All Ages!

by Ian McNulty

One of the clichés trotted out about New Orleans is that people here "love to have a good time," as if there were other communities where people just love to get together to sulk. I grew up in New England, and I can confirm that such group urges are confined only to a few coffeehouses. But still, there is clearly something to this image of fun-loving New Orleans. It's real, and as a transplant it has helped cement me to this city.

What drew me back to New Orleans after the Katrina levee failures was my belief that as long as I live here I need not fear growing old. That is a long-play proposition and a powerful gift, and I feel it's there for anyone in New Orleans to embrace.

In a lot of other places, it seems like if you're not young, hot, or rich then you're marginal to the city's story. Here, however, the older people grow, the better they are at the really great things about this city. They've had more experience as New Orleanians and that makes their lives richer and, yes, more fun.

There are lots of old cities with interesting histories and distinctive folkways. But in New Orleans, history and related customs aren't just cultural assets to be exhibited, studied, and remembered. They remain the basis for relentless and extraordinary fun. I think the difference is that ideas about what makes a good time here spring less from pop culture and more from resilient family traditions and the interactions of people from different generations and social realms. New Orleans surely falls for fads, but the most enduring ways that locals pursue and cultivate pleasure are developed over time and from the very specifics of this place. That's also how they are best enjoyed.

As usual, Mardi Gras provides a quintessential example. Carnival time gets better for me with each passing year because I know more people on the streets and in the parades, I have a more deeply developed personal ritual of where I go and whom I see, and I feel that I understand the whole context a little better.

The identity of this city is so strong that living here feels like participating in something bigger than yourself, and for me that's hugely rewarding. Some people look forward to retirement or the day Social Security benefits kick in. I look forward to the days when I can blow away whippersnappers with stories about Mardi Gras past, about the Christmas Day when it snowed in New Orleans, and about that season of night after Katrina when we filtered back to a ruined city and began rebuilding.

Maybe we could have started over somewhere else, and if enough people chose that path then New Orleans would be dead today. We would have wept as an emptied city receded into modern myth, and then slowly we would learn the histories and traditions of our new homes. We would have built new lives. But I know they really would not have been as much fun.

Hind Quarter

by Lee Meitzen Grue

I don't remember what year the rents went up in the Quarter. This is not history. It is poetic memory which exists somewhere on the edge of sleep. I had quit my day job and gone back to college full time, so it had to be around 1962. The apartment I took was downtown on Burgundy Street, in what today is called the Marigny Triangle, across Esplanade Avenue from the French Quarter.

My apartment was the back-half of half-of-a-shotgun double: that's a New Orleans description. To get to my apartment I walked past a bare chain-link fence on the neighbor's side, down a side alley where I had to step over a set of concrete steps that led into somebody else's apartment, on down the alley to concrete steps that led into mine. My apartment consisted of two good-sized rooms, a small furnished kitchen, and a bath with a claw-foot tub.

I was single, and I hung out at The Ryder Coffee House on North Rampart Street. The apartment cost forty dollars a month. I was going to a state school which had cheap tuition. I lived on my meager savings and a part-time job as the world's worst typist for an auto repair at a dealership, where I recorded the repairs of cars on index-file cards. They hired me out of pity.

We called our part of the city Hind Quarter because we had been ousted from paradise—the French Quarter—by high rent. We were the young writers, painters, and service workers of the Quarter. We rode bicycles and had rent parties to gather funds for next month's rent. My backyard was huge. A great space for a party. I would ride my bicycle with a dingy dog called Puppy following along to Schwegmann's on St. Claude Avenue. It was called a supermarket but had the narrow aisles and neighborhood chaos of a mom-and-pop corner store.

I didn't like to talk to the butcher. He made me nervous, but chicken hearts were only ten cents a pound. He sold me five pounds. I bought a few onions, bell peppers, and a small can of cayenne pepper. Out of this I made a huge pot of dirty-rice jambalaya. The chicken hearts were cut to look like mushrooms, then sautéed in bacon grease with the cut onions and bell peppers. Mixed with pounds of boiled rice, salt and peppered, this was food fit for the gods. One gallon of red wine to go with and we had a party.

The other necessity was a good doorman—Jack Husband—to collect the rent. The guests were providing the rest of the wine, but I provided food and music. Earl Tillman was there on vibes, a flute—Eluard Burt, Uganda Roberts on congas, and whoever else showed up on guitar. It was a mixed neighborhood; nobody cared about the noise as long as they were invited. We usually went on dancing until four or five a.m. It took that long to collect the thirty or forty dollars I needed to get my rent together.

A Streetcar of Solace is Back in New Orleans

by Adam Nossiter

Like the rolling tide to seacoast residents, the low rumbling of the streetcar is a nearly internal sound for citizens here in New Orleans.

The St. Charles streetcar line is that most valued local commodity, an unbroken link to the past: the same green tin boxes rocking at the same slow speed down the same tree-shaded avenue, unchanged since the early 1920s.

"It's all very, very much the way it's been for a very long time," said Robert Michiels, a shipbuilding engineer who paid $1.25 to ride it the other day, just for the pleasure of riding it again, down the avenue.

The streetcar has represented something else besides the connections through time and space: the city's living room, a privileged spot for tentative social encounters across lines of race, class, and nationality, in a place not otherwise given to them.

Before the storm, the St. Charles streetcar was at least an image of the social ideal. Uptown lawyers in seersucker sat by weary-looking housekeepers going to the downtown hotels. Noisy schoolchildren jostled for space with tourists from France, Rome, and Australia wondering about the solemn fellow on the column at Lee Circle. (That would be Robert E. Lee.) Prim suburbanites visiting from Nashville and Atlanta, and encountering public transportation for the first time, smiled nervously past muttering bums. No other city in the South entertained such a mix.

In the worn wooden interior, bathed in the smell of sulfur and the soothing racket of clanging machinery, the fractures in the stratified city melted, slightly. And what would be deficiencies in other places—improbable premodern slowness, the occasional surly conductor, unexplained lengthy halts between stops—were virtues. The conductor sang out, ingeniously mispronounced, the names of the Greek muses that double as street names here: MEL-Po-MEEN! (Melpomene) TERP-Si-Core! (Terpsichore) You were getting somewhere, slowly. Complicated reading could be accomplished.

Excellent, as a rider named Cherry Gardon put it the other day, "if you're not in a rush to get to work"—a widely held ethic.

For those who have come back, the memory of the old social model remains powerful. "The streetcar is not just something convenient," said Manuel García-Castellón, riding it recently to his job as a professor of romance languages at the University of New Orleans.

He struggled to explain why something so irrational could also be so indispensable. "Sometimes, I think I'm in the salotto of my house," he said, using the Italian word for parlor.

In July and August, the streetcar effects a miracle: benign contact with the superheated New Orleans air. All the windows come down, the sweet, thick air rushes in, and you are in a truce with the beast of the South Louisiana summer.

Like other elements that have struggled to come back, this one—in the telling of the riders, at least—has an intimate connection with the biographies of everyone who is asked about it.

"Me, personally, I been taking it all my life," said Derek Batiste, who was going to his job at Wendy's. "I took it to school, that's how long I been taking it. Not just for tourists, no. The streetcar, it's like part of my family." A computer technician, Samps Taylor, savoring his ride, said, "It brings it back to where you were."

In other places, citizens move on, leaving the historic artifacts people here believe make up the urban fabric. The ties are personal. Past proposals to build new cars for the line have been vehemently rejected.

"Whole lot of history," said Henry Carter, riding the streetcar to a construction job. "I been catching this streetcar since '69. Been catching it a long time."

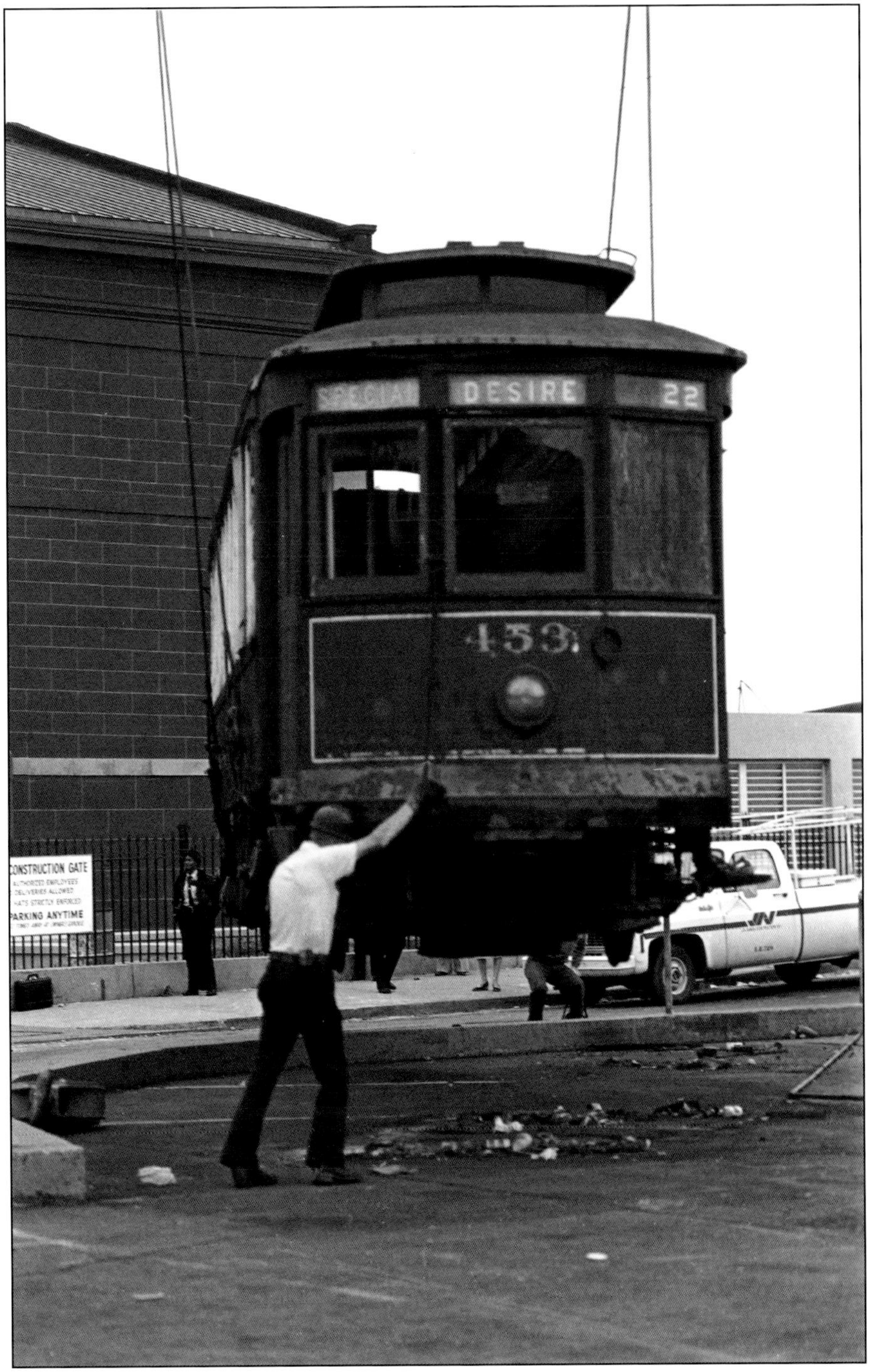
SPECIAL
DESIRE
22
453
CONSTRUCTION GATE
PARKING ANYTIME

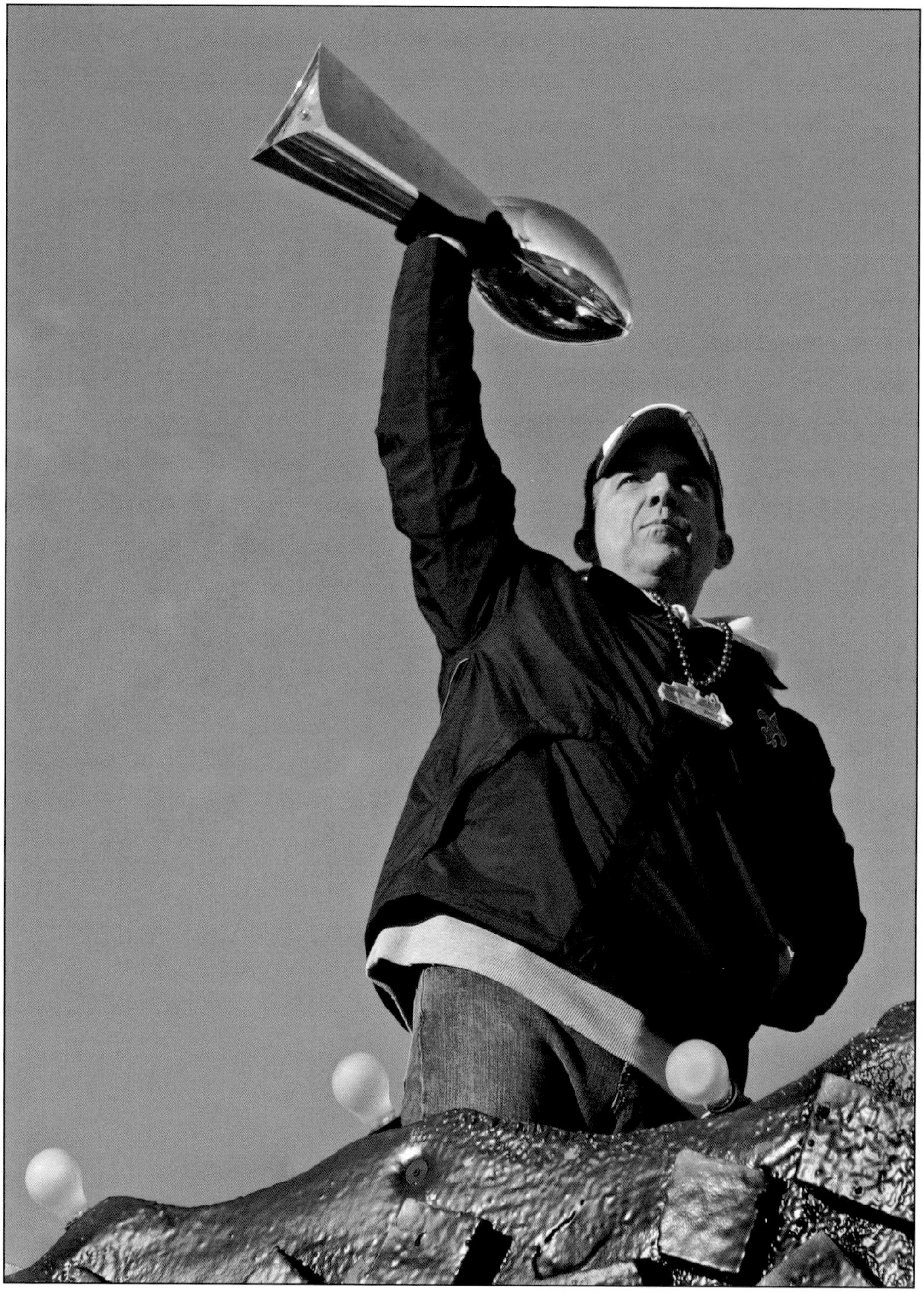

What We Can't Lose

by Marda Burton

Referring to the nightmare called Katrina, a visitor asked: "Has the city come back yet?" My answer: "It never left."

Even after that horrifying catastrophe the spirit of New Orleans stood steadfast. The great levee flood caused terrible loss of life that will never be forgotten; it broke hearts and neighborhoods, but it did not break a life force so strong that New Orleans never lost its glorious contradictions or its talent for joy. Although the city's ineffable persona lay dormant for a heartbeat, in shock and grief, buried beneath mud and flotsam and wretched heat, it soon gathered itself together and burst forth again with defiance.

What we called "survivor's guilt" preyed on those who evacuated and watched the flood's horror unfold on television, unable to contact loved ones without means of communication. Soon after my return, concerned that it might seem frivolous yet believing New Orleanians were longing to reconnect with one another, I hosted a salon in the largely undamaged French Quarter. People cried and cheered when Roy Guste read his essay, "I Am Creole." They laughed at Chris Champagne's FEMA-put-down poetry. They danced to the familiar music of Tom McDermott's piano and Tim Laughlin's clarinet and savored actress/singer Lila Hay Owen's performance. Champagne flowed. Everyone said thanks for bringing us back together, for re-creating a semblance of life before the storm.

All over the city, returning New Orleanians did the same. Desperate for a taste of normal, those living on the second floors of their flooded homes pooled their unappetizing MREs (Meals Ready to Eat) and organized block parties. Chefs immediately mobilized, feeding both appetites and spirits. Soon their restaurants were back with vigor; today New Orleans has more restaurants than it did before the hurricane. Musicians missed only a few beats before resuming their essential roll; and when Jazz Fest came along in April, huge crowds gathered to enjoy and honor them.

A mere six months after the deluge, Mardi Gras 2006 was poignant beyond belief, as costumed celebrants swarmed over the streets, living a few days in a carefree and badly needed alternate reality. Mardi Gras Indians, who had nailed their drowned feathers and sequins to the fronts of their devastated homes, returned to parade in vivid new suits sewn in Atlanta or Detroit or Dallas. One of the fabulously feathered Big Chiefs told me: "We came back to kick Katrina in the ass."

New Orleans recovery found its icon when legendary musician Fats Domino was almost lost to the flood. When he retired, the seventy-seven-year-old Fats had returned to his home in the Ninth Ward, where he was trapped for three days and believed dead. His rescue brought hope to the deeply damaged city. After declaring his performing days were over, two years later Fats put on his gold jewelry and his yellow-checked coat and his wonderful smile and returned to Tipitina's to perform all his hits to wild acclaim—a beloved symbol of the city's stamina and courage.

After the flood, the Superdome was saddled with not only a macabre hurricane history but grievous structural wounds, and the city was in grave danger of losing another icon. But the New Orleans Saints' owners decided to stay and join the recovery. A scant year later the perpetually underdog football team came back to a resurrected Dome and their loyal army of "Who Dats"—a passionate mass of humanity of all ages, races, and economic levels. As if to prove the city's resilience, the team proudly shouldered the task of personifying their healing city, playing out the analogy all the way to Miami and the 2010 Super Bowl. Winning the NFL Championship and the Super Bowl for the first time, the Saints not only sent their city into paroxysms of celebration but became national heroes.

Thus New Orleanians continue to show the world our city's unquenchable spirit—a city that refused to die—a collective reality we can't afford to lose.

Jewish-New Orleans Art?

by Jonathan Freilich

Over the last sixteen years, playing with the New Orleans Klezmer All-Stars, I have had a close view of what a hybridized New Orleans-Jewish art form might be and, more interestingly, what forces in any locale might contribute to the alteration of certain sounds in music.

The common definition of Klezmer music is usually given by the translation of the word coupled with the origins of the sound. The word Klezmer is from two words, *kley* and *zemer*, meaning vessel of song. Some go on to say that this describes the musician who is the vessel who channels the melodies that in a sense are already out there in a metaphysical space given by God. From a cultural or ethno-musicological standpoint, Klezmer denotes Eastern European Jews playing the secular music of those regions but with an instrumental inflection from the liturgical singing style of the *Chazzans* or synagogue cantorial soloists of those regions.

It is interesting how people begin to identify with phenomena such as sounds and places and relate to those things as being their own. Since this band started playing the bars of New Orleans in the early nineties, the energy of that world began to seep in. People wanted to dance, and they wanted rhythmic, ecstatic music that lasted for hours into the night. That was their idea of New Orleans music at that time. People who saw that element said that we were New Orleans players—that we played New Orleans Jewish Funk. On the other hand, many said that we were keeping alive a traditional Jewish form—that the sound was Jewish—and they seemed proud that we were giving public voice to an unsung tradition in New Orleans.

What was happening on the inside? The beauty of these melodies and styles that we heard on record or distantly remembered from our childhood fascinated us. However, we decided to play them without limiting any of the other ways in which we played. We wanted to play the melodies responding to the energies and immediacies of the moment rather than confining ourselves to a preconceived framework. One could say it was like the energy you might see delivered by one of the young local brass bands of the time. In this way we were vessels, but for the collective energy of the city at that time. The song melodies from another place and time were transformed into a delivery system for an underlying local spirit.

What is this spirit? New Orleans is often described as spiritual. The word spirit comes from Latin where *spiritus* meant to breathe. How the city does seem to breathe—even under water as the world discovered towards the end of 2005. Music, similarly, is equated with spirituality and the breath.

Although we breathe approximately 21,600 times a day, no two breaths are exactly the same. Change happens moment by moment; can we ever decide that the breath is ours? Try holding it in. What happens to "your" breath? Perhaps it is the same as the attempt to claim ownership of any phenomena that breathes—like music or even a remarkable city. To whom do sounds or communities belong?

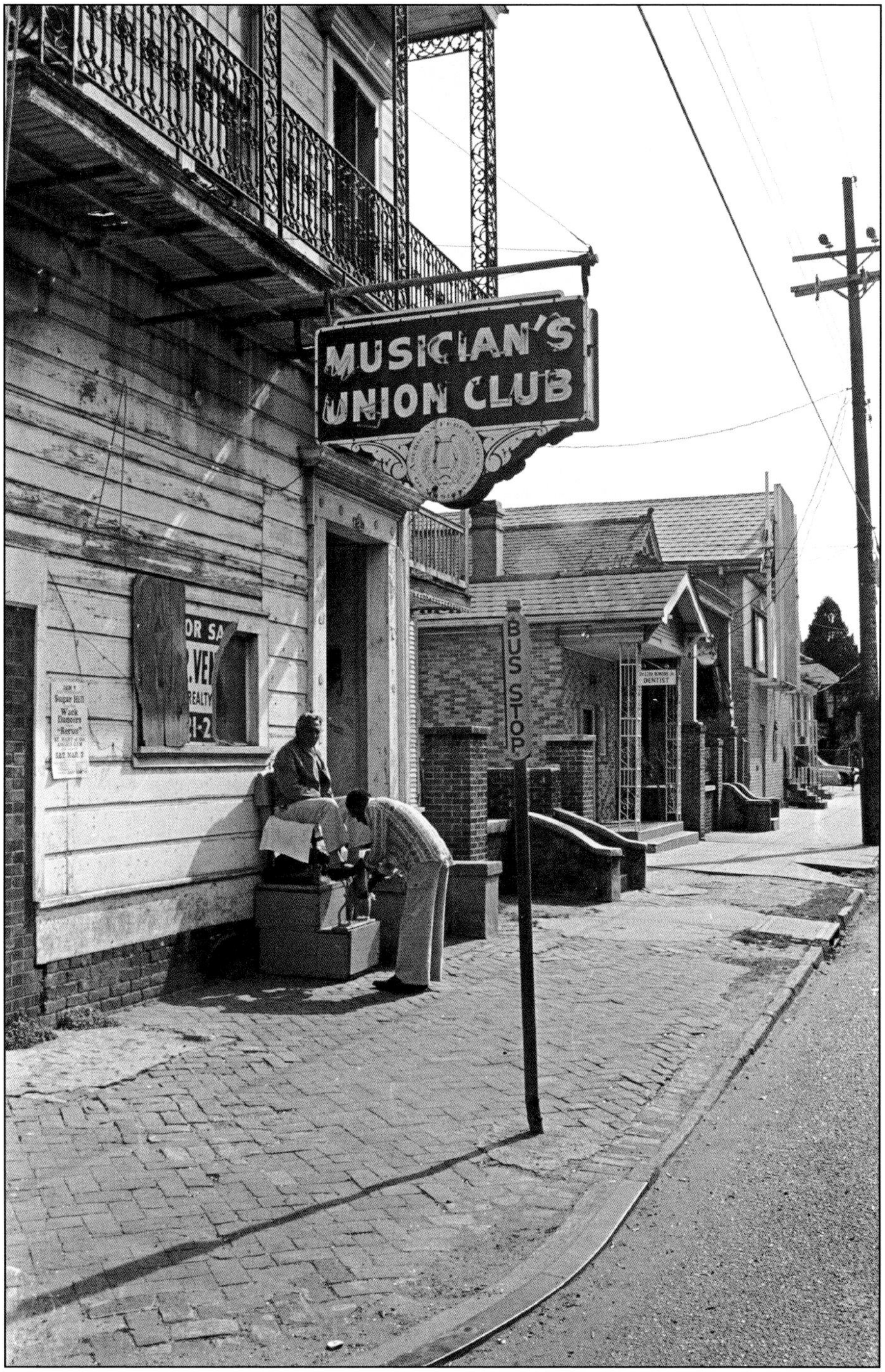
MUSICIAN'S
UNION CLUB
BUS STOP
DENTIST

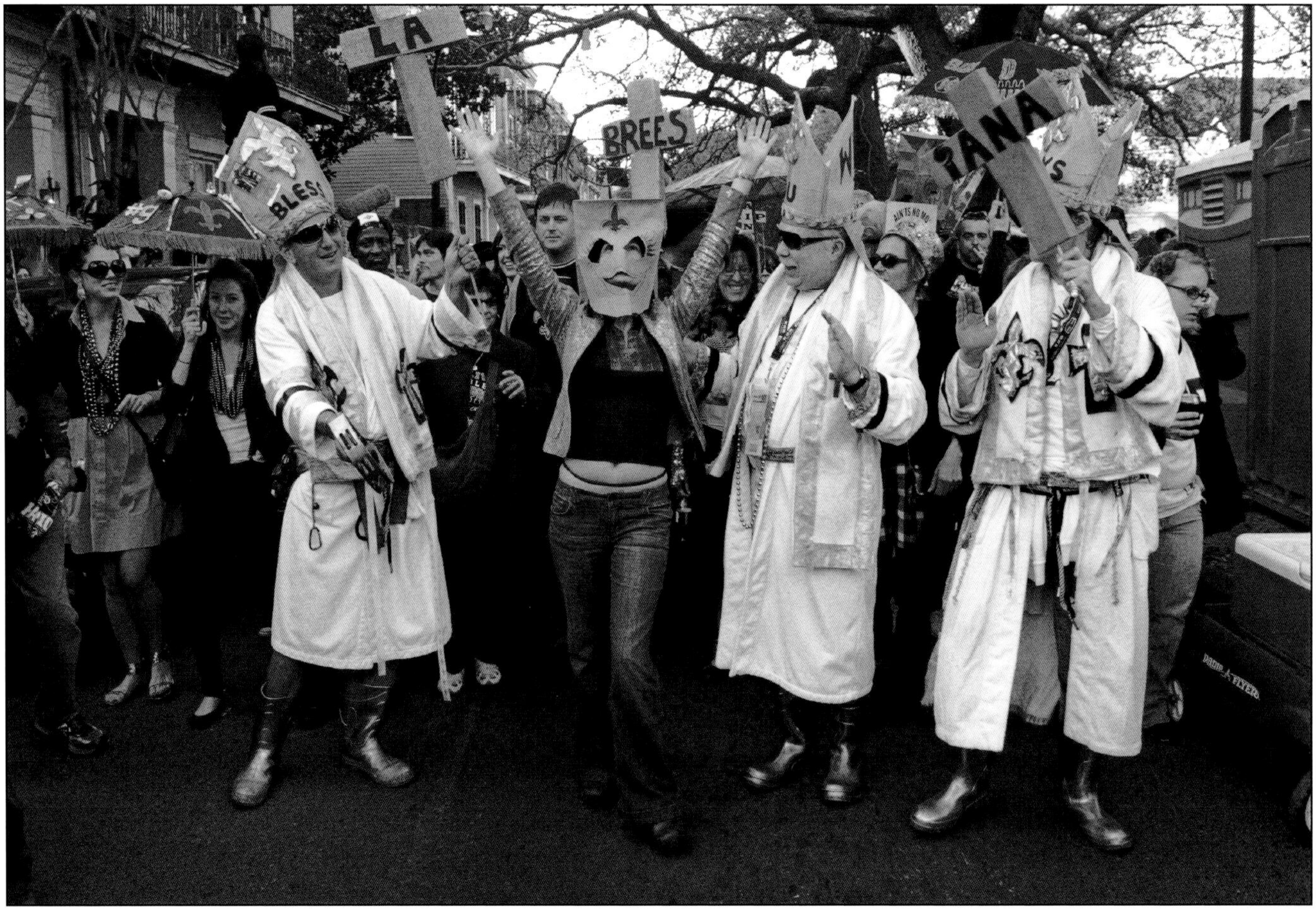
LA
BREES

No Parking Parade Route

by Ann Marie Coviello

At Mardi Gras time everyone wants to see the parades, and everyone wants to catch some beads, pennies from heaven. Parade connoisseurs value all aspects of the parade: the live music (the more the better); the beauty of the floats; the way the parade's theme amuses, inspires, and holds the parade together. Each parade is the art of the captains, supported by their krewe members. They work tirelessly to assemble the mind-boggling details, from police permits to flambeaux carriers. They have jobs, families, and bills to pay, yet they put on grand spectacles, in relative anonymity, with enormous expenditures of time and money, asking nothing in return. I sing the praises of these intrepid parade geniuses.

I sing, too, the praises of the little parades, the ones that travel the backstreets like fire-breathing dragons. The Young Men Olympians, the Black Men of Labor, the Jolly Bunch, the Prince of Wales, the Lady Buck Jumpers, the Big Nine, the Big Seven, the Money Wasters, and all the other social aid and pleasure clubs put on second line parades thirty-nine Sundays a year. La Societé de Saint Anne and Krewe du Vieux keep parading alive in the Bywater, Marigny, and French Quarter. Barkus is the dog parade. The Krewe of O.A.K., The Pussyfooters, Box of Wine, Julu, the Krewe of Joyful Noise, and the Royal Revelers of Discordia all pop up in odd places during Mardi Gras. There's the Southern Decadence Parade, New Orleans' twisted answer to Labor Day. The Irish Parades roll the week of St. Patrick's Day, and the Mardi Gras Indian Parades come out around St. Joseph's Day.

The Grand Marshal for Life of Box of Wine, smallest of the small parades, says that when we put on parades we are like Tibetan monks making Sand-Mandalas, intricate designs made with colored sand which take days to create. When they are finished, the monks sweep them away to celebrate the impermanence of all creation. In New Orleans, we paint the wheel of life with glitter and feathers, with brass and drum, with high steps and waving arms. A parade which has taken months to pull together is over in a few hours: ephemeral, transcendent, transformative, holy.

My Mother's House Is the River

by Andy Young

From the other side of the Mississippi River, New Orleans is a mirage, its lights spill in a reflection that scatters and forms itself again, revealing the city's ephemeral nature. Not always appearing to flow in one direction, the river dances and swirls, swishes up and back, or sometimes seems to meander with no direction at all. We live in an arc of her winding spine, in the crook of her curves, beside her open mouth. She is the reason the city is crescent. Here you see boats from Panama, France, Morocco drift past like huge, impossible buildings.

On my birthday one year, I walked her banks, the city beside me like a friend, and saw a man catch a fairytale catfish almost as long as me, a testament to the hidden mystery of her depths. She connects us to the rest of the country and carries what drifts down to the sea, reminds us of its vastness, and that we are mostly made of water, too.

So many afternoons—a warm, sunny winter afternoon, a summer day hot as a tongue—I have come to watch her eddy and flow, to let my worries or sadness flow out and into her to be swallowed. The Yoruban words to a prayer for Oshun, the spirit of the river, often stream through my head. *Iya Mile Odo.* My mother's house is the river. When my aunt died, when my friend did, when I needed to purge my ragged heart, it was here I came to sit and watch her, constant and constantly changing. And in gratitude, it is here I come to bring oranges and blooms, to light little boats of fire and watch them drift out and away toward the Gulf, the world.

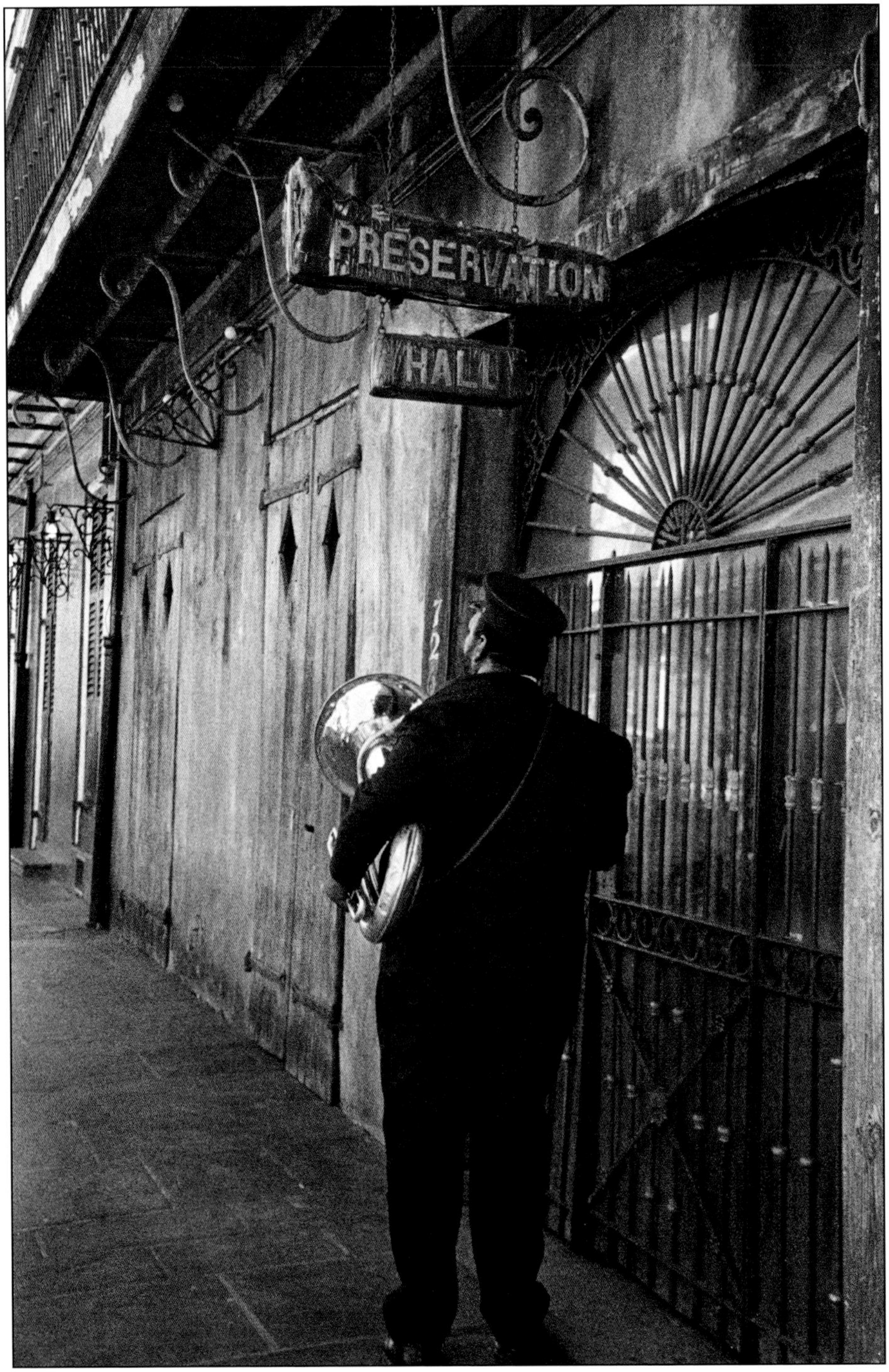
PRESERVATION
HALL

A Prayer for Preservation Hall

by Jennifer Odell

Some glad morning a generation ago, a new spring day bloomed, settling its sun thickly upon Jackson Square. A handful of young men gathered by the cathedral—tuba, sax, couple a trumpets, snare drum, baritone horn. They sported bushy haircuts, jeans, tennis shoes. A pouf of someone's brown curls refused to be tamed by the encroaching heat. My father watched him work out a tune on his horn, this teenager who had grown up around the corner on 726 St. Peter Street, learning the language of the Bruniouses, Barbarins, Sweet Emma Barrett.

Leaving the culture they were born into back North, the kid's parents had migrated here in the '60s, following their passion as folks did back then. They weren't meant for the cold winters or concrete skylines of Philadelphia. Their hearts had grown roots in the Crescent City. Their love had borne the fruit of protection. The ghosts in the cracks of the French Quarter sidewalks were whispering their names. *Make a sanctuary for what you love.*

And so hugged by the moisture and trusting the spirits, Allan and Sandra Jaffe came to St. Peter Street. There, they built a bassinet for traditional New Orleans jazz in the music's very cradle.

"Whss, whss, whss-whss, when this life is o-ver, *whisss whis-whis-whis . . .*"

My father used to whistle as he'd tap out triplets with his foot and push cloves of sizzling garlic around a pan in our kitchen while familiar notes drifted from his cassette player. I'd pull the drawer in the music bench as wide open as it would go, my dad's DNA comforted by the sight of methodically aligned rows of Preservation Hall Jazz Band tapes. That same DNA finding small joy in big swing.

One day, I sang in my ten-year-old heart, *I'll fly away. The streets will steam with sound, and I'll find a home where it's enough to know your own desire. I'll smell the clear fragrance of jasmine as I shuffle-hop my feet down the street. I'll feel the creak of warped boards beneath my bouncing limbs and the pulsing sst-ssst-ssst of a snare drum that's aching to wake up and move.*

My father felt it, too. So we packed our things one August and pointed the car south, driving through tobacco fields, Blue Ridge Mountains, wide swaths of dry land cut through with spindling spires of Tennessee wildflowers. We drove down into the deliciously languid belly of the Gulf. And when we landed—safely six feet under—my father and I marched straight to St. Peter Street. We waited in line for a fifteen-year-old's eternity to pile inside Preservation Hall and climb up on that rickety back windowsill. It's where I still stand to hear the sanctity of tradition, my tail-feathers now better seasoned for shaking as I rattle the walls, moving my hips to that big swing, swaying eardrums drunk on history.

Hallelujah, my father's spirit has flown. Allen Jaffe has passed this church on to his son. And suddenly it's three a.m. and my sister and I are thumping those floorboards, singing loud and proud. A grown man with a pouf of brown curls nods his head on the two and the four.

"I'll fly away, oh glory, I'll fly away!"

We lift our voices up in unison, down to our roots and out into space, where Sister Gertrude Morgan sang and where John Brunious led a second line.

"I'll fly away, oh glory, I'll fly away!"

New Orleans, and All That It Implies

by Rick Bragg

It is not the only place.

I love others.

I love Miami, where the light and the women have a golden quality to them, where Spanish comes flying at you like machine gun bullets, and the *café con leche* tastes better than those ingredients should naturally allow.

I love the foothills along the Alabama-Georgia line, love the fog-shrouded mountains and jade-colored streams and rugged pastures studded with wicked blackberry islands, the places I traveled as a boy in a time before blood pressure pills, and financial disclosure forms.

I love the Alabama coast, where you watch the sun set over what seems to be Biloxi, where the red snapper out in the Deep Blue seem to line up at your hook, and an old house waits for me with my name on the uncollected mail, for a month, forever?

I love Manhattan, when it's cold, and Boston, when it's not, and big ol' Atlanta, when the traffic moves. I loved Africa, for the romance of what it used to be, and London, for the way the working people talk, and Haiti, for its magic, and its will.

But I love New Orleans deeper, stronger, meaner, more.

Places tweak your heart, gentle it, or stir it.

New Orleans reaches from the grave, and snatches it from your chest.

I have written that I love it the way some men love women, and people said that was a pretty thought. But I don't think they quite understood.

If New Orleans was a woman, and some say she is, she would seize your heart, break your heart, steal your money, ruin your reputation—as if that needs any help—and leave you penniless walking through the French Market, looking for an orange to steal.

I guess some people would say I love an idea, but that's alright, too.

I only lived here about four years, but I dreamed about living here most of my life. As

243

a boy I filled my head with its romance, with stories of its fencing academies and pistol fights, of Marie Laveau and Jean Lafitte, of zombies, and Cities of the Dead.

As a young man it was a playground, a place where you rode the ferry to Algiers with a young beauty in your arms, half-drunk, with fireworks painting the blackness above your head.

And as a sore-kneed, burnt-out, forty something, I learned to love it not for any of that—well, there is always room for beauty—but for everything else. I loved it not for witches but for the Uptown ladies, who made their groceries, and took their mommas to a ladies lunch at Ye Olde College Inn. I loved it not for zombies but for clip-joint bars on Bourbon, where I suffered a two-drink minimum of watery whiskey to hear an old black man beat an electric guitar half to death, conjure it from a broke-string nothing, and whup it some more. I avoided the Cities of the Dead—you get uneasy around cemeteries, the older you get—and spent my time in celebrations of life. I haunted the Upperline, Commander's, Dunbar's, and became great, great friends with the Lucky Dog man.

I was not oblivious to its tragedies and its agonies—the flood made sure of that, if I had any doubts. I knew that people suffered here long before the waters came, knew that drugs were its new curse, its real curse, and the nine millimeter its new demons.

But that was how it always was, light and dark, pain and pleasure, bunched together, like those big yellow stalks of bananas they used to unload off the docks, by hand. You just knew, as one New Orleans writer once said, there was a snake coiled inside.

And you love it anyway, because nothing good for you will ever be any goddamn fun.

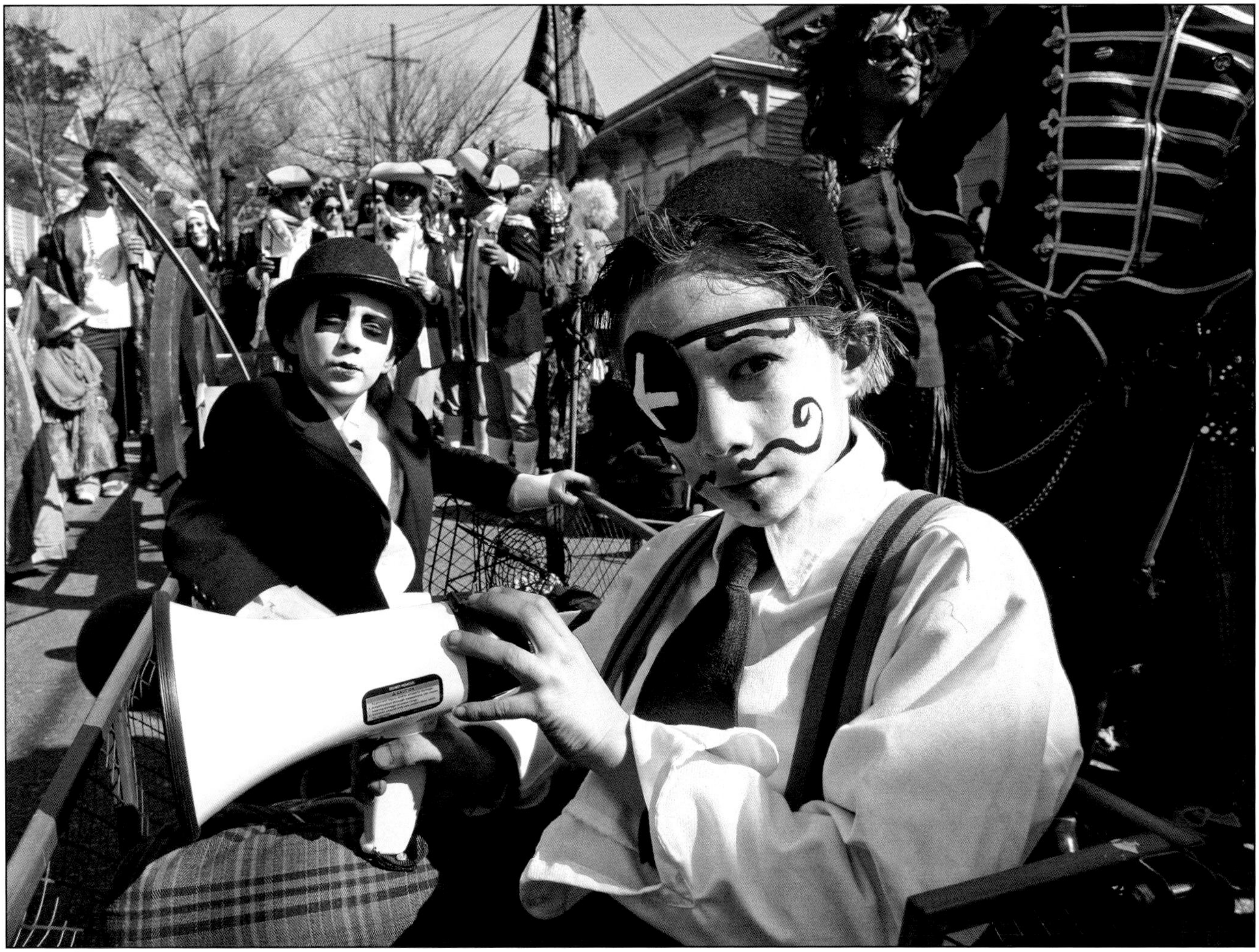

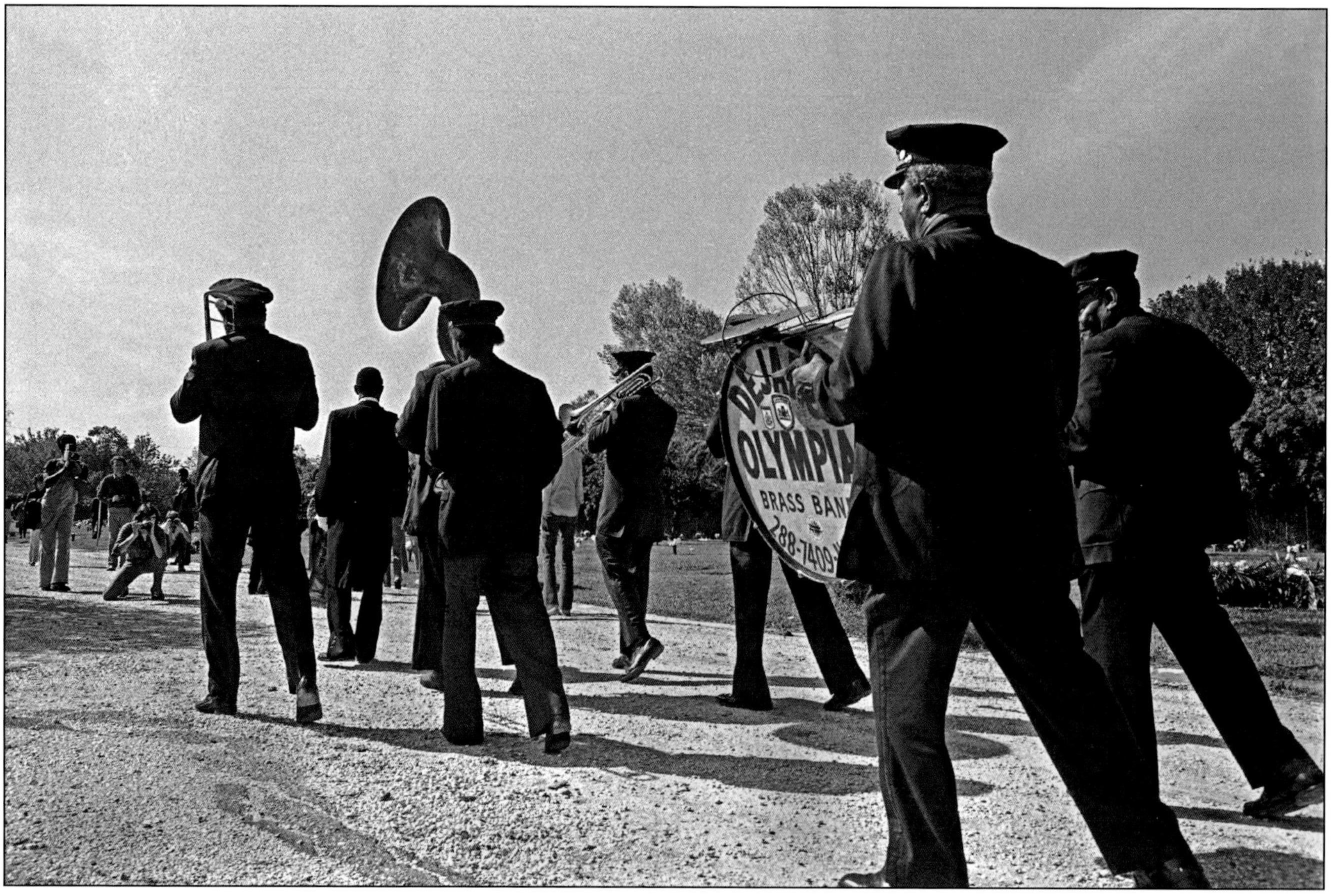
OLYMPIA
BRASS BAN

Afterword

by Joshua Clark

The wealth of the world is here unworked gold in the ore. The paradise of the South is here, deserted and half in ruins. I never beheld anything so beautiful and so sad.

—Lafcadio Hearn, 1877

Finally I cry. When for so long there was no time but to hold tight to the smile. Four years after the planes fell out of an ordinary September sky and the fire came to America, the water came to New Orleans. This time, sky shook the Earth, ocean rose above the land, and water filled eight-tenths of our city like it does the human heart.

Clouds shifting through attic roofs, through all the holes that could only have been made with little fists from the inside. The moaning houses, once homes, people crawling through them, collapsed like cardboard boxes, upon their first return. An amethyst sky holding its line against ash land once towns, barren and deserted as the Mojave. August 29, 2005, giving us all the greatest stories of our lives. Months later, the first squirrel, the evening pulses, cicadas, taking them for granted now. A man who blew his heart out with a shotgun last week in Plaquemines Parish. Robert on Christmas morning, four months after the levees failed, recognizing the skeleton because it wears the same clothes he dressed his mother in that Sunday morning in August. Returning the day after Christmas, shifting through still more debris because he needs to find her jawbone for the coroner to release her.

For the humor, the smiles in their eyes, for the man who tells me, "Life is good. It *really* is," and means it, as his dog curls up on his concrete-slab foundation where its favorite couch once was, and sleeps. For how good life can be here. For the fact that still, after two days in any other U. S. city I sincerely pity the people who live there, in America, because they don't know what life can be like. Upon this fastest disappearing earth on Earth.

And the small airplane's engine that lulls me to sleep somewhere over Barataria Bay, a row of dead cypress like skeleton hands reaching up toward me in the sky, what was once farmland now only patches of marsh like torn rags, last shards of remaining marsh marbling into open water, and I wake in the sky above only ocean lit with sky like mercury. See it. The setting sun crimson, horizon ringed pink, stars burning overhead, Mississippi curling brown from its delta into that ocean lit like quicksilver, and Plaquemines Parish, dark sliver of the world's end, shining endless debris back at me, this final confluence of nature's beauty, man's destruction.

Stakes sticking out of the water a thousand feet beneath me. Tens of thousands of them, miles from land, outlining what was once land. The ghost of Louisiana, water now, the reason so many died that August morning. No marsh, no swamp, no wetlands to abate the unprecedented surge, higher than the Indian Ocean tsunami a year earlier. Robert's mother slipping from his grip into the water. The white dress he had dressed her in, ballooning into the water, strange hyacinth, then gone.

And the strongest, wildest, once-longest river on Earth narrowly constrained by the largest human creations on Earth, its levees, dumping the sediment of the entire American valley uselessly off the continental shelf into the Mexican Gulf.

The river is all. The river brought this sediment, this newest land on the continent to the continent's oldest white and black cultures. From the Montana Rockies to the Appalachians, the Dakota plains down through the Ozarks, the deserts of New Mexico to the hills of upstate New York, we live on tiny pieces of every American landscape. Above us, in America, it is the people who are dynamic, their land a fixture. Here, the opposite.

Here it is a city that is the fragile thing, nestled into a nook of the great river's great motherly arm. A city cooing to us. And biting the river that feeds it. River scoffs and river scolds. And people are murdered.

Our culture was not an accidental confluence of arts. That part of culture is indeed ephemeral. It is the place—land and water—the river, a unique ecosystem birthing a unique culture. Yes, our literature, our music, art, dance, food, is all that remains once those very same things are gone. But our culture is more basic. It is how we live, and how we live beside this river. The land, the water define us. Something that should, and could, be lasting, but has been made too more ephemeral every minute, vanishing, as if we are accidental now, and not our art.

Six countries' flags have flown over southern Louisiana, and it may be argued that each of those countries used us more than we used them. If America wants to continue doing so—our oil, gas, seafood, the largest port in the world—it must help us reclaim that territory, now ocean, once land, it took from us. Help us rebuild our wetlands, shield us from the next flood. Oil refineries' flames dancing in wind like candles.

And down there, finally, our fragile city, three centuries of fire and flood, plague and war, but only now a new American landscape, one hardly changed since the levees failed because the wetlands were not there to stop the surge. Place in much of New Orleans has become a shadow of what we once knew. The splintered viscera of everyday existence that people outside, in America, take for granted. The human details are there, the stories still here. Break into these homes, stare at that sky through that hole in the attic that could only have been made by a tiny fist from the inside. Rage and weep and rejoice, hope and pain for the future. Navigate and map these new landscapes of the city and heart. And tell it.

Time here once turned like a wheel. Round and round, each rotation taking us back to where we were, days, years, once little changing but for fleeting strokes of sun and sister stars, now changed forever. For water. Beginning and end of life in New Orleans.

Wonder at this fragile earth in the great river's arm. Ocean straining to caress its dim glow, to forever extinguish it as it did that August morning. We live here now not *because* of the city's myriad virtues that fill these pages, but *despite* its faults. A definition of love. We have lost our oldest generation. We are suddenly shocked to find ourselves the storytellers, the history makers and keepers, creators. Keepers of the fire. Of the water. The land.

Contributors

The Editor

Proud to call New Orleans home, LEE BARCLAY lives in Faubourg St. John, down a bend of the bayou from 600-year-old oaks, pelicans, ibises, and blue herons. She is devoted to the preservation of New Orleans through community education and collaboration and the performance of New Orleans culture—in kitchens and down backstreets; through trumpets and voices; on page, stage, and sidewalk; and when any time, for any reason, a parade rolls by.

The Writers

PAGE 1NE, New Orleans native, stand-up comedian, poet, and gymnastic instructor, has amazed audiences with his acrobatic performances in the French Quarter in New Orleans, for circuses, NBA half-times, festivals, and private venues around the world since 1983. Page 1NE was a 1997 winner at the Apollo and starred on the 2008 hit-NBC television series *America's Got Talent*. He is currently at work writing his eighth album (and counting) and performing across the Gulf South.

SUNDAY ANGLETON is a poet, prose writer, artist, and teacher. She was born and raised in South Texas, where she developed an uncommon affection for vivid characters and jalapeño peppers. In 2001 she moved to New Orleans, where she developed hurricane-survival skills and a new appreciation for street revelry. A graduate of Loyola New Orleans, she now teaches at Lusher Charter High School, one of the nation's top high schools for arts and sciences. She lives and writes in Mid-City, just inches above the flood line.

Born May 3, 1947, WAYNE M. BAQUET, SR., represents a third generation in the restaurant industry in New Orleans. Active in the restaurant business since he was nineteen years old, in 1980 he became the operator of his father's restaurant, Eddie's, located at 2119 Law Street and established in 1966. Since then he has owned and operated twelve successful restaurants in New Orleans. Post-Katrina, he has been featured in the *New York Times*; *O: The Oprah Magazine*; and on NPR. He is the current owner of Lil Dizzy's Café —two locations in New Orleans: 1500 Esplanade Avenue in the Tremé and 610 Poydras Street—serving breakfast and lunch Monday through Saturday.

JASON BERRY has published seven books, including a novel, *Last of the Red Hot Pop-*

pas, and two landmark investigations of the Catholic Church crisis: *Lead Us Not into Temptation* in 1992 and *Vows of Silence* in 2004, which spurred a Vatican prosecution of one of the most powerful priests in Rome. He produced an award-winning documentary based on the latter book which has aired in several countries. He is coauthor of *Up from the Cradle of Jazz*, a New Orleans music history. His play *Earl Long in Purgatory* won a Big Easy Award for best original drama. A recipient of Alicia Patterson and Guggenheim fellowships, Jason writes for many outlets and is often interviewed in the national media.

SIMONETTE BERRY, a painter specializing in murals in New Orleans homes, is also a freelance writer and photographer. She graduated from Benjamin Franklin and the New Orleans Center for the Creative Arts and went on to Tulane University to complete her bachelor's degree in Visual Arts. The proud daughter of writers Jason Berry and Lisa LeBlanc Berry, she published her first article in *Gambit Weekly* at age nine. She is a contributing writer and associate editor at *Louisiana Homes and Gardens Magazine*. A voracious reader and costume designer, Simonette has a passion for New Orleans music, art, and culture.

JOHN BIGUENET wrote *The Torturer's Apprentice: Stories* and the novel *Oyster* (Ecco/HarperCollins) and such award-winning plays as *The Vulgar Soul*, *Rising Water*, and *Shotgun*. He edited or coedited *Foreign Fictions* (Random House), *The Craft of Translation and Theories of Translation: An Anthology of Essays from Dryden to Derrida* (University of Chicago Press), and *Strange Harbors* (Center for the Art of Translation). An O. Henry award winner for short fiction and *New York Times* guest columnist as well as past president of the American Literary Translators Association, he is the Robert Hunter Distinguished University Professor at Loyola University in New Orleans.

CRISTINA BLACK is a journalist, arts critic, fiction writer, and musician based in New York City. Her work appears regularly in *Village Voice*, *Nylon*, and *Time Out New York*, where she was music critic from 2005 to 2007. A former full-time resident of New Orleans, she worked as writer for Mayor Ray Nagin from 2002 to 2004 and contributed arts and entertainment coverage to various regional publications such as *Louisiana Life*, *New Orleans Magazine*, and *offBeat Magazine*. She is a three-time New Orleans Press Club Awards nominee, placing first in 2005 for a *Gambit Weekly* cover story. She is currently the entertainment editor at *Foam Magazine*.

AMANDA BOYDEN is the author of two novels, *Pretty Little Dirty*, released in 2006, and *Babylon Rolling*, a tale set in pre-Katrina New Orleans (Pantheon, 2008). She has lived in the city fifteen years and calls it home.

RICK BRAGG is the best-selling and critically acclaimed author of five books, including *All Over but the Shoutin'*, *Ava's Man*, and *The Prince of Frogtown*. A one-time resident of New Orleans, he lives with his family in Alabama.

Born in '67 and raised in New Orleans, DAVE BRINKS' blood is Acadian French and Choctaw. Brinks is editor-in-chief of *YAWP: A Journal of Poetry & Art*, publisher of Trembling Pillow Press, director of *17 Poets! Literary & Performance Series*, and founder of The New Orleans School for the Imagination. His works have appeared in dozens of magazines, newspapers, journals, and anthologies throughout the U. S., Canada, and overseas. Additionally, they have been featured by NPR, *NewsHour with Jim Lehrer*, *National Geographic Traveler*, and *Louisiana Cultural Vistas*. Brinks has authored six books including the acclaimed *The Caveat Onus* (Black Widow Press, 2009).

POPPY Z. BRITE has published eight novels, most recently *Liquor*, *Prime*, and *Soul Kitchen*, which are set in New Orleans' restaurant world. She has also published four short-story collections, most recently *Antediluvian Tales*. Brite lives in New Orleans with her husband, the award-winning chef Chris DeBarr.

Over a forty-year career as an award-winning freelancer specializing in the arts and worldwide travel and photography, MARDA BURTON has produced hundreds of feature articles for many national newspapers and magazines. For *Veranda* magazine she has been a contributing editor for twenty years. She has contributed essays and short stories to several anthologies and in 2004 coauthored *Galatoire's: Biography of a Bistro*. A native of Laurel, Mississippi, she has lived in the French Quarter since 1986. She spends summers in the mountains of North Carolina, where she is writing fiction and memoir.

ROBERT OLEN BUTLER has published eleven novels and five collections of short stories, including the Pulitzer Prize-winning *A Good Scent from a Strange Mountain*, about the Vietnamese in New Orleans. His stories have twice won a National Magazine Award. His latest work is the novel *Hell*, set entirely in that place. His book on the creative process, *From Where You Dream*, is widely used in writing workshops. He teaches creative writing at Florida State University.

GARNETTE CADOGAN is at work on a book about rock-reggae superstar Bob Marley. He is also coeditor, with Shirley Elizabeth Thompson, of the forthcoming *The Oxford Handbook of the Harlem Renaissance*.

JULIA CAREY lives in New Orleans where she leads a double life managing restaurants and writing, oftentimes writing about restaurants. Her writing can be found in *Louisiana: In Words*, *Dudley Review*, *Revisions*, the *Double Dealer Redux*, and on the website juliacarey.com. She has held editorial positions for a creative-writing publication out of Harvard University and the *New Orleans Review* and is at work on her first novel.

CHRISTIAN CHAMPAGNE is a lifelong resident of New Orleans and a graduate of Orleans Parish Schools and the University of New Orleans. He is a poet, satirist, and performer and has performed at venues all around New Orleans and the United States. He is the author of *Roach Opera*, a book of poetry published by Portals Press. He is the author of numerous satirical works dealing with the unique political landscape of New Orleans, *Mike Ditka in Love* and *Ray Nagin: The Musical*, among them. As poet Bill Myers says of Chris' work, "This is poetry on the cloven hoof—nothing but pure, psychotic, associative human beauty."

LEAH CHASE is a proprietor of the renowned Dooky Chase Restaurant, a bastion of Creole cuisine and culture in New Orleans, founded in 1939 as a po' boy stand by her husband, Edgar "Dooky" Chase II. Chase is the recipient of the Candace Award, the Times-Picayune Loving Cup Award, and the Lifetime Achievement Award of the Southern Foodways Alliance. Additionally, she has been inducted into the Lafcadio Hearn Hall of Honor and the Chef John Folse Culinary Institute.

TARA JILL CICCARONE turned thirty-four on September 11, 2009. Her fiction and non-fiction can be found in the *New Orleans Review*, the *Alaska Quarterly*, *Louisiana: In Words*, *Soul Is Bulletproof*, and on the floor of her shotgun apartment. A writer and photographer, she continues to chronicle New Orleans experiences that are sometimes mysterious, often mundane, yet always of gigantic proportion. Her struggle to complete a collection of short stories titled *The Cyanide Hole* has followed her from the Faubourg Marigny, to Gentilly, to Bayou Saint John where she lives, protected by a small dog, Guadalupe, whose devotion remains unrivaled.

JOHN P. CLARK is the Gregory F. Curtin Distinguished Professor in Humane Letters and the Professions and Professor of Philosophy at Loyola University New Orleans. Books he has written or edited include: *Max Stirner's Egoism*; *The Philosophical Anarchism of William Godwin*; *The Anarchist Moment*; *Renewing the Earth*; *Environmental Philosophy*; *Anarchy, Geography, Modernity*; *A Voyage to New Orleans*; and *The Possible Impossible* (forthcoming). For many years he has been active in the green movement and has worked on a small ecological restoration project along Bayou LaTerre in Hancock County, Mississippi.

JOSHUA CLARK is the author of *Heart Like Water: Surviving Katrina and Life in Its Disaster Zone*, a finalist for the National Book Critics Circle award. His work has appeared in many newspapers, magazines, and anthologies. The founder of Light of New Orleans Publishing, he has edited such books as *French Quarter Fiction*, *Southern Fried Divorce*, *Louisiana: In Words*, *How You Can Kill Al Qaeda (in 3 easy steps)*, and *You Are Your Own Gym*.

MORGAN CLEVENGER grew up among the musicians, artists, and writers of New Orleans' French Quarter and Tremé. For over thirty years, she's been a participant and early advocate for New Orleans' culture and its creators; a member of Social Aid and Pleasure Clubs; collaborator with Black Men of Labor; organizer of Jazz Funerals; founder of New Orleans Jazz Legacy Foundation; a Costume Designer; Art Director and Producer in film, television, and special events; and ten years with New Orleans Jazz Fest working with hundreds of musicians. In October 2005, Morgan and Fred organized Chef Austin Leslie's Jazz Funeral—a historic, spiritual event symbolizing the renewal of New Orleans culture.

ANDREI CODRESCU's (www.codrescu.com) most recent books are *The Posthuman Dada Guide: Tzara and Lenin Play Chess* and *Jealous Witness: New Poems*, with a CD, *Storm Songs*, by the New Orleans Klezmer All-Stars. He edits *Exquisite Corpse: A Journal of Letters & Life* (www.exquisitecorpse.org), is a commentator on National Public Radio, and winner of the Peabody Award for the film *Road Scholar*. His work has been widely translated, and he received National Endowment for the Arts fellowships for poetry, and editing, the Romanian Literature Prize, the ACLU Freedom of Speech Award, and the Ovidius Prize.

ANN MARIE COVIELLO and a group of friends invented the Box of Wine Parade on their way to see Bacchus in 1995. In August of 2005, with Shelly Loughnane and L. J. Goldstein, she helped found the 6t'9 Halloween Parade as a safe and fun way for kids of all ages to celebrate Halloween in the downtown neighborhoods. Ann Marie has taught English in Kenya, Prague, and New Orleans. She is currently a school librarian, the mother of two beautiful boys, and a resident of the Historic Seventh Ward.

MARCI DAVIS is a bicoastal author/auteur/alchemist immersed in the junction where spirit and body collude, where culture conjoins community, where nurture is natured—the plexus of the nexus as pertains to the sexus. New Orleans is a sacred spot in her peregrinations, a second home of the soul.

Since 1993, LLOYD DENNIS has written a weekly "Love Doctor" column, and from 1999 to 2003, he shared insights about family and community on the *The Love Doctor Show*, which aired weekly on local radio. Since 2002, he has cohosted *Between the Lines*, an issue-oriented television talk show. He also wrote *His Way Works*, a humorous book of essays designed to encourage and support family living. Lloyd Dennis founded the Silverback Society, a volunteer organization that group-mentors eighth-grade boys. Today Lloyd is a public speaker, journalist, photographer, filmmaker, and webmaster of multimedia-rich websites.

LUCAS DÍAZ-MEDINA, born in Santo Domingo, Dominican Republic, immigrated to Louisiana in 1977. He completed his BA from Loyola New Orleans and MFA in Creative Writing from the University of New Orleans. Díaz-Medina lives in New Orleans and is the author of *Passing Unseen: Stories from New Domangue*, a collection of short stories set in a fictional town south of New Orleans. He received positive reviews from the *New York Times* and the *Chicago Tribune* for his narrative of *Strange Fruit*, Irvin Mayfield's 2005 epic jazz release. Currently he directs Puentes New Orleans, a community-development nonprofit.

JOEL DINERSTEIN is an Associate Professor in the Department of English at Tulane University, where he also directs the American Studies program. He is the author of *Swinging the Machine: Modernity, Technology, and African-American Culture between the World Wars* (2003), an award-winning study of the relationship between jazz and industrialization. He is currently working on a cultural history of the origins of the concept of cool in American culture.

LOUIS EDWARDS is the author of three novels: *Ten Seconds, N,* and *Oscar Wilde Discovers America.* A devoted son of Louisiana, he was born in Lake Charles, graduated from LSU in Baton Rouge, and lives in New Orleans, where he works for Festival Productions, Inc., which produces the New Orleans Jazz & Heritage Festival and other special events.

LOLIS ERIC ELIE is a writer and filmmaker. His most recent film, *Faubourg Tremé: The Untold Story of Black New Orleans,* was featured at the Tribeca and San Francisco International Film festivals. After fourteen years as a columnist for the *New Orleans Times-Picayune,* Lolis Eric Elie joined the writing staff of the HBO series, *Treme.* He is the author of *Smokestack Lightning: Adventures in the Heart of Barbecue Country* and the producer of a film based on that book. His food writing has also appeared in *Gourmet, Bon Appetit, Food Arts,* the *Oxford American,* the *New York Times,* and the *Washington Post.*

GINA FERRARA is a fifth-generation New Orleanian. In 2006, her chapbook, *The Size of Sparrows,* was published by Finishing Line Press. Her poems have appeared in numerous journals, including: *The Poetry Ireland Review, The Briar Cliff Review,* and *Callaloo.* She was awarded a grant from The Elizabeth George Foundation for her work in poetry. Her book, *Ethereal Avalanche,* was published by Trembling Pillow Press in October of 2009. She has work forthcoming in *Louisiana Literature* and *Orpheus 2,* and she is currently working on a collection of poems titled *Unearthed.*

ALISON FENSTERSTOCK has lived in New Orleans since 1995. From 2006-2009, she was the music critic for *Gambit Weekly;* she is now a contributing writer at the *New Orleans Times-Picayune.* Her coverage of New Orleans roots music and hip-hop has appeared in *Vibe, Paste, Q, Spin.com, MOJO,* and the *Oxford American.* In April 2009, she had her wedding reception at the Mother-in-Law Lounge.

RICHARD FORD is a novelist, story writer, and essayist. He was born in Jackson, Mississippi, and spent part of his childhood in New Orleans.

DENNIS FORMENTO is a poet and the publisher of Surregional Press. A native of New Orleans, he lives, Post-K, in Slidell on the North Shore of Lake Pontchartrain, where crawfish build their mudhuts in the moonlight. He edited *Mesechabe: The Journal of Surregionalism* and is the author of seven chapbooks. Currently, he's chronicling the life of the late New Orleans poet, playwright, and coffeehouse proprietor, Robert Borsodi.

JONATHAN FREILICH has been fascinated with the culture of the city since first finding a Professor Longhair album at sixteen. A New Orleans musician since 1989, Jonathan was trained by and has played alongside some of the most wonderful artists in the city. He is a founding member of the New Orleans Klezmer All-Stars which has formed a New Orleans-style rhythmic approach to Yiddish music. He also maintains an avid interest in the many types of "mysticism" surrounding the field of yoga and is a certified "Iyengar" instructor.

A New Orleans native, SCOTT GARVER is a graduate of Jesuit High School, Class of 1983. He earned a BA in History from LSU in 1988. As a freelance artist he has collaborated with Manuel Ponce in assisting Henri Schindler in designing floats and artwork for the Krewe of Hermes. He cites, as literary influences, Baron Corvo, Lafcadio Hearn, and Henri Schindler. He is a recreational student of Anglican liturgy, including the Coronation Service.

QUO VADIS GEX BREAUX is a New Orleans poet. She has published in local, national, and international journals and anthologies including *Furious Flower, Trouble the Water: 250 Years of African American Poetry, African American Review, Quimera*, and *Life Notes*. Ms. Gex Breaux edited two commemorative books for the National Black Arts Festival: *The Ark of the Spirit* (1996) and *Art Beyond Borders* (1998). She was a Visiting Writer in Residence at Tulane University in 2000. She has an MFA in Creative Writing from the University of New Orleans, and a BA in English and Communications from Tulane University/Newcomb College. She lives and writes in New Orleans.

GIO was the "Burlesque Queen of New Orleans" from 1988 to July 2005. Halfway through an illustrious world-traveling career, she chose Bourbon Street to re-introduce the Art of Striptease with a modern, erotic, performance-art sensibility. Now a systemic psychotherapist, GiO was educated at the Pratt Institute of Technology in New York, from which she graduated in 1975 with an honors degree in Industrial Design, and the University of New Orleans where she acquired a Master of Counseling degree in 2002. GiO lives in the Marigny, has had short essays published intermittently, and sometimes reads at the *17 Poets! Literary & Performance Series* open mike.

GABE GOMEZ received a BA in Creative Writing from the College of Santa Fe and an MFA in Creative Writing from St. Mary's College of California. He has taught English at the University of New Orleans, Tulane University, the College of Santa Fe, and the College of Contemporary Indian Arts. He is the Director of External Relations for the Southwestern Association for Indian Arts, which produces the Santa Fe Indian Market. His poetry, prose, and essays have been published in various literary journals and anthologies. His first collection of poetry, *The Outer Bands*, won the Andres Montoya Poetry Prize and was published in 2007 by the University of Notre Dame Press.

LUTHER GRAY is one of the leading percussionists in Louisiana. He has formed two major musical groups, Percussion Incorporated and Bamboula 2000. In addition, Luther is the primary drummer with the Guardians of the Flame Mardi Gras Indians. They have toured Ghana, India, Singapore, Sri Lanka, the United Arab Emirates, France, Mexico, Martinique, Trinidad, and Tobago. Luther founded the Congo Square Foundation in 1989 that has been instrumental in the resurrection of drumming and cultural activities in Congo Square. In 1997, the Congo Square Foundation was successful in placing Congo Square on the National Register of Historic Places.

LEE MEITZEN GRUE writes about New Orleans street life and anything else that strikes her fancy. Her books are *Trains and Other Intrusions: Poems*; *In the Sweet Balance of the Flesh* (poetry); *French Quarter Poems*; *Goodbye, Silver, Silver Cloud: New Orleans Stories*; *Downtown* (poetry), recently released by Trembling Pillow Press; and a spoken word CD with jazz accompaniment: *Live! On Frenchmen Street*. She is currently teaching fiction and poetry at the Alvar Library supported by a grant from Poets and Writers, Inc.

HERREAST J. HARRISON is the widow of the late Donald Harrison, Sr., founder of the Guardians of the Flame Mardi Gras Indian group, and holds an MA in Museum Studies. She is a fifth-generation quilter known for incorporating intricate beaded motifs and symbols into her works. She has traveled to Africa, Asia, Europe, the Caribbean, and throughout the United States to make presentations on the indigenous African American cultural traditions of New Orleans. Mrs. Harrison is currently the Program Director of the Guardians Institute.

ESTER "HUMPHREY STANDARD" HITCHENS II began performing his unique style of poetic prose at the *17 Poets! Literary & Performance Series* at the Gold Mine Saloon in New Orleans in the fall of 2004. "To perform in front of an audience is a yearning that became a part of my existence. It has become the incessant pursuit of imagery that sustains my life today. I am deeply honored that so many people have aligned themselves with me and have become supporters of my work. I wish I could shake hands with you all. In closing, thank you to all my fans and the Academy."

When SARAH K. INMAN'S not hanging upside down or hula hooping, she writes. Her first novel, *Finishing Skills*, was published by Livingston Press in 2005. In addition to contributing to NOLAFugees.com, her writing has appeared in anthologies such as *Soul is Bulletproof, Year Zero, Life in the Wake, Louisiana: In Words, Do You Know What It Means to Miss New Orleans*, and *Tied in Knots: Funny Stories from the Wedding Day*. She lives in the Bywater with her cats, husband, and son.

MARLON JAMES was born in Kingston, Jamaica, in 1970. His first novel, *John Crow's Devil* (Akashic Books, 2005) was a finalist for the Los Angeles Times Book Prize, the Commonwealth Writers Prize, and was a *New York Times* Editors' Choice. His second novel, *The Book of Night Women* (Riverhead 2009), was nominated for the National Books Critics Circle Award.

He has taught at the Gotham Writers Workshop in New York City and was a judge for the PEN Beyond Margins Award. Marlon James teaches Literature and Creative Writing at Macalester College, St. Paul, Minnesota.

FRED J. JOHNSON, JR., a native of New Orleans' Seventh Ward, first masked Indian at age thirteen with legendary Big Chief Tootie Montana of The Yellow Pocahontas, serving as Spy Boy for seventeen years. As a community mentor with Tambourine and Fan for twenty years, Fred advocated cultural participation as an alternative to drugs. Professionally, as Outreach Specialist and now CEO of New Orleans Neighborhood Development Foundation, Fred's helped hundreds become first-time homeowners. A founder of The Black Men of Labor Parade Club, Fred has served as President since 1995. Fred and BMOL Members stayed through Katrina, performing search and rescue. Post-K, Fred is committed to rebuilding New Orleans.

JULIE KANE, a native of Boston and longtime resident of Louisiana, is the author of three collections of poetry: *Jazz Funeral*, the winner of the 2009 Donald Justice Poetry Prize; *Rhythm & Booze*, a National Poetry Series winner and finalist for the 2005 Poets' Prize; and *Body and Soul*. With Kiem Do, she coauthored the Vietnam memoir *Counterpart: A South Vietnamese Naval Officer's War*, which became a History Book Club Featured Alternate. She teaches at Northwestern State University in Natchitoches, Louisiana.

KARISSA KARY is a writer and producer whose travels and work in the Missouri Ozarks, Europe, Asia, and South America still leave her feeling most at home in New Orleans. A cofounder and management consultant for Greenlight Operations, focused on artists and businesses emphasizing social responsibility, she was the Associate Director with the celebrated Tennessee Williams/ New Orleans and Saints and Sinners Literary Festivals. She is the cofounder and Producing Managing Director for Halifax Theatre Company, a regional touring company that most recently toured *The Kingfish* and opened The Bayou Playhouse seeking to showcase the rich culture and heritage of Louisiana.

DAVID KUNIAN is an award-winning radio producer, musicologist, and freelance writer. He has produced radio programs about James Booker, Earl King, James Black, Guitar Slim, Chris Kenner, Michael Ward, Everette Maddox, Jonathan Freilich, and popular Mardi Gras songs. He writes for *DownBeat*, *Gambit Weekly*, and *offBeat*. His late-night jazz program "Jazz Lunatique" has been on WWOZ for over fifteen years of craziness. Currently, he is working on radio programs about Lee Dorsey and Danny Barker.

ERROL LABORDE is the Editor-in-Chief of Renaissance Publishing Company. In that capacity, he serves as Editor/Associate Publisher of *New Orleans Magazine* and Editor/ Publisher of *Louisiana Life Magazine*. Laborde is producer and a regular panelist on *Informed Sources*, a weekly news-discussion program broadcast on public-television station WYES-TV, Channel 12. The winner of over twenty New Orleans Press Club awards, Laborde is a three-time winner of the Alex Waller Award, the highest award given in print journalism by the Press Club. Laborde's most recent book is *Krewe: The Early Carnival from Comus to Zulu.*

KATHERYN KROTZER LABORDE is a writer of prose, both fiction and literary nonfiction. A recipient of a Louisiana Division of the Arts Fellowship, her work has appeared in *Callaloo, Poets & Writers,* and *CrossRoads: A Southern Culture Annual.* Her book *Do Not Open—The Discarded Refrigerators of Post-Katrina New Orleans* (McFarland) will soon hit the shelves. She teaches at Xavier University of Louisiana.

With respect to his Big Chief Edgar Jacobs, Council Chief RONALD W. LEWIS of the Choctaw Hunters is a longtime member of the Big Nine Social and Pleasure Club, Krewe du Jieux, and is Gatekeeper of the Northside Skull and Bones. He retired from the Regional Transit Authority in 2002 to concentrate on his museum on Tupelo Street in the Lower Ninth Ward, The House of Dance and Feathers, which displays and preserves the heritage of Black Mardi Gras Indians, Social Aid and Pleasure Clubs, Bone Gangs, Baby Dolls, and Parade Clubs.

LOUIS MAISTROS is the author of the critically acclaimed New Orleans novel, *The Sound of Building Coffins.* A longtime resident of the New Orleans' Eighth Ward neighborhood, he is a former forklift operator and self-taught writer with no formal training. His work has appeared in publications such as the *New Orleans Times-Picayune* and the *Baltimore City Paper,* among others. He is currently at work on his second New Orleans novel, tentatively titled *Holy Meaux.*

Musician ALEX MCMURRAY was born and raised in Red Bank, New Jersey. He moved to New Orleans to attend Tulane University, where he received a BA in English and Philosophy in 1991. He has been playing guitar and singing professionally in New Orleans since the late eighties, though music has brought him around the country and the world. Mr. McMurray moved to New York nearly a year before Hurricane Katrina and returned on February 1, 2006. For further information about Alex McMurray, go to: www.alexmcmurray.com.

IAN MCNULTY is the author of *Season of Night: New Orleans Life after Katrina* (2008) and the forthcoming *Louisiana Rambles: Exploring America's Cajun and Creole Heartland* (2010). He lives in Mid-City.

PATRICE MELNICK lives in Grand Coteau, Louisiana, with her husband Olan. She own Casa Azul Gifts (http://casaazul.homestead.com) which hosts an open-mic series. Melnick writes essays, teaches Creative Nonfiction online for UNO, directs nonprofit programs, and does a little gardening in-between.

MARIA MONTOYA is a reporter for the *New Orleans Times-Picayune.* She moved to

New Orleans in June of 2001 from Washington, D.C., where she worked for *USA Today*'s "Life" section. A graduate of the University of Florida, Ms. Montoya met and fell in love with her husband during Mardi Gras. The couple lives in Algiers with their children and three dogs.

In the early 1990s New Orleans native STANTON MOORE founded New Orleans-based "steam-roller" funk band Galactic. Their seventh studio release, *Ya-Ka-May*, features collaborations with many NOLA luminaries. Moore launched his solo career in the late '90s with the album *All Kooked Out!* and continued with *Flyin' the Koop*, *III*, and *Emphasis! (on parenthesis)*. His latest solo project *Groove Alchemy* is a multimedia project (DVD, book, and CD) and focuses on his approach to grooves and the creative process. Stanton has performed and recorded with Tom Morello, Charlie Hunter, Leo Nocentelli, Maceo Parker, Irma Thomas, Dr. John, John Medeski, and Corrosion of Conformity, to name a few.

JAMES NOLAN'S latest book is *Perpetual Care*, a collection of short stories set in New Orleans, which won the 2009 Next Generation Indie Book Award. The manuscript of his novel *Higher Ground* was awarded the 2008 William Faulkner-Wisdom Prize. His books of poetry include *Why I Live in the Forest* and *What Moves Is Not the Wind* (Wesleyan University Press). He is a frequent nonfiction contributor to *Boulevard*, and recent essays have appeared in *Utne*, *North American Review*, the *Washington Post*, and the *Gastronomica Reader* (University of California Press). A fifth-generation New Orleans native, he lives in the French Quarter.

ADAM NOSSITER has been, since 2009, the West Africa Bureau Chief for the *New York Times*, based in Dakar, Senegal. Nossiter has been a reporter for the *New York Times* during Katrina, the Associated Press, the *Atlanta Journal-Constitution*, the *St. Petersburg Times*, and the *Anniston Star*. His publications include *The Algeria Hotel: France, Memory and the Second World War*; *New York Times Book Review* "Bear in Mind" column; *Of Long Memory: Mississippi and the Murder of Medgar Evers*; and the *New York Times Book Review*, "New and Noteworthy Paperbacks" column. His articles have appeared in: the *Nation*, the *New York Times Book Review*, *Le Monde*, the *National Journal*, the *Washington Post*, and the *Chicago Tribune Book Review*.

A music writer for publications including *DownBeat*, *People*, and *CMJ* magazines, JENNIFER ODELL has written extensively about New Orleans music since earning her MS in Journalism at Columbia University, where she focused on cultural reporting and graduated with high honors. She is an alumna of numerous arts and music organizations in the Crescent City and owes her love of music, her addiction to the smell of night-blooming jasmine, and her life to the city of New Orleans. Her portfolio can be downloaded at www.jennieodell.com.

Grammy-winning singer/songwriter, ANDERS OSBORNE, has recorded and produced records for over twenty-five years. His discography includes, but is not limited to, *American Patch-*

work; *Which Way to Here*; *Live at Tipitina's*; *Ash Wednesday Blues*; *Bury the Hatchet*, a collaboration with Big Chief Monk Boudreaux; and Grammy-nominated *Living Room*. He received a Grammy for Keb' Mo's album *Slow Down* (1998). Osborne has been working as a professional songwriter for Polygram and Universal Music Publishing since 1994. His song, "Watch the Wind Blow By," was recorded by country music star Tim McGraw, hitting #1 on the country charts for two weeks and selling over four million albums.

JORIN "JAHN BE" OSTROSKA, thirty-nine years old, is an original member of two highly regarded Social and Pleasure Clubs in New Orleans: The Revolution and Keepin-It-Real. A poet, artist, music-video director, and Second Line dancer, he discovered Second Line parades in 1992 and has immersed himself in this uniquely New Orleans subculture of talented musicians and dancers ever since. He is a regular contributor to *Mineshaft*, a literary/arts journal. You can catch him on the fourth Sunday in March every year parading with the Revolution, or on the sidelines rolling behind a tuba on any given Sunday during Second Line season—ONLY IN NEW ORLEANS, BABY!

KAMI PATTERSON is proud to call New Orleans home. Her work has appeared in *Hip Mama*, *Deep South Mouth*, and *Rag Cooperative*.

TOM PIAZZA is the author of nine books, including the novel *City of Refuge*, which won the 2008 Willie Morris Award for Southern Fiction, and the post-Katrina classic *Why New Orleans Matters*. A well-known writer on American music as well, Tom won a 2004 Grammy Award for his album notes to *Martin Scorsese Presents The Blues: A Musical Journey* and is a three-time winner of the ASCAP-Deems Taylor Award for Music Writing. He is currently writing for the upcoming HBO series *Treme*, and is at work on a new novel. He lives in New Orleans.

VALENTINE PIERCE is a poet, performance artist, photographer, and graphic designer. Her book, *Geometry of the Heart*, was published by Portals Press in 2007. Two poems, "Womb Poem" and "First-born," were recently published in the *Maple Leaf Rag IV*. She is a member of the Alvar Fiction Writers group and the Women's Caucus for Art. These days she spends some of her "spare" time on her crocheting and sewing—two things she has enjoyed since childhood. However, she'll be cutting those loose temporarily to prepare for her one-woman show, *Cozy Cottages and Beatific Bungalows*, where Fannie Fleur-de-lis Boudreaux, aka Fanatical Fannie, describes life in a FEMA trailer.

CHRIS ROSE is a writer, actor, lecturer, and comedian in New Orleans. His accolades and awards include a Pulitzer Prize for Public Service in 2006, and his book, *1 Dead in Attic*, a collection of stories, anecdotes, and observations of life in New Orleans in the aftermath of Hurricane Katrina, was on the *New York Times* "Best-Seller" List for four weeks in 2007. A native of Washington, D.C., Rose is a graduate of the University of Wisconsin School of Journalism and lives in New Orleans with his three children.

New Orleans writer, filmmaker, and educator, KALAMU YA SALAAM is codirector of Students at the Center, a writing program in the New Orleans public schools (http://sacnola.com). He is also moderator of Breath of Life, a Black music website (http://www.kalamu.com/bol). Kalamu blogs at (http://kalamu.posterous.com). Salaam can be reached at kalamu@aol.com or on Twitter (http://twitter.com/neogriot).

DR. MONA LISA SALOY, New Orleans native, Folklorist, is currently Associate Professor and Director of Creative Writing, Director of Honors at Dillard University in New Orleans; she is author of a love song to New Orleans in the award-winning collection: *Red Beans and Ricely Yours: Poems* (Truman State University Press, 2005); the audio book premiers in 2010. For more information, go to: www.monalisasaloy.com.

For the past twenty-seven years, MICHAEL SARTISKY, PhD, has been President and Executive Director of the Louisiana Endowment for the Humanities. He has been a Trustee of Sarah Lawrence College, on the Rhodes Scholarship Selection Committee for Louisiana, and directed the first statewide Louisiana literacy conference in 1990. As the founding editor of the award-winning quarterly magazine *Louisiana Cultural Vistas*, Dr. Sartisky three times has won the Ashton Phelps Memorial Award for Editorial Writing as well as six first- and second-place awards for editorial writing from the New Orleans Press Club.

As an acknowledged authority on the history of Mardi Gras, HENRI SCHINDLER has become synonymous with the annual New Orleans celebration. A curator for the Louisiana State Museum's Presbytere Mardi Gras exhibit, Schindler also has made his mark as a celebrated float, costume, invitation, and jewelry designer for the Mistick Krewe of Comus, the Rex Organization, The Krewe of Hermes, and Le Krewe D'Etat. His series, *Mardi Gras Treasures*, showcases four aspects of the celebration: *Mardi Gras Treasures: Jewelry of the Golden Age, Mardi Gras Treasures: Invitations of the Golden Age, Mardi Gras Treasures: Float Designs of the Golden Age*, and *Mardi Gras Treasures: Costume Designs of the Golden Age.*

REBECCA SNEDEKER is an award-winning filmmaker whose work supports human rights, creative expression, and her native city, New Orleans. Her directorial debut, *By Invitation Only* (2006), premiered at the Full Frame Documentary Film Festival and screened on PBS stations nationwide. Currently, she is producing *Witness: Katrina* (National Geographic Channel, 2010) and coproducing *Land of Opportunity* (Arte France, 2010). She has contributed to numerous documentaries including *A Village Called Versailles* (2009), *Faubourg Tremé* (2007), and *Desire* (2006). Snedeker serves on the board of Patois: New Orleans International Human Rights Film Festival, and she is an active member of New Day Films.

NED SUBLETTE is the author of *The Year Before the Flood: A Story of New Orleans*

(Lawrence Hill Books); *The World That Made New Orleans: From Spanish Silver to Congo Square* (Lawrence Hill Books); and *Cuba and Its Music: From the First Drums to the Mambo* (Chicago Review Press). He is the founder of the Institute for Postmambo Studies.

An NEA-award recipient and Louisiana Theater Fellow, JOSÉ TORRES-TAMA, was awarded a 2009/10 Creation Fund from the National Performance Network for the commissioning of *Aliens, Immigrants & Other Evildoers*, a sci-fi Latino noir and multimedia solo exploring the rise in hate crimes against immigrants in the United States. His critically acclaimed post-Katrina performance *The Cone of Uncertainty* chronicles his dramatic escape from the flooded city on a stolen school bus three days after the levees breached. (torrestama.com)

SHIRLEY ELIZABETH THOMPSON is the author of *Exiles at Home: The Struggle to Become American in Creole New Orleans* and coeditor with Garnette Cadogan of *The Oxford Handbook of the Harlem Renaissance*. She's currently at work on a book about African American conceptions of property and ownership and a memoir which traces the afterlife of slavery in the U.S. South through her family's history. She lives with her husband and son in Austin, Texas, where she is a professor in the Department of American Studies and the John L. Warfield Center for African and African-American Studies at the University of Texas at Austin.

BARBARA TREVIGNE received her Master's degree from Tulane University's School of Social Work. Barbara is a licensed tour guide, visual artist, playwright, storyteller, actor, cultural historian, genealogist, and published author. A descendent of Marie Laveaux through the Crocker line, Barbara is often called upon to present the history of the Tignon, an eighteenth-century headdress worn by women of color. On May 11, 2007, Alliance Françoise honored her for the preservation of Creole culture. In 2009, she received The Danny Barker Award for artistic and humanitarian efforts. Through her efforts, the Family Tomb of Marie Laveaux, the St. Ann Shrine, and the St. Roch Chapel are under study by the Louisiana Landmark Commission.

JERRY W. WARD, JR., Professor of English at Dillard University, is a poet, critic, and Richard Wright scholar. He taught for thirty-two years (1970-2002) at his alma mater, Tougaloo College, in Mississippi and has lived in New Orleans since 2003. Ward, author of *The Katrina Papers* (UNO Press, 2008), compiled and edited *Trouble the Water: 250 Years of African American Poetry* (1997) and is the coeditor of *The Richard Wright Encyclopedia* (Greenwood Press, 2008) and the *Cambridge History of African American Literature* (Cambridge University Press, forthcoming). His works-in-progress include *Reading Race Reading America*, a collection of essays, and *Richard Wright: One Reader's Responses*.

DR. MICHAEL WHITE is a leading figure in New Orleans jazz. He is a clarinetist and historian who has had many international performances, recordings, and film appearances. White holds the Keller Endowed Chair in the Humanities at Xavier University, where he has taught Spanish and African American Music for thirty years. He rebounded from devastating Katrina losses with a recent recording of original compositions, *Blue Crescent*. White has received numerous honors and awards, including the French Chevalier of Arts and Letters, and a NEA National Heritage Fellowship Award. He was named Humanist of the Year in 2010 by the LEH.

MISSY WILKINSON is a Baton Rouge native and, since 1998, a proud New Orleanian. She is Special Sections editor at *Gambit Weekly* and has an MFA in Fiction from the University of New Orleans. Recently, she completed a novel, *Life During the Plague Years*, which was a finalist in the 2008 and 2009 Faulkner-Wisdom competitions.

KELLY WILSON received her MFA in Creative Writing from the University of New Orleans and her BA in English Literature from Tulane University, where she was honored with the John Kennedy Toole Scholarship for emerging writers. Wilson spent several years as an Instructor of English at Loyola University in New Orleans and now works as a freelance writer. She lives with her family in Algiers Point in New Orleans.

CHRISTINE WILTZ, a native New Orleanian, is the author of four novels, *The Killing Circle, A Diamond Before You Die, The Emerald Lizard*, and *Glass House*, all set in New Orleans, and a biography, *The Last Madam: A Life in the New Orleans Underworld*, about French Quarter legend Norma Wallace. She also cowrote and coproduced the TV documentary *Backlash: Race and the American Dream* about David Duke and his followers, first aired on PBS in 1992.

ANDY YOUNG is the coeditor of *Meena Magazine*, a bilingual Arabic-English literary journal, and teaches Creative Writing at NOCCA. Her work was recently featured in *Best New Poets 2009* and has been used in jewelry designs, electronic music, a flamenco play, and on buses in Santa Fe.

The Photographer

CHRISTOPHER PORCHÉ WEST is a photographer and artist who has been documenting the people and culture of New Orleans for thirty years. A native Californian with Franco-European roots in Louisiana, Porché West first came to New Orleans in the late 1970s on a fellowship from the University of California at Santa Cruz. Captivated by the city, he returned in 1981 to undertake a self-directed photo-documentary on the daily lives and cultural activity of contemporary New Orleans Creoles of Color and African Americans, including the elaborate costumes of Mardi Gras Indians, passing rites, community occurrences, neighborhood scenes, and jazz funerals.

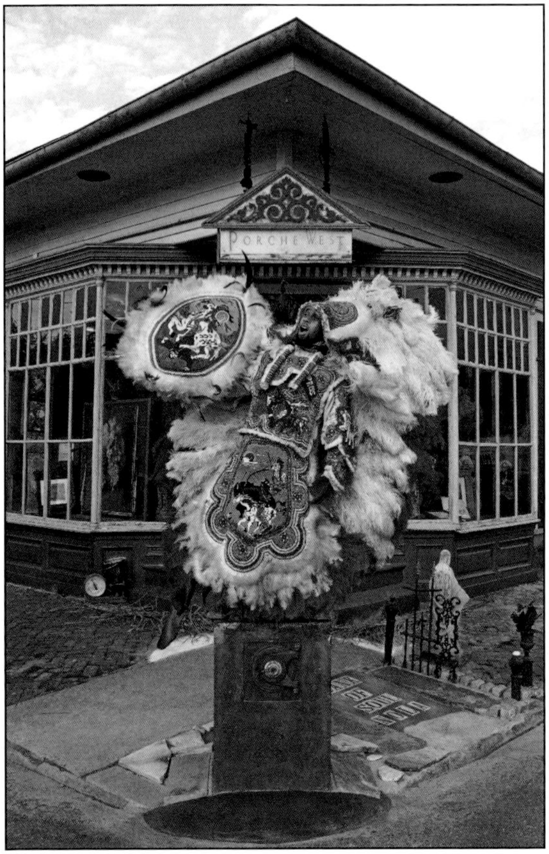
PORCHE WEST

In 1995 he established a temporary studio to accommodate solely formal portraiture in a controlled environment for individual members of many different tribes of the Black Mardi Gras Indians—the first and only time that the Indians themselves were part of the process of their own documentation.

For the past decade, Porché West has explored new mediums of creative expression while also expanding the thematic focus of his work beyond New Orleans' Franco-Creole culture. Recycling scraps of wrought iron, aged cypress, window frames, and other found materials from the streets of New Orleans, Porché West began creating handcrafted, one-of-a-kind ensembles through which to view his imagery. He currently lives and works in one of New Orleans' oldest neighborhoods, Bywater, founded in 1809, where he continues to document and preserve the culture and life of New Orleans and its people.

Index of Contributors

Permissions

The following essays are included in this compilation through the gracious permission of the author and the original publisher:

"Who We Are" by Chris Rose first appeared in the *New Orleans Times-Picayune*, September 6, 2005, as "Louisiana ambassadors say hello, y'all;" it was also published in *1 Dead in Attic* (New York: Simon and Schuster, 2007).

"Olive Oil and Alligator Pears" by James Nolan appeared as "Huile d'Olive et Poires Alligator" (Mane, Haute Provence, France: Oliviers & Co., 2001); it also appeared as "Aceite de oliva y peras caiman" in Nolan's collection of essays, *Fumadores en manos de un dios enfurecido* (Madrid: Enigma Editores, 2005).

"Architectural Distinction and Identity" by Michael Sartisky from *Louisiana Cultural Vistas* (Summer 2002).

"The Rhythm of the City" by Christine Wiltz from *Glass House* (Baton Rouge: LSU Press, 2001).

"What to Do with Your Goat in a Drowning World" by Andrei Codrescu appeared in *Jealous Witness: Poems by Andrei Codrescu* (Minneapolis: Coffee House Press, 2008).

"End of the World" by Joshua Clark is adapted from "Disaster is Only One Marsh Away," which appeared in the *Boston Globe*, August 29, 2007.

"A Lifetime Addiction" by Ronald W. Lewis from *The House of Dance and Feathers* by Rachel Breunlin, Ronald W. Lewis, and Helen Regis (New Orleans: Neighborhood Story Project and the UNO Press, 2009).

"We Cry at Birth and Rejoice at Death" by Morgan Clevenger and Fred Johnson first appeared in November 2005 in a catalogue presented by Louisiana Folk Roots in collaboration with PROJECT HEAL and the Acadiana Arts Council.

"The Queen of Canal and Broad" is adapted from "Glitter Goddess," which appeared in the *New Orleans Times-Picayune*, February 25, 2006.

"Mid-City Rock 'n' Bowl" by Patrice Melnick from *Turning Up the Volume* (New Orleans: Xavier Review Press, 2005).

"Forgive Us if We Make Lemonade and Refuse to Cry" by Lloyd Dennis from *Data News Weekly*, 2006.

"The New Orleans of Possibility" by Michael Sartisky from *Louisiana Cultural Vistas* (Fall, 2005).

"A Streetcar of Solace is Back in New Orleans" by Adam Nossiter appeared in the *New York Times*, December 30, 2007.

Editor's Acknowledgments

I would like to honor all of those who speak the breath of our ancestors in the preservation and creation of New Orleans culture, paying special tribute to all Black Mardi Gras Indian Tribes. Those whose incredible contributions to culture appear on these pages are: Big Chief Donald Harrison, Sr., of the Guardians of the Flame (page 181); Big Chief Allison "Tootie" Montana of the Yellow Pocahontas (page 131); with respect to his Big Chief Edgar Jacobs, Council Chief Ronald W. Lewis of the Choctaw Hunters (page 129); Spyboy Roy "Buck" Varnardo of the Geronimo Hunters (page 155); Wildman Lionel "Bird" Ouibichon of the White Eagles (page 126); and with respect to his elders, Felton, Jake, Big Foot Joe, Nat Flagboy Nelson, and Bird, Spyboy Demond Melancon of the Seminole (page 266).

This book is for New Orleans, an offering of deep gratitude, respect, love, and reverence.

For going the extra mile for this book, special thanks go to Erik Whitfield, Joshua Clark, Garnette Cadogan, Jason Berry, Jennifer Odell, Gwen Richardson, Jason Wiese, Karissa Kary, John Clark, Dave Brinks, Fred Johnson, Morgan Clevenger, Leah Chase, Henri Schindler, Jerry W. Ward, Jr., Herreast Harrison, Barbara Trevigne, David Kunian, Poppy Z. Brite, Lee Meitzen Grue, L. J. Goldstein, Katheryn Krotzer Laborde, Kelly Wilson, Ember Soberman, Julia W. Harris, Bill Harris, J. W. Nickels, Whitney Wall, Craig Szakaly, Monique Rhodes, Anders Osborne, Page 1NE, Christopher Alfieri, Dino Gankendorff, Adam Shipley, James Huck, Thomas Thayer and d.b.a., Hubig's Pies, Christophe Szapary, Lena D. Giangrosso, Steve O'Keefe, Lucille Regina Wilson Brown, Elliot Hyett Wilson Brown, everyone at Sweet Home New Orleans, Preservation Resource Center, the Louisiana Endowment for the Humanities, and my new superhero, James D. Wilson, Jr., of the University of Louisiana at Lafayette Press and the Center for Louisiana Studies.

Sincere and heartfelt thanks go to those upon whose support I have relied since this book was only scribbles in my hands: my family, my friends, and my sacred city.

To Christopher: I can't thank you enough for the chance you took, for the time you have dedicated to the people and places of New Orleans, for the way you love them, for your patience, your authenticity, your creativity, and your amazing eye.

To my eight-eight keys: for answering that call or e-mail and believing in this book, or for saying yes that afternoon at the post office or book signing or panel discussion, *thank you.* Your exceptional contributions of talent, time, creativity, and endurance—and your devotion to your city and to each other—made this possible.

To the people and places on every page in this book, to the New Orleanians scattered across the country, to those who protect this city with love or loyalty or rolled-up sleeves, and to those we have lost but will never forget, wherever you are, this is your book.

Sweet Home New Orleans

SWEET HOME
NEW ORLEANS

Proceeds from *New Orleans: What Can't Be Lost* will be donated to Sweet Home New Orleans in thanks for their work preserving New Orleans culture.

Sweet Home New Orleans is a nonprofit organization whose mission is to support the individuals and organizations that will perpetuate New Orleans' unique musical and cultural traditions. They began their work immediately after the levees broke in 2005, and they have provided millions of dollars in financial assistance to thousands of members of the city's music community. They help New Orleans musicians, Mardi Gras Indians, and Social Aid & Pleasure Club members get on their feet, get to work, and revitalize their communities and the cultural economy of New Orleans.

www.sweethomeneworleans.org

Your New Orleans Photograph

Your New Orleans Story

Your New Orleans Story (cont.)